Jack Clayton

CW01429555

MANCHESTER
UNIVERSITY PRESS

BRIAN MCFARLANE, NEIL SINYARD *series editors*

ALLEN EYLES, PHILIP FRENCH, SUE HARPER,
TIM PULLEINE, JEFFREY RICHARDS, TOM RYALL
series advisers

BRITISH FILM MAKERS

already published

Lance Comfort   BRIAN MCFARLANE

forthcoming titles

Terence Fisher   PETER HUTCHINGS

Pat Jackson   CHARLES BARR

Launder and Gilliat   BRUCE BABINGTON

J. Lee Thompson   STEVE CHIBNALL

Jack Clayton

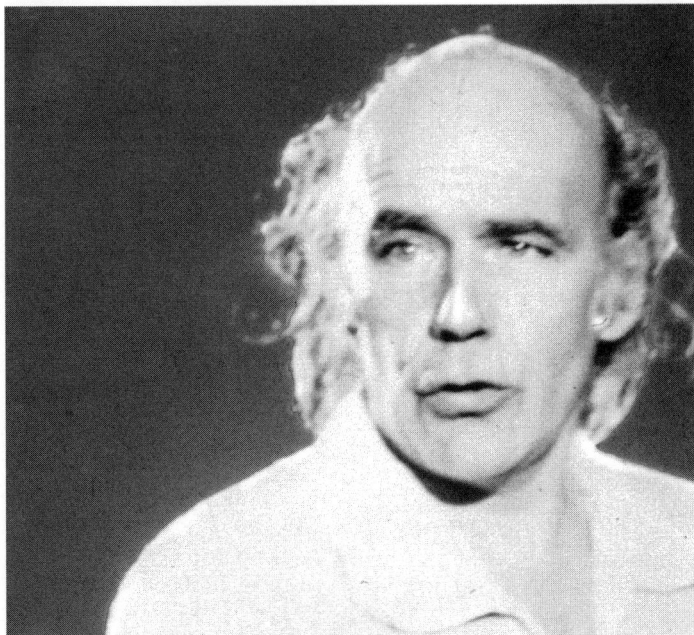

NEIL SINYARD

Manchester University Press

MANCHESTER AND NEW YORK

distributed exclusively in the USA by St. Martin's Press

Published by Manchester University Press
Oxford Road, Manchester M13 9NR, UK
and Room 400, 175 Fifth Avenue, New York, NY 10010, USA
http://www.manchesteruniversitypress.co.uk

Distributed exclusively in the USA by
St. Martin's Press, Inc., 175 Fifth Avenue, New York,
NY 10010, USA

Distributed exclusively in Canada by
UBC Press, University of British Columbia, 2029 West Mall,
Vancouver, BC, Canada V6T 1Z2

British Library Cataloguing-in-Publication Data
A catalogue record for this book is available from the British Library

Library of Congress Cataloging-in-Publication Data applied for

ISBN 0 7190 5504 0 *hardback*
     0 7190 5505 9 *paperback*

First published 2000

07 06 05 04 03 02 01 00   10 9 8 7 6 5 4 3 2 1

Typeset in Scala with Meta display
by Koinonia, Manchester
Printed in Great Britain
by Bookcraft (Bath) Ltd, Midsomer Norton

For Haya

also by Neil Sinyard

Journey Down Sunset Boulevard: The Films of Billy Wilder (with Adrian Turner) BCW Publishers, 1979

All-Time Box-Office Hits (general editor), Gallery Books, 1985

Classic Movies, Hamlyn, 1985, reissued 1993

Directors: All-Time Greats, Gallery Books, 1985

The Films of Richard Lester, Croom Helm, 1985

Filming Literature: The Art of Screen Adaptation, Croom Helm, 1986

The Films of Alfred Hitchcock, Admiral/Multimedia, 1986, reissued 1994

Zinnemann (with A. Goldau and H. Prinzler), Verlag Filmland Presse, 1986

The Films of Steven Spielberg, Hamlyn/Bison, 1987

The Films of Woody Allen, Magna Books, 1987

The Best of Disney, W. H. Smith, 1988

The Films of Mel Brooks, Hamlyn/Bison, 1988

Marilyn, Magna Books, 1989

Silent Movies, W. H. Smith/Magna, 1990

The Films of Nicolas Roeg, Charles Letts, 1991

Classic Movie Comedians, Bison, 1992

Children in the Movies, Batsford, 1992

Mel Gibson, Bison, 1992

Clint Eastwood, Bison, 1995

Contents

LIST OF PLATES   *page* ix
SERIES EDITORS' FOREWORD   xi
ACKNOWLEDGEMENTS   xii

1   Introduction: lonely passions – the cinema of Jack Clayton   1

2   Early career: *Naples is a Battlefield* (1944); *The Bespoke
    Overcoat* (1955)   20

3   Sex, realism and Yorkshire pudding: *Room at the Top*
    (1959)   37

4   Pearl of ambiguity: *The Innocents* (1961)   81

5   Woman on the verge of a nervous breakdown:
    The Pumpkin Eater (1964)   109

6   Forbidden games: *Our Mother's House* (1967)   130

7   Clayton in America: *The Great Gatsby* (1974);
    Something Wicked This Way Comes (1983)   144

8   God's lonely woman: *The Lonely Passion of Judith
    Hearne* (1987)   174

9   Death makes a call: *Memento Mori* (1992)   190

10 Unfinished business: the unrealised projects of
    Jack Clayton   206

11 Conclusion   224

APPENDICES: SOME WRITINGS OF JACK CLAYTON
   'You Can't Declare Peace' (1944–45)   229
   'On the Prevention of War' (1946)   234
   The *Queen* interview (1960)   237
   'Abstract on Vision' (1977)   239
   Short story: 'The Enchantment' (1985)   241

FILMOGRAPHY   261
SELECT BIBLIOGRAPHY   272
INDEX   277

List of plates

1 A thoughtful Jack Clayton on the set of *The Great Gatsby*   *page* 67

2 Jack Clayton as sketched by John Huston at the Beverly Hills Hotel, 1953   68

3 Clayton as a child actor with Peggy Ashcroft in Carl Zuckmayer's *The Golden Toy*, London Coliseum, 1934   69

4 Clayton as a bespectacled young third assistant director on the set of *Wings of the Morning* (1937), the first British Technicolor film. The stars in the centre of the photograph are Henry Fonda and Annabella, in her role as a heroine dressed as a boy   70

5 Sex comes to British cinema: Laurence Harvey and Simone Signoret in *Room at the Top*   71

6 The price of wealth: Mary Peach, Laurence Harvey and Donald Houston in *Room at the Top*   72

7 Unhappy is the groom: Laurence Harvey and Heather Sears in *Room at the Top*   73

8 The famous preview card of *Room at the Top* that Clayton displayed in his office   73

9 Deborah Kerr and Jack Clayton on the set of *The Innocents*   74

10 Clayton's sketch of the last scene of *The Innocents*   75

11 Clayton, Haya Harareet and James Mason arrive for the
    screening of *The Pumpkin Eater* at the Cannes Film
    Festival, 1964   *page* 76

12 Clayton at Jurassic Park: directing the scene on the
    boating lake in *Our Mother's House*. Photograph by
    Eve Arnold. Reproduced by courtesy of Eve Arnold and
    Magnum Photos, to whom grateful thanks   77

13 Dirk Bogarde and Pamela Franklin in *Our Mother's House*   78

14 Clayton directs Robert Redford and Mia Farrow in *The
    Great Gatsby*   78

15 Mr Dark in Disneyland: Jonathan Pryce and Jack Clayton on
    the set of *Something Wicked This Way Comes*   79

16 Clayton shares a joke with his favourite film composer,
    Georges Delerue, 1987   79

17 Maggie Smith in *The Lonely Passion of Judith Hearne*   80

18 Clayton at home, with his pigeons. Photograph by Haya
    Clayton   80

Unless otherwise indicated, all stills are from the personal collection
of Haya Clayton, to whom we offer our grateful thanks

Series editors' foreword

The aim of this series is to present in lively, authoritative volumes a guide to those film-makers who have made British cinema a rewarding but still under-researched branch of world cinema. The intention is to provide books which are up-to-date in terms of information and critical approach, but not bound to any one theoretical methodology. Though all books in the series will have certain elements in common – comprehensive filmographies, annotated bibliographies, appropriate illustration – the actual critical tools employed will be the responsibility of the individual authors.

Nevertheless, an important recurring element will be a concern for how the oeuvre of each film-maker does or does not fit certain critical and industrial contexts, as well as for the wider social contexts, which helped to shape not just that particular film-maker but the course of British cinema at large.

Although the series is director-orientated, the editors believe that a variety of stances and contexts referred to is more likely to reconceptualise and reappraise the phenomenon of British cinema as a complex, shifting field of production. All the texts in the series will engage in detailed discussion of major works of the film-makers involved, but they all consider as well the importance of other key collaborators, of studio organisation, of audience reception, of recurring themes and structures: all those other aspects which go towards the construction of a national cinema.

The series will explore and chart a field which is more than ripe for serious excavation. The acknowledged leaders of the field will be reappraised; just as important, though, will be the bringing to light of those who have not so far received any serious attention. They are all part of the very rich texture of British cinema, and it will be the work of this series to give them all their due.

Acknowledgements

Writing a book, like making a film, might be the ultimate responsibility of the author (or 'auteur'), but it is a task that cannot be
brought to fruition without the help of a great many people. It gives
me great pleasure to acknowledge the assistance of the following:
Andrew Higson of the University of East Anglia, for kindly supplying
me with a transcript of an interview he had conducted with Clayton in
1985 on the subject of *The Innocents*; Brad King, the Public Services
Officer of the Imperial War Museum, for his help in enabling me to
see *Naples is a Battlefield*; Jeanie Sims, Clayton's long-time script
editor, for generously allowing me access to some of her papers; John
C. Tibbetts, from the University of Kansas, for sending me his article
on Ray Bradbury adaptations with particular relevance to *Something
Wicked This Way Comes*; Adrian Turner, for seeking out an obscure
Sight and Sound reference and for helping me with a Robert Bolt
query; Jim Welsh, from the University of Maryland, for sending me
relevant material from the excellent *Literature/Film Quarterly* journal
which he edits; my fine film friend Gil West, for loaning me a better-
quality tape of *Our Mother's House* than the one I had; and my talented
research student, Melanie Williams, for turning up a *Films and
Filming* piece I had overlooked. Jacqui Thomson had the daunting
task of typing up my indecipherable manuscript: my sympathy and
my sincere thanks.

My friends and colleagues in the English Department at Hull
University as always provided a stimulating, pleasurable environment
in which to think and write. I would particularly like to thank the
Head of English, Rowlie Wymer, for his stalwart support and Angela
Leighton for being an unfailing source of positive advice and valuable
friendship. I am very grateful to the Faculty of Arts, particularly the
Dean, Dr Alan Best, and the Deputy Dean, Professor Peter Beardsell,

for their support for this book. The help provided in terms of teaching relief and financial support for research expenses was invaluable. Matthew Frost and Lauren McAllister of Manchester University Press are everything one could ask of academic editors: always supportive and, above all, patient. Brian McFarlane is also the friendliest and most helpful and constructive of co-editors.

The book could not have been written without the love, support and understanding of my wonderful family – my wife Lesley, and my children Natalie, Jessica and Joel. If writers, as they say, suffer for their art, writers' families suffer for their suffering. I am eternally grateful to them all for their tolerance of my absences, even (as my good friend Adrian would say) when I was present.

Much of the research for this book was done in Jack Clayton's summerhouse in Marlow. Whilst I was methodically working my way through his papers in a meticulously filed set of boxes, I could not but notice and absorb the contents and atmosphere of the room, which was adorned with framed and signed portraits from his casts and crews, plaques of his film awards, and, not least, a diploma for his first prize (out of a field of 171) in the Marlow Pigeon Race of 20 May 1991. On the table lay his collection of knives, the 1950s telephone out of *Memento Mori*, and copies of scripts, some of which had cigarette burns on them. (John Mortimer could recall seeing Jack, so absorbed in his work, absent-mindedly putting a cigarette out on himself.) The study was lined with an eclectic selection of books whose topics ranged from jazz to American Indian Art, from biographies of favourite collaborators, such as Truman Capote and Maggie Smith, to Bertrand Russell's *History of Western Philosophy* and a Freud Reader; from Zane Grey to George Orwell, Coward to Le Carré, *Middlemarch* to *The Manchurian Candidate*, and from Picasso to *Pigeons of the World*. For a music lover like myself, the collection of old records was fascinating: Dave Brubeck at Carnegie Hall, the Gerry Mulligan Quartet, Billie Holliday, Ella Fitzgerald and André Previn doing Gershwin, Dorati conducting *The Rite of Spring*, Ormandy's version of Sibelius's Symphony No. 2, Klemperer's account of Brahms's Second Symphony, David and Igor Oistrakh playing Bach and Vivaldi, Richter's version of Rachmaninov's Second Piano Concerto, a rare recording of the Beethoven Piano Concerto No. 3 by Glenn Gould, with Bernstein and the New York Philharmonic. Soundtrack collectors would have been enthralled by priceless recordings of the Delerue music for *The Lonely Passion of Judith Hearne* and, particularly, for *Our Mother's House*, a score which so floored Steven Spielberg that its traces are to be heard over the soundtrack of *The Color Purple*.

The privilege of being able to consult these materials in these surrounds was entirely due to the generosity of Clayton's widow, Haya Harareet Clayton. Filmgoers will know her as the beautiful actress who played the role of Esther opposite Charlton Heston's Ben-Hur in William Wyler's great film. In our first telephone conversation, she had told me that she and Jack had met at a pre-Oscar party on 4 April 1960, hosted by Laurence Harvey, when *Room at the Top* and *Ben-Hur* were in contention for the top awards. (Indeed, it was *Room at the Top* that prevented *Ben-Hur* from making a clean sweep of twelve awards from twelve nominations, for it was the British film that won the Oscar for best-adapted screenplay.) Jack had sent her a bouquet of roses the next day; a deeply loving relationship developed that was to endure for thirty five-years until Clayton's death in 1995. Whilst I have no doubt that Haya might disagree with some of my interpretations of the films, I am also sure that my memories of those afternoons will have coloured some of the writing. As we talked about him and his films, or discussed poetry (Haya is an extremely gifted poet) or listened to some of Georges Delerue's score for *Something Wicked This Way Comes*, which the Disney Organisation rejected and which Haya would hear with tears in her eyes, the spirit of Jack Clayton seemed very near. I arrived already with a devotion to the films. I came away with a deep affection for a man whom I never had the good fortune to meet. This book is dedicated to Haya: her company and kindness will be my most treasured memory of the writing of it.

I once came upon a friend of mine who had just finished reading Henry James's *The Portrait of a Lady* and was crying her eyes out. 'It's really sad, isn't it?' I said. 'It's not that,' she replied. 'I'm just so sorry it's ended.' I feel a bit like that on finishing the writing of this book. Needless to say, the errors and imperfections are all mine.

Introduction: lonely passions – the cinema of Jack Clayton

> Jack Clayton is out of fashion at the moment. Best remembered for *Room at the Top*, his incisive but impersonal craftsmanship almost counts against him in an age when directors have to be flamboyant projections of their own movies' obsessions. Clayton's time will come again. (Alexander Walker, *Hot Tickets*, 30 April 1998, p. 12)

> The British cinema that interests me is a cinema which produces great films – films which are masterpieces. (Peter Wollen, *Sight and Sound*, April 1998, p. 22)

> If you care for what you are doing more than your own life, you have to be ready to fight. (Jack Clayton, quoted in *The Great Gatsby* press book, April 1974)

Why write a book on the films of Jack Clayton? The answer is simple: I love them, and wanted to communicate and justify that feeling to an interested reading audience in the hope of reaching fellow Clayton admirers and of persuading others that there might be more in these films than meets the eye. Connected with that hope, then, is a conviction that the films are not as well known as they should be and, in some cases, not as highly esteemed as they deserve. These facts in turn have something to say about the state of British film culture, and how it has changed and developed over the forty years or so since Clayton began directing feature films. In one sense, the career seems to me a triumph in terms of the calibre of work he produced: not for nothing did Fred Zinnemann talk of him as a 'director's director ... greatly admired by colleagues and very much a member of our "Directors' Imaginary Society of Mutual Admiration"'.[1] In another sense, the career is a disappointment, particularly in relation to the comparatively meagre output (Clayton directed only nine films in forty years of film-making) but also in relation to its commercial and, in some cases, critical reception. But this too has much to tell us about what Christian Metz termed the machines of cinema – in this case the industrial and the writing machines.[2]

Why did Clayton make so few films? Why, except with the spectacular exception of *Room at the Top*, did they fail to find a large audience? Why did they generate the kind of criticism – sometimes adulatory but sometimes dismissive and even condescending – that they did? All these issues are addressed in this book. The answers might throw light on certain tendencies and developments within the film industry and of film criticism – the British film industry and film criticism in particular.

In discussing the films, I have attempted to pay due attention to the actors, writers, composers, editors, cameramen, sound recordists, designers, etc. who have all made invaluable contributions to this body of work. Clayton would have been the first to acknowledge the cinema as a collaborative medium and to pay tribute to his cast and crew (not to mention key personnel behind the scenes such as, for example, his indispensable script editor, Jeanie Sims, and his casting director, Irene Lamb, whom he credited for such triumphant casting coups as Simone Signoret in *Room at the Top* and Renée Asherson in *Memento Mori*). The regard was mutual. 'It would be hard to think of a director who inspired greater devotion from actors or crews,' Karel Reisz said of him (*Guardian*, 25 March 1995). A mock clapper board in his study signed by the whole crew of *The Great Gatsby* was dedicated simply to 'The Great Clayton'. No one seemed to doubt or question who was the governor on all these films, the main inspirational creative force. As Peter Finch said about his experience of working with Clayton on *The Pumpkin Eater*: 'He has his own absolutely vivid style as a director, which you could see after only three days' work'.[3] Clayton himself said that directing a film was the only form of dictatorship he approved of.

So it is puzzling that the word 'impersonal' crops up quite regularly in critical discussion of Clayton's work. In his grouping of directors in his seminal study of American cinema, Andrew Sarris (writing in 1968) consigned Clayton to the ignominious category of 'Strained Seriousness' – alongside other estimable directors, it must be said, such as Richard Brooks, Stanley Kubrick, Richard Lester, Sidney Lumet, Karel Reisz and Robert Rossen – and remarked that 'the only Clayton constant is impersonality but such studied impersonality seems out of date'.[4] Writing about Clayton a decade later, Roy Armes claimed that 'good intentions in no way compensate for lack of real passion or concern'.[5] Even the complimentary quote from Alexander Walker that heads this chapter talks of 'impersonal craftsmanship': admittedly, it is coupled with 'incisiveness' and Walker is contrasting such crafts-manship favourably with modern, modish self-indulgence, but there is still the ghost of an impression of a reticent stylist who is typically and predictably English in the restraint of his filmic personality.

Yet the idea of Clayton's work as, in Armes's phrase, 'lacking real passion' is hard to reconcile with what one knows of the man and his career. This is a man who could not take on a project unless he believed in it with every fibre of his being and loved all the characters: this was one of the principal reasons why his output was so small. Clayton was someone who felt so deeply about his work that he sometimes went on a film set with a knife strapped to his leg and who, for example, was so distraught when the shooting of *The Great Gatsby* was over that, rather than join the farewell party for cast and crew, smashed windows and pictures in a corridor of Pinewood in what he called an 'explosion of sorrow'. Film-making was never a chore or an entertainment: it was an all-consuming obsession, or nothing. 'Kid, you do have a temper don't you?' Clayton was told on his first meeting with John Huston, whom he rapidly came to revere; and it was from Huston that he learnt courage: 'stick by your guns and never compromise, regard-less of producers or money'.[6] Meticulously courteous with his cast and crew, he was famously ferocious with producers and the front office. In his *Guardian* obituary, Karel Reisz told the story of how

Clayton threw a chair at the producer of *Gatsby*, David Merrick, after a fierce row: the chair shattered, and the next day Clayton sent Merrick the bill – seemingly in no doubt where the blame lay. At the BAFTA memorial service for Clayton, his close friend the writer Mordecai Richler told of Clayton's immortal response to a producer who vowed never to work with him again: 'Yes, but how can I be sure you'll keep your word?'

Admittedly, it is one thing to have a passionate nature: it is quite another to translate that emotion onto the screen. I can only say that, in writing this book and in the process of recollecting the impact of the films, I have had to struggle against using unavoidable adjectives such as 'moving' or 'poignant' too often: far from being passionless, the films strike me as being emotionally overwhelming. I am aware that this might be saying as much about me as about Clayton; and there is something about the Clayton universe – this fearsomely fatherless zone, this exorcising through cinema of the most individual kind of a personal distress rooted in an unsettled childhood – to which I strongly relate and which has a very special resonance. But it is not that so much as his precise preparation of context and his supreme visual craftsmanship that make moments in his films so spine-tingling: like Pamela Franklin's haze of disillusionment at a key point in *Our Mother's House*; or the panic terror in Bob Hoskins's eyes during the clumsy last embrace in *The Lonely Passion of Judith Hearne*; or, particularly, that bone-chilling moment at the end of *The Innocents* when Deborah Kerr's governess throws her head back in wild abandon and screams 'Miles!' into the night air as she suddenly realises what she has done – or to borrow Henry James's wonderfully apt phrase, 'what it truly was that I held'.

Indeed, far from seeming impersonal, Clayton's films have always struck me as idiosyncratic to the point of quirkiness. How else to account for the almost Dickensian *Our Mother's House* at the height of the so-called 'Swingin' Sixties'? How else to explain his refusal to exploit his new-wave success with *Room at the Top* with other projects in the same vein and his defiance of any genre orthodoxy, which makes his films difficult to place (and arguably, sell)? Unlike, say, the producer/director partnership of Michael

Relph and Basil Dearden, who had a preference for a particular kind of film (the thriller with a social/moral conscience, like *The Blue Lamp* or *Victim*) but who would keep a continuity going by working on less congenial material, Clayton held no preference for any particular type of film and was unwilling and, I would say, constitutionally unable to make a film simply for the sake of it. His film credo, as expressed in the Spring 1959 issue of *Sight and Sound* (quoted at the beginning of Chapter 4) was an idealistic one. His films had aspirations, pretensions. This was not a director predictably English in the reticence and restraint of his filmic personality but one who in the climate of the 1960s seemed set to situate himself at the core of European art cinema. He used French composers on his soundtracks (Auric, Delerue) and even some of his films had a Gallic flavour, *The Innocents* stylistically evoking the Cocteau of *Beauty and the Beast* and *Our Mother's House* thematically recalling the Clément of *Jeux Interdits*. *The Pumpkin Eater* might have been unjustly pilloried for aspiring to Antonioniesque flights of alienation, but what other British films of the time were aiming so high? This was not anonymous so much as unorthodox, unclassifiable film-making.

The idea of anonymity is further belied by an underlying consistency of style and theme that suggests that, however varied the material, there is an individual vision that gave coherence and unity to the *oeuvre*. The 'found footage' film-makers Christophe Girardet and Matthias Müller have done a marvellous film essay on Hitchcock, *The Phoenix Tapes* (1999), that assembles a mosaic of the director's obsessions, repetitions, tics: one would love to let them loose on Clayton's imagery. Although Clayton made a religion, as he said, of not repeating himself, there is an insistent structuralist/auteurist line that can be traced through his works; there are certain features that are common to nearly all of them. One might mention, on a thematic level, the fascination with feminine feeling, with childhood innocence and experience, with issues of class: deeper beneath the surface, one notes a recurrent subtext of religious oppression and frequent tension between dream and reality. There are stylistic signatures such as the co-existence of past and present within the same frame; the counterpoint of sound and image; the frequent use of slow dissolves; and a visual emphasis on details such as hands, flowers, photographs, animals, rings. Far from the impersonal craftsmanship ascribed to him by Alexander Walker, however incisive he finds it, Clayton's work seems to me to justify more Otto Plaschkes's description of the director as a 'great stylist',[7] and one of the most visually distinctive directors of post-war British cinema. For those who know the style, the first five minutes of *Judith Hearne*, say, could not possibly have been directed by anyone else. Of course, a recognisable and distinctive style does not of itself guarantee quality or eminence, but it does surely challenge the notion of 'impersonality'.

In his aforementioned assessment of Clayton, the word Andrew Sarris used of his direction was 'academic'. It is an odd word to use of a man who was self-educated and who always claimed to make up in intuition for what he lacked in intelligence. (Clayton was being modest: anyone who has read through his working notes on a script could only marvel at his astute insights into narrative form.) 'Every project must find its appropriate style,' said Sarris disparagingly, articulating what he meant by Clayton's academicism and why he felt it was literal and wrong. Yet the strategy Sarris quotes so slightingly seems to me a perfectly laudable one and was precisely the approach of someone like John Huston, at once the most literary and yet one of the most individualistic of all great Hollywood directors. 'He had an unbelievably wonderful pictorial eye,' Clayton would say of Huston, and one suspects that when Huston lined up Clayton to take over the direction of *Under the Volcano* and *The Dead* in case his health failed him, Huston was repaying the compliment.

Clayton's pictorial eye has sometimes antagonised critics: they often take exception to some aspect of his *mise-en-scène*. *Sight and Sound* dislikes the shot of Anne Bancroft's feet during her walk through Harrods in *The Pumpkin Eater*, feeling it is visually too self-conscious and distracting; but does it not effectively convey in visual form the character's mental weariness, the burden of her progress, her low self-esteem (in the novel, the self-effacing Judith Hearne has a similar habit of looking down at her shoes), the inability/fear at that moment of squarely facing the world around her? The *Monthly Film Bulletin* has qualms about the veiled shot of Pamela Franklin at a key moment in *Our Mother's House*, just as the critic Janet Maslin guffaws at a reflected image of Gatsby and Daisy in the swimming pool during their modern-day romance in *The Great Gatsby*. In both cases, I believe these critics are wrong; I have offered a defence of these moments in discussing the films (see pp. 139 and 157). Neither seems to me the mistake of an 'impersonal director' but rather the instinctive decision of a film stylist who has an intuitive sense of where he wants the camera to be at a crucial dramatic moment.

If one is looking for a guide to what a director does, there is no better introduction than chapter 35 of John Huston's autobiography, *An Open Book*, which concisely distils a lifetime of screen direction experience into half a dozen pages of wisdom and expert advice. At one stage he contrasts the method of the conventional film-maker, whose way of covering a scene is through a full shot, followed by medium shots, close-ups, etc. from which the scene will later be assembled in the cutting room, with a less conventional approach where the director finds the one shot that serves as an introduction to the scene and allows the rest to flow naturally. 'There's a grammar to it,' Huston writes. 'Once you write your first declarative sentence, the narration flows.'[8] The key is to search out that first shot, he says, and sometimes it is not easy to find, particularly when you are surrounded by people; but without it you are lost. 'Look for something that has style and visual energy, something in keeping with your ideas for the picture as a whole.'[9] My view is that Clayton's approach to a scene was often similar to that, an approach picked up from Huston and applied imaginatively to his own work. Think, for example, of the under-the-table shot of the children's legs, some not touching the floor, which opens the scene of the reading of the will in *Our Mother's House*: how touchingly that conveys the sense of a situation too big for them to comprehend; how wittily it supplies a clue to Clayton's whole style for material which is, as he put it, 'slightly feet off the ground'.[10] Or think of the close-up of the huge and beautiful rose that opens the scene in *The Innocents* when the governess is first to see the ghost of Quint on the battlements. The scene's movement from beauty to apprehension is exquisitely plotted: the almost impossible largeness of the rose seems to correlate to a tendency in the governess for magnification of everything; and because roses in the film are subtly associated with the uncle, the shot can subliminally suggest the prominence of the uncle in the governess's mind at that point in the narrative, an idealised image that is then to be undercut, perverted and displaced by the misty, monstrous masculinity at the top of the tower. It is both visually imaginative and absolutely true to the spirit of the Henry James original.

All of Clayton's films have been adaptations and this has obscured perceptions of his originality. Because his work has been drawn exclusively from prior literary sources, he has been considered a respectful servant of his material rather than a creative personality in his own right. This is implied in Roy Armes's placement of Clayton in what he patronisingly termed 'a certain tradition of pseudo-serious British cinema'.[11] (There is nothing pseudo about Clayton's seriousness.) 'He is, in fact, a "literary director",' wrote Brian McFarlane, 'in general so respectful of his sources in rendering their surfaces that the films themselves sometimes seemed overwhelmed by their art direction.'[12] In his famous paper of 13 March 1969, 'British Cinema: The Unknown Cinema', for a British Film Institute seminar, Alan Lovell named the dominance of the literary tradition as one of the reasons for the British cinema's neglect and undervaluation. But again the comparison with Huston might be instructive here, where the basic literary material is reshaped into an individual filmic vision rather than the story simply being told in pictures. What is immediately striking about Clayton's choice of sources is its variety and eclecticism: from Gogol to Gloag, from Braine to Bradbury, from Fitzgerald to Spark, from Penelope Mortimer to Henry James. The fact that, within that variety, he has found material that speaks with especial meaning to him seems to make his work more personal rather than less. (He said he had never found an original screenplay that had had that effect.)

In a previous book, *Filming Literature* (1986), I have argued that great film adaptations of literature tend to have one or all of three characteristics: that they go for the spirit of the original; that they use the camera to interpret and not simply illustrate the text; and that there is some kind of creative empathy between the author of the original text and the director of the film. My own view is that Clayton's films are models of screen adaptation in this respect, giving a sense of the quality and character of the original but at the same time being deeply personal and having an underlying concept and approach that both enriches an understanding of the text and provides a stimulating piece of cinema in its own right. In conceptual and narrative terms, there are moments, I would argue, when the films actually improve on Spark, Fitzgerald, Mortimer, Bradbury, and when they certainly improve on Braine and Gloag. Also the complex literary sensibilities of F. Scott Fitzgerald, Henry James and Brian Moore have never been better served on film than by Clayton. Penelope Gilliat had a fine phrase for this when discussing *The Great Gatsby* in the pages of the *New Yorker* (11 April 1974): 'Clayton', she wrote, 'has a shapely comprehension of an author's intelligence'.

Something of this comprehension is evident in the opening of *The Lonely Passion of Judith Hearne*, which establishes characters and themes with masterly precision. The critic Brian McIlroy offers a fine analysis of this sequence, showing the way the opening suggests that, even from childhood, Judith is 'enslaved in institutions unsuited to her'[13] and how therefore the problems in her later life can be deduced from this introduction. The sequence is full of significant detail: the young Judith's dipping her hand in the holy water, which is to contrast so strikingly with the older Judith's angry gesture later in the film when her faith is crumbling; the aunt's gesture of holding Judith's hands tightly to her to stop her giggling, in what McIlroy calls a 'forced togetherness' that portends their relationship in adulthood; the shot of the tabernacle, followed by the dissolve to the adult Judith which again is a forewarning of her later crisis when she is to break down in church and try to pull open the tabernacle door. The details, then, are woven into a sequence that is both eloquent and evocative in its own right but also premonitory of, and crucial to, the narrative/

thematic thrust of the film. None of this is in the original novel: all of it is 'faithful' to the author's intentions but conceived in cinematic terms.

Why, then, the current unfashionability of Jack Clayton? And where does he fit in a profile of post-war British cinema? A descriptive label often given to him was 'maverick' – a term frequently applied to offbeat directors who give producers a hard time and whose orneriness often precludes any continuity to their career. Clayton's name has often been linked to other such British mavericks as Thorold Dickinson (for whom he worked on *Queen of Spades*), Alexander Mackendrick, Lindsay Anderson, Karel Reisz and Nicolas Roeg. Like these, Clayton was a talented, temperamental individualist who refused to be typecast or pigeonholed in an industry where commercial conformity is not simply the norm but vital for survival. Along with the other directors mentioned, Clayton was also affected by the cultural climate in which he was obliged to operate. In this regard, I would like to make one or two personal observations about the British film scene of the 1960s: that is, the period when Clayton's directing career began to develop.

Clayton had come to prominence with *Room at the Top*, around the time of the British 'Free Cinema' movement (involving directors like Reisz and Anderson) and immediately prior to the so-called British 'new-wave' films of the early 1960s from directors such as Tony Richardson and John Schlesinger. The impact of Clayton's film within that context is discussed in greater detail in Chapter 3 but it might be worth emphasising again that, with *Room at the Top*, Clayton had had neither the intention nor the desire to launch or associate himself with any 'new wave' or 'social realist' movement in British film. Also, after its success, he had no inclination to capitalise on it by making films in a similar vein. Indeed, I suspect the artistic achievement of *Room at the Top* took the producers, John and James Woolf, a little by surprise, as the rather lurid advertising of the film seemed to place it in the sensationalist melodrama category for which they were at that time better known. It was Clayton's direction that lifted the film onto a different plane and made it an unexpected trend-setter of a kind the critical establishment had been looking for. In some ways, *Room at the Top* is Clayton's least typical film whose reputation and popularity he sought to distance himself from: the reputation a bit misleading (Clayton was no angry young man) and the popularity a little excessive (he made other films equally, if not more, deserving of success). At the same time the many devout critical admirers of *Room at the Top* might have been a little dismayed at the direction Clayton's career was to take. He never achieved a comparable commercial success, and it was to be over thirty years before he achieved a comparable critical one.

Then there was the critical attitude to British cinema in the 1960s. For all the international prestige of *Room at the Top* and the films that followed in its wake, the new critical intelligentsia of the cinema had little time for anything British. This was the heyday of auteurism and, by the side of the big names of Europe and Hollywood, it was felt that British film had little to offer. The notorious May 1962 issue of the influential new magazine *Movie* classified British cinema in the manner of Sarris and Hollywood, and found only one English director, Seth Holt (and even he was born in Palestine), who qualified as 'talented'. Clayton was consigned to the 'Competent or Ambitious' category, which was marginally above 'The Rest'. In some ways, this set the intellectual tone of the debate about British film for the rest of the decade. It culminated in three symbolic events: in 1968, Tony Richardson's refusal to allow a trade screening for the British press for his new film, *The Charge of the Light Brigade*, in protest at the way his films had been treated;[14] in 1969, Alan Lovell's aforementioned description of British cinema as 'unknown', despite the fact that, at one stage during the decade, Britain had seemed the cinema capital of the world and had been attracting *cinéastes* of the calibre of Polanski, Truffaut and Antonioni; and in 1970, the critical drubbing handed out to British cinema's most honoured elder statesman, David Lean, for *Ryan's Daughter*, an experience that left Lean feeling ashamed and in a state of shock.[15]

In any book on British cinema these days it has become almost obligatory to quote Francois Truffaut's mischievous assertion that there is a certain 'incompatibility' between the terms 'Britain' and 'cinema',[16] and to take Truffaut to task for such a hostile and sweeping generalisation. Yet, when in 1998 I asked Nicolas Roeg about this comment (and Roeg had been photographing Truffaut's *Fahrenheit 451* round about the time Truffaut was expressing this opinion), he told me that, in his view, at the time he made the comment, Truffaut was right. There were no film schools to speak of in Britain. When Clayton was interviewed by the *Oxford Mail* (24 February 1962), he expressed the view that the British film industry 'suffered sadly from union restrictions on intake and from the lack of a proper film school: both made it very difficult to develop new talent'. Film was still considered inferior to theatre and literature. There was a lingering Leavisite educational hostility to film that took a long time to eradicate (has it ever entirely gone?), and from which people of my generation, who had an educational commitment to film, probably still bear the scars. Colin McArthur has written trenchantly about the educational context in which film teachers in this country had to operate at this time in his valuable British Film Institute monograph on *The Big Heat* (1992). My own most vivid memory from this period is proposing a course on film at a reputable educational institution and being greeted with derisive laughter from my head of department – a response all the more remarkable from a man who had hitherto reputedly laughed less often than Swift (who could only remember laughing three times in his entire life).

If cinema generally was having to fight for intellectual and educational respectability in this country, specifically *British* cinema was having to struggle even harder for recognition. It is not surprising then that British film-makers in this context might be prone to self-doubt; might wonder whether the work that they were doing was being properly appreciated; might wonder indeed if they were in the wrong profession. When talking of his association with Joseph Losey, which produced masterpieces like *The Servant* (1963), *King and Country* (1964) and *Accident* (1967), Dirk Bogarde would insist, emotionally, that 'we were doing it for Britain'[17] – the implication being that he and Losey were endeavouring to create art cinema in Britain of a standard that would rival their great contemporaries in Europe. But Bogarde's emotionalism when he said this always came over not only as patriotism but as exasperation – that is, they were doing it for Britain in spite of the British and whether the British cultural establishment wanted it or not.

Like John Schlesinger, Karel Reisz, Peter Yates and others, Clayton had looked to America in the 1970s to continue his career. The reason was fundamentally an economic one: the bottom had fallen out of British film production at the end of the 1960s anyway. But it is hard not to conclude that it was something to do with the cultural climate as well. It is one thing to be a prophet without honour in your own country, as Ken Russell used to say of Edward Elgar: it is even worse to be a prophet without profit in your own country, particularly in an industry as commercially oriented as cinema. But I would say that the problem for the British film-maker was as much to do with the critical as the commercial climate: the sense of not being valued. Critics such as Raymond Durgnat, Jeffrey Richards, Anthony Aldgate and Charles Barr were beginning to take up the cudgels on behalf of British film in the 1970s. A rather overlooked volume of *Framework* magazine (in its Winter 1978/79 issue) concentrated much of its attention on British cinema, pronouncing it 'ideologically fascinating' if not aesthetically challenging. But as late as the Autumn of 1977, Philip Simpson could still lament that, as far as film education went in this country, far more expeditions were being made to John Ford's Monument Valley and the Magic Factory than to Ealing Green.[18] Peter Harcourt's *Movies and Mythologies* (1977) quotes Raymond Durgnat's rebuke of British critics for failing to show the same level of aesthetic sympathy to English directors like Lindsay Anderson and Peter Watkins, even if they don't like what they have done, as they would to Jean-Luc Godard or even Sam Peckinpah. 'The standard of criticism in England is lower than what the English are doing creatively,' said Durgnat, 'and I think this has always been the case. England has always had a lot of first rate artists, but the critics have never actually fought for them.'[19] As an example of that, one need only cite the case of David Lean. In the 1999 British Film Institute survey of the hundred best British films ever made, Lean had no fewer than four in the top eleven and three in the first five. Yet, as I write, there has still not been a single critical volume written on the aesthetic achievement of his films by a British film academic. When Lean died in 1991, Philip French wrote an elegant obituary in the *Observer* (21 April 1991), concluding that Lean belonged in the company of such cinematic giants as John Ford, Ingmar Bergman and Akira Kurosawa, which is all very well except that I am sure Lean would have preferred reading that when he was alive, and particularly round about the time of the reviews of *Ryan's Daughter.*

Which brings me back to Jack Clayton, the problematic progress of his career and where to place him in the context, or tradition, of British film. I think it is clear from what I have said why someone of Clayton's maverick individualist temperament, with a penchant for literary subjects with a deceptively personal slant, would find it difficult to make headway within a conformist industry and a hostile critical and cultural climate. A further aggravation would be that Clayton was consistently making, or aspiring to make, 'arthouse' films in a country with a limited arthouse outlet (so the problem is also one of distribution and exhibition) and that did not really believe in film as an art form, and within a national cinema that (as Dirk Bogarde recognised) even critics who did believe in film as an art form felt was beyond its capabilities. It became easy therefore to attack Clayton for 'academicism' or 'pretentiousness' or 'pseudo-seriousness' or any other synonym that comes to hand when a British critic wants to take a British film-maker to task for attempting to be as ambitious as his European counterparts. In some ways, in claiming Clayton as temperamentally an 'arthouse' director, I am conscious of making more serious claims for him than he might have made for himself: I think he was making his films for popular consumption and not for an arthouse elite. At the same time the kind of films he made were not, for the most part, those that mass audiences attend. *Room at the Top* might be the exception that proves the rule, but that film tapped providentially into the shifting tastes of the times, whereas in a film like *Something Wicked This Way Comes* there is a real disjunction between the Clayton style and the Disney expectation and ethic:

small wonder Clayton found the experience of making it so traumatic.

In fact, in trying to define the Clayton style, I was surprised to find how closely it corresponds in many respects to David Bordwell's classic formulation of the mode of discourse of the art film.[20] Bordwell was writing mainly of what one might call the modernist masters of European cinema – Federico Fellini, Michelangelo Antonioni, Jean-Luc Godard, Ingmar Bergman, among others – in their 1960s heyday and making some shrewd generalisations about their cinematic characteristics. Yet nearly everything he says about their cinema can be applied to Clayton's cinema, particularly up to and including *The Pumpkin Eater*. For example, he itemises 'realism', 'authorial expressivity' and 'eroticism' as vital dimensions of art cinema's mode of practice: all of these are strongly present in, say, *Room at the Top* and *The Pumpkin Eater*. Bordwell writes of narratives that drift rather than are goal-oriented, that are dissections of feeling and emphasise reaction more than action, and have a hero or heroine 'shuddering on the edge of breakdown'. Again that can be applied directly to Clayton's films such as *The Innocents*, *The Pumpkin Eater* and *The Lonely Passion of Judith Hearne*. Bordwell also defines one of the characteristics of art film as 'a commitment to both objective and subjective verisimilitude': in some ways one could say that this is one of the defining features of Clayton's style. One sees it, for example, in the shift from an objective observation of Judith Hearne's drinking to a spinning camera movement that simulates her drunken dizziness and loss of control; or in Jo Armitage's walk through Harrods in *The Pumpkin Eater* – her consciousness of her feet, and the subjective blurring of vision immediately prior to uncontrolled weeping and breakdown. 'Deviations from the classical canon,' writes Bordwell, 'an unusual angle, a stressed bit of cutting, a prohibited camera movement, an unrealistic shift in light or setting – in short, any breakdown of the motivation of cinematic space and time by cause effect logic – can be read as "authorial commentary".'[21] As we have discussed already, these are often the most controversial aspects of Clayton's *mise-en-scène* (the close-up of James Mason's mouth in *The Pumpkin Eater*, for instance, is either aesthetically expressive or authorially intrusive, according to taste), but they are vital to his style. He is not aiming for an invisible naturalism: the director's role, in his films, is a consciously expressive, editorialising one.

A final point Bordwell makes on the art cinema's mode of practice is the importance of 'ambiguity' and an open ending that leaves an audience thinking. Again the applicability to Clayton seems evident: *The Innocents* is one of cinema's key texts of ambiguity, and Clayton's endings – from *Room at the Top* to *Judith Hearne* – are classically 'open'. It is not until *Memento Mori* that he manages a 'happy' ending in his films (though there again, the very last shot after the end titles pulls you up with a start): the others, like those of a director he much admired, Fred Zinnemann, end not with closure but with a question mark or a dying fall.

The fact that Clayton's films fit Bordwell's paradigm of the art film is one explanation, I suppose, why producers had difficulty with him and why mainstream cinema found his work hard to place and assimilate. The fit is not simply a generic one, however: it is because Clayton was, in my view, a film artist. The case I make for Clayton in this book is finally, and primarily, an aesthetic one. This might antagonise some readers, and I am not unaware of the dangers of talk of 'great art' and 'masterpieces' against an intellectual/theoretical/cultural/critical background that could cite in opposition the 'death of the author', the industrial constraints of the film industry, Clayton's dependence on literary sources, accusations of cultural elitism, and much else besides. I would entirely endorse Richard Dyer's assertion in his characteristically astute introduction to the *Oxford Guide to Film Studies* that

> the aesthetic and cultural cannot stand in opposition. The aesthetic dimension never exists apart from how it is conceptualized, how it is socially practised, how it is received ... Equally, the cultural study of film must always understand that it is studying film, which has its own specificity, its own pleasures, its own way of doing things that cannot be reduced to ideological formulations.[22]

Nevertheless, if there is one piece of recent film criticism that has thrilled me more than any other, it is the entirely unexpected conclusion that Peter Wollen wrote for his *Sight and Sound* article on the 'spiv' cycle of late 1940s British cinema:

> As I read through copious new accounts of British studios or genres or periods or representations of gender and national identity, I begin to wonder where aesthetics fits into the agenda of research and rediscovery. Perhaps the point has come when we need to step back for a moment and make some broad judgements about British cinema, to look at it again as an art form. Which are the films that really count, the films we wouldn't mind seeing again and again? ... The British cinema that interests me is a cinema which produces great films – films which are master-pieces.[23]

On hearing Leonard Bernstein's recording of Mahler's First Symphony with the Concertgebouw, the record critic Edward Seckerson said he had been waiting for this performance for twenty years; I have been waiting for a statement like Peter Wollen's for thirty years. (It has all the more impact, of course, because Wollen's brilliant text of 1969, *Signs and Meaning in the Cinema*, had done as much as any other book to send film studies spinning away from aesthetics and towards semiotics, ideology, psychoanalysis, politics, theory of representation, and the like). Even in the invaluable re-evaluation of the British cinema that has taken place over the last two decades, the aesthetic case has been tentatively handled. But it is in that spirit that this study of Clayton is offered. How the films came to be made, how they were appreciated, the industrial and cultural context of their production and distribution, where Clayton fits in British cinema, how characteristic or idiosyncratic he is compared with his peers: all these and more, I trust, will figure in the argument. But the central thrust of the argument is that, for any person who cares about the art of the cinema, these films deserve attention.

There is one final thing. In describing Clayton as 'a great stylist' in his tribute in *Direct*, Otto Plaschkes crucially added that Clayton 'was much more than that. He was a great humanist, something much rarer ... It showed in his work, it showed in his eyes'. Where that humanity came from in Clayton would be hard to pinpoint: his 'making good' after a troubled childhood, his experience in the Second World War, his recovery from a serious stroke. But I agree entirely with Plaschkes that it showed in his work. Clayton's films are beautiful aesthetic constructs but what really touches you about them is their sense of human dignity. They pay tribute to the courage with which ordinary people live their lives, often in adversity. In *Something Wicked This Way Comes*, Jason Robards's Mr Halloway talks at one stage of the 'soul's midnight' and that is what Clayton explored in many of his characters, from David Kossoff's haunted tailor in *The Bespoke Overcoat* to Maggie Smith's Catholic in crisis, Judith Hearne. These characters endure. As Anne Bancroft was to say of Clayton (and it is a key observation to which I will return), he did not make films about larger-than-life heroes but about the small victories of unheroic people – 'a tougher but higher aspiration', as she put it. Defining the experience of a Clayton film, I would cite George Eliot's view of the *moral* purpose of all art: that it enlarges human sympathies. This quality is also present in the Clayton short story 'The Enchantment' with which the book closes – a story which, in its simple directness and compassion, calls to mind the 'social sympathy' of the great Russian realist Gogol, from whom Clayton's directing career, as it were, began.

Notes

1 Quoted in the programme accompanying the retrospective of Clayton's work at the National Gallery of Art, Washington, DC, 9–23 September 1998.
2 See Christian Metz, 'The Imaginery Signifier', *Screen*, Vol. 16, No. 2, Summer 1975, pp. 14–76.
3 *Films and Filming*, June 1964, p. 7.
4 Andrew Sarris, *The American Cinema: Directors and Directions, 1929–1968* (New York, E. P. Dutton & Co., 1968), p. 191.
5 Roy Armes, *A Critical History of British Cinema* (London, Secker & Warburg, 1978), p. 244.
6 Lawrence Grobel, *The Hustons* (London, Bloomsbury, 1990), p. 405.
7 Otto Plaschkes, 'Jack Clayton Remembered', *Direct*, Summer 1995, p. 15.
8 John Huston, *An Open Book* (London and Basingstoke, Macmillan, 1981), p. 363.
9 *Ibid.*, p. 366.

10 *Films and Filming*, April 1974, p. 12.

11 Armes, *Critical History*, p. 248.

12 Brian McFarlane, 'A Literary Cinema: British Films and British Novels', in *All Our Yesterdays: Ninety Years of British Cinema*, ed. by Charles Barr (London, BFI Publishing, 1986), p. 137.

13 Brian McIlroy, 'Tackling Aloneness: Jack Clayton's *The Lonely Passion of Judith Hearne*', *Literature/Film Quarterly*, Vol. 21, No. 1, 1993, p. 34.

14 Tony Richardson explains his reasons for his action, and describes the reaction, in his autobiography, *Long Distance Runner: A Memoir* (London, Faber & Faber, 1993), p. 200. For a lively response to Richardson's action, see *Films and Filming*, June 1968, p. 18.

15 See Kevin Brownlow's *David Lean* (London, Faber & Faber, 1997), p. 588.

16 *Hitchcock by Francois Truffaut* (London, Secker & Warburg, 1968), p. 100.

17 Interview with Margaret Hinxman, *Sunday Telegraph*, 22 February 1970. Quoted in the booklet on Dirk Bogarde for the John Player Lecture Series, 8 November 1970.

18 Philip Simpson, 'Directions to Ealing', *Screen Education*, No. 24, Autumn 1977, p. 5.

19 See 'Hollywood England – The British Cinema in Search of Itself', in Peter Harcourt, *Movies and Mythologies* (Toronto, Toronto Canadian Broadcasting Corporation, 1977), p. 106.

20 David Bordwell, 'The Art Cinema as a Mode of Film Practice', in *Film Criticism*, Vol. 4, No. 1, 1979. Repr. *Film Theory and Criticism: Introductory Readings*, 5th edn, ed. Leo Braudy and Marshall Cohen (Oxford, Oxford University Press, 1999), pp. 716–24.

21 Bordwell, 'Art Cinema as a Mode of Film Practice', p. 720.

22 Richard Dyer, 'Introduction to Film Studies', in the *Oxford Guide to Film Studies*, ed. by John Hill and Pamela Church Gibson (Oxford, Oxford University Press, 1998), p. 9.

23 Peter Wollen, 'Riff-Raff Realism', *Sight and Sound*, April 1998, pp. 18–22.

Early career: 2
Naples is a Battlefield (1944);
The Bespoke Overcoat (1955)

Jack himself had never been to school. He grew up not knowing a father, never settled in one place for long, in the company of pets and nannies. (Karel Reisz, *Guardian*, 25 March 1995)

I was about this tall when I wrote an embarrassingly amateurish letter to Alexander Korda and, to my amazement was granted an interview. He was about 6 foot 4 and sat behind the biggest desk I've ever seen. After talking who knows what gibberish to his questions, I walked out very proud. I went home and said to my mother, 'I have been appointed as third assistant director'. (Jack Clayton, *The Daily Breeze*, 30 December 1987)

Jack Clayton was born in Brighton on 1 March 1921. Brought up by his mother and not knowing his father, he had an unsettled, solitary childhood. Karel Reisz always thought that *The Innocents*, an adaptation of Henry James's *The Turn of the Screw*, was the perfect subject for Clayton, precisely because he would understand so acutely the feelings of the young boy Miles who finds the adult world so frightening and untrustworthy. Without wishing to turn Clayton's films into disguised autobiographical statements, I would add that, as will be explored later, there is a conspicuous absence of father figures in them, and the family set-ups are invariably odd or dysfunctional in some way, with a missing parent figure (generally a father) and a proliferation of aunts and uncles who may or may not be supportive. If Graham Greene felt that childhood was the 'bank balance' of the writer (BBC *Arena* documentary, January 1993) and Dennis Potter thought that 'for any writer the first fourteen years of his or her life are the crucible, no matter what you do' (Channel 4 interview with Melvyn Bragg, 5 April 1994), I also believe that Clayton's childhood was crucial to the formation of his artistic personality and a vital determinant in his choice of film subject.

His early interests, it seems, were photography and skating: indeed, at one stage it was thought he had a good chance of being picked for the skating Olympics, but the interruption of war put an end to that ambition. (When he returned to England after the war, one of the first things he did was to buy a new pair of skates and try them out on Richmond ice rink, but after two circuits, he realised he had lost the skill and edge that before might have made him a champion.) His schooling was erratic and intermittent; the one time he did complete a term was at the Arnold House School, St John's Wood, in the summer of 1932, and his school report is sufficiently interesting and adulatory to warrant quoting in full:

Summer Term 1932

Name	*John Clayton*
Form	*III Arnold House School, St John's Wood*
	No. of boys in form: 10
Reading	*Very good*
Writing	*2nd Excellent*
Spelling	*75% Very good*
English Literature	*He enjoys books and all they contain.*
Essay	*1st 81% Excellent*
Verse Speaking	*Good and distinct*
History	*78% Keen and always interested. He has done a good term's work.*
Geography	*Very good. He is both interested and interesting.*
Arithmetic	*Has worked hard and done well.*
Algebra Geometry	*2nd 86% Most encouraging work.*
French	*He has worked really hard and made definite progress.*
Latin	*Has done very well in a subject in which he is much below standard.*
Sports	*A neat high jumper. He is very keen.*

Elementary Science	*A keen and very interested worker.*
Class Singing	*Has reached a high standard of vocal technique. Enthusiastic, acquiring a wide appreciation of the subject.*
Games	*Most promising wicket-keeper. Very keen.*
Scripture History	*Very good indeed.*
The Head's Remarks	*Excellent for his first term. An intelligent and cheerful boy – a pleasure to have in a form.* A.M. Hanson

Next term will begin on Tuesday 20th September 1932

Any educationalist would recognise this as a report on a student with a real hunger and aptitude for learning. If Clayton had followed a conventional educational pathway, Haya told me, he would probably have been a biologist or botanist. But he never returned to the school.

By his own account, he was a voracious reader in his youth, and in interviews he would always cite three novels that had a profound impact on him: Henry James's *The Turn of the Screw*, F. Scott Fitzgerald's *The Great Gatsby* and Horace McCoy's *They Shoot Horses, Don't They?* It might be more than coincidence that he was to film two of these novels and have the opportunity of filming the third (see Chapter 10 for an account of what happened to *They Shoot Horses, Don't They?*). At the age of 12 he appeared on the West End stage in a production of Carl Zuckmayer's *The Golden Toy* at the Coliseum, Charing Cross Road, in February 1934. Presumably his mother must have been instrumental in landing him this role; and Maggie Smith always felt that the experience gave him an insight into the handling of actors which was to stand him in good stead in later years. His co-stars included Peggy Ashcroft, Ernest Thesiger, Wendy Toye (later to become a fine film director in her own right, of course) and Wilfrid Lawson, who was to play Joe Lampton's uncle in *Room at the Top*.

By this time, however, Clayton had set his sights on getting a job in films. Having run away from school three times, he was told by his mother that if he landed a job with Alexander Korda's London Films at Denham studio (not far from where they were living at the time), she would not send him back to school. After the interview with Korda (see epigraph), he was offered a job as third assistant director. It sounded grand but basically consisted of making tea, running errands, buying biscuits and calling the artistes when they were needed on the set. It was in this latter capacity that he first met Deborah Kerr when she was making her screen début in Gabriel Pascal's film of G. B. Shaw's *Major Barbara* (1941); twenty years on, Clayton would direct her in what is arguably her greatest screen performance, as the governess in *The Innocents*. He was to work in a similar capacity with such directors as Victor Seastrom (on a 1937 swashbuckler, *Under the Red Robe*) and Michael Powell (on *The Spy in Black* in 1939). He was also the co-ordinating second assistant director on all three shooting units of Korda's classic, *The Thief of Baghdad* (1940).

After volunteering for the Royal Air Force in 1940 and being recruited as a flight mechanic, he was assigned to the RAF Film Unit in the capacity of cameraman, editor and director, and eventually became a commanding officer. He directed one film during that time, *Naples is a Battlefield* for the Ministry of Information. After the war, he was an assistant director on Anthony Asquith's film version of a Terence Rattigan play, *While the Sun Shines* (1946); the production manager on Korda's film version of Oscar Wilde's *An Ideal Husband* (1947); and the second unit director on Gordon Parry's *Bond Street* (1948). However, his most interesting project of the late 1940s was undoubtedly as associate producer on Thorold Dickinson's film version of the Pushkin story, *The Queen of Spades* (1948). Dickinson's evocation of the Russian atmosphere and, in particular, his use of suspenseful soundtrack to suggest ghostly visitation undoubtedly had an influence on Clayton's style in both *The Bespoke Overcoat* and *The Innocents*. (He was also to use Dickinson's composer, Georges Auric, for both films.) 'One reel of it is as good as anything you could ever see,' Clayton told Brian McFarlane;[1] I feel sure he was referring to the sequence when Anton Walbrook's Herman is being tormented by some sinister supernatural threat, a scene analysed in detail in Karel Reisz's classic text *The Technique of Film Editing* (1953).[2]

The turning point in Clayton's career came in the 1950s, when the brothers John and James Woolf, who owned Romulus Films, were looking for a good production manager and associate producer for their new film, *Moulin Rouge* (1952), to be directed by John Huston. Clayton and Huston got on like a house on fire, and Clayton was to be associate producer (and uncredited supervising film editor) on Huston's next film, the spoof thriller *Beat the Devil* (1954). Huston then offered Clayton the tempting opportunity to be producer on his next four films, but ironically, it was Huston more than anyone who had given Clayton the taste for direction. With some sadness Clayton turned down the offer in favour of the opportunity to direct *The Bespoke Overcoat* (1955) for the Woolfs. When the film won awards and was a success on the festival circuit and after Clayton had served an agreed two more years for the Woolfs in a production/administrative capacity (his part of the bargain for being allowed to direct), the Woolfs offered him the chance of directing his first feature, *Room at the Top* (1959). The rest, as they say, is history.

It would be unwise to scrutinise Clayton's production credits too closely for clues to his subsequent directing career. As he told Gordon Gow, 'I've always been a good organiser and being an associate producer is basically that. I didn't care if the film was bad because I didn't really want to make it … But I always had a great kick out of doing the very best that I could personally do with the job'.[3] Generally the connection between Clayton's production experience and the films he went on to direct has more to do with continuity of technical personnel than with, say, continuity of theme. Huston's script editor on *Moulin Rouge* and *Beat the Devil*, Jeanie Sims, was to become Clayton's script editor on all his films; the editor of the Huston films, Ralph Kemplen, was to edit *The Bespoke Overcoat* and *Room at the Top*; the camera operator on *Beat the Devil*, Freddie Francis, was to be Clayton's director of photography on *Room at the Top* and *The Innocents* (which I will recklessly declare as the finest piece of black and white cinematography ever seen in a British film). In *Moulin Rouge*, in the scene where Toulouse Lautrec (Jose Ferrer) and Maria (Colette Marchand) have their final argument and he calls after her unavailingly as she disappears into the night, composer Georges Auric uses a musical motif that will appear only once in the score but which would reappear as the main theme of *The Bespoke Overcoat*. Huston's film was photographed by Oswald Morris, who would be Clayton's cameraman on *The Pumpkin Eater*; and, incidentally the important role of 'La Goulue' in *Moulin Rouge* was played, and superbly (particularly in her last scene of drunken reverie about her former glory and fame), by Katherine Kath, who was at that time married to Clayton.[4] In *I am a Camera* (1955), a surprisingly leaden comedy given the poise of director Henry Cornelius's work on previous films such as *Passport to Pimlico* (1949) and *Genevieve* (1953) and also given his knowledge of the milieu through his association with Max Reinhardt in 1930s Berlin, there are few laughs but one line that startlingly looks ahead to Clayton's *Gatsby*: 'penniless people', says the narrator, 'should avoid contact with the rich'. In *Beat the Devil*, one of that film's many in-jokes is that Bernard Lee plays a police inspector called Jack Clayton.

These are all incidental connections with Clayton's subsequent directing career. However, the case of *The Story of Esther Costello* (1957), which Clayton produced, is rather more intriguing. According to Otto Plaschkes, who was the third assistant director on the film, when the shooting had finished and star (Joan Crawford) and director (David Miller) had returned to America, it was found necessary to shoot some additional scenes with Heather Sears (as Esther) and Rossano Brazzi (as Carlo Landi). 'Jack directed these himself', Plaschkes wrote, 'and suddenly one became aware of what directing was about: a magisterial but very human relationship with the actors, an air of easy but complete authority on the set and a quite brilliant camera technique. Watching David Miller and Jack Clayton directing the same film was like going from a clapped out old Mini to a Lamborghini.'[5] What is fascinating about this account is that it suggests that Clayton, and not Miller, was responsible for what is incontestably the film's most powerful scene: the rape of Esther by Landi which, because of the shock, has the effect of restoring Esther's sight and speech. (It is almost an anticipation of the similar situation in Dennis Potter's *Brimstone and Treacle*.) It is noticeable that the scene is in a different style and on a different level of intensity from the rest of the film, and it does have something of the look and feel of a Clayton scene, with its careful preparation of atmosphere (the violent storm outside), the emphatic visual detail (the lingering shot of the Braille manuscript), the intensifying camera angle (the low-angle shot of Landi's kiss) and the visual symbolism (the shutter being blown violently open at the point of rape). It also has that shift from objective to subjective visual presentation mentioned in the introduction as one of Clayton's particular stylistic signatures – in this case represented by a marked heightening of the soundtrack and a visual graininess to suggest the return of Esther's hearing and her sight. Even the theme of the traumatic shock that both triggers and then unlocks a heroine's silence seems to prefigure *Silence*, the film which Clayton laboured to make in the 1970s until its last-minute cancellation. As another of these strange coincidences, one might mention the comment about the media circus surrounding the heroine in *Esther Costello* that is made by the newspaperman played by Sid James. 'The biggest thing since *Ben-Hur*,' he says, anticipating a film that was to play a major part in Clayton's life, since it was to star his future partner, Haya Harareet, and was to be the main Oscar competitor against his own *Room at the Top*, the sensational début feature film that was to make his name. In fact, although *Room at the Top* was his first feature, Clayton had earlier directed two short films discussed below.

Naples is a Battlefield (1944)

> I was never aware at the time of the awful miseries or, in fact, terrors of war. One was always prepared, one thought death was almost inevitable.
>
> [...]
>
> I was very young when I started with the R.A.F. and so many of my lovely friends died and for some reason I didn't die. It rather troubled me at the time. I felt guilty. (Jack Clayton, *The Stage and Television Today*, 2 April 1992, p. 20)

Assigned to the RAF Film Unit in 1941, Clayton's sole experience as director came as a result of his arrival in Naples at the time of the Allied liberation and his idea to make a film of the experience. He shot what he described as 'a good three quarters' of the material, which was then edited in England by another member of the RAF Film Unit, Peter Bayliss, and subsequently released as a Ministry of Information film.

Lasting for thirteen minutes, *Naples is a Battlefield* gives a documentary account of the wartime destruction of the city of Naples and then its reconstruction, which symbolises the role of the United Nations as an agency charged with the responsibility for rebuilding (both physically and politically) post-war Europe. The first part of the film shows the destruction resulting from what the narration calls 'Mussolini's war' wreaked both by the Allies, who had 'bombed everything that enabled the enemy to carry on the war', and by the Nazis, who, when forced to evacuate the city, laid waste everything they thought might give succour to their adversaries. Thus, when the armies of liberation entered Naples on 1 October 1943 they found a city with no power, gas or water and, for a lot of the population, no homes. The film creates a sense of dramatic anti-climax here: the expected triumphal entry is muted (perhaps as a reminder that most Italians had supported the Fascists during the war) and what greets the soldiers is a situation of chaos, the new enemies being disease, famine and plague.

Prior to their evacuation the Germans had booby-trapped the city, and the camera is in place to capture the terrible event of 7 October when the post office was suddenly blown up, the hidden bomb killing a hundred people and injuring many others. There are brief, distressing shots of the dead and injured, but the task of restoring the city is promptly renewed and music and editing quicken in tempo to match the resurgence of energy and hope. A shot of a gushing water pipe appears like a purification of an earlier image of diseased water from the sewers that had been causing typhoid. The film concludes with shots of the people in a city that, battling hard against starvation and poverty, is now slowly coming back to life and tasting freedom.

Technically the film is very accomplished, edited with a sensitivity to pace and rhythm. The music, as Cocteau used to say of all good film music, seems simultaneously to drive the film forward and to be driven forward by the film. The raw photography prefigures post-war neo-realism, where Italian film-makers like Rossellini and De Sica will explore the social consequences of the war and echo the comment made at the end of Clayton's documentary: that this rebuilding process is only a beginning. (One is reminded of the tentative return of the children to the city that movingly concludes *Rome – Open City*, shot immediately after the Allies had liberated Rome.) The more overtly dramatic moments are effectively timed: for example, the shock cut to the bomb explosion at the post office is prefaced by a terse narration saying that 'the Nazis had not yet finished with Naples', and there is a suspenseful montage of still shots of the silent city prior to the switching on of the power supply, an action which risked triggering another Nazi booby trap.

Naples is a Battlefield is a film that occasionally elicits a high level of emotional involvement but is also, in some ways, remarkably objective. This is no jingoistic polemic and it has something of the dignified restraint of the great war documentaries of Wyler and Huston: it seeks neither to glorify nor demonise. The Allies are referred to throughout as 'they'. The film does not insist on the fact that Italians had supported a Fascist regime, which might impinge on an audience's sympathies. Although made by a British crew, it does not stress the role of the British over its allies in this programme of recovery. There is even latent irony in some of the visual and verbal information. For example, the film clearly senses the faint absurdity of the Allies' arrival to rebuild a city they had spent part of the early years of the war destroying. Even the commentary notes that the supplies now coming in to Naples are food and munitions 'to fight the war and to feed Naples': that is, supplies needed simultaneously for peace and war, renewal and destruction. In addition to its unusual objectivity and irony, the documentary is also modest about its own achievement. A report lodged in the Imperial War Museum describes the sequence of the post office bombing as 'one of the masterpieces of on-the-spot motion picture photography' and suggests that this 'might very well have been played up as such to a great extent'.[6] One suspects, though, that Clayton would have been horrified at the prospect of 'playing up' so tragic an event as a technical *tour de force*.

Tested on selected audiences in New York, Chicago and San Francisco, *Naples is a Battlefield* drew a very positive response. Negative comments were relatively minor: some confusion about the passage of time in the film; complaints about the lack of political perspective, notably the absence of any reference to Italy's role in the war (though this may well have been a deliberate elision); and occasional comments that some moments look 'staged' (like the tense grouping of shots before the power is turned on), or unduly manipulative (the shot of the dead child amidst the rubble of the post office bombing) in a way that undercuts the documentary realism. The overwhelming impression conveyed is that the film succeeds through not overstating its case; that its covert propagandist purpose to encourage home-front sacrifice for the rebuilding of cities such as Naples is achieved; and that a moving and convincing picture is conveyed of the magnitude of the work of reconstruction.

It would be wrong to draw many conclusions about Clayton's subsequent development from a film made within such tight constraints of budget, circumstance and purpose. Perhaps one can say that the film's impressive professional finish is an augury of Clayton's future technical skill. As this film foretells, his work will remain rooted in the tradition of realism – but as a starting point, not as an end in itself. More significantly, this documentary's unstrident humanity (one notices, for example, the shots of black American soldiers as part of the liberating forces) will be a feature of Clayton's work throughout his career. *Room at the Top* will contain some interesting reflections on the war but within the context of that film's observations of class conflict and changing social stratification.

Maybe the epigraph gives the largest clue to a future aspect of Clayton's work: the omnipresence of death. Whether the war experience alone is responsible for that is impossible to say, but it is striking, for a director who never worked in the most violent film genres, how often death scenes occur and are given great visual, thematic and/or structural prominence. One thinks of the burial that opens *The Bespoke Overcoat*; the shocking off-screen death of Alice in *Room at the Top*; the traumatic death of Miles that closes *The Innocents*; the death of Jo's father in *The Pumpkin Eater*; the death of the mother that opens *Our Mother's House* and the killing of the father that closes it; the murder and suicide that conclude *The Great Gatsby*. Small wonder that in Clayton's last film, Death will not simply be prominent but the leading character.

The Bespoke Overcoat (1955)

> The theme seemed to offer wonderful opportunities to express the strength of the simple friendship between its two main characters and presented an interesting problem in its use of fact and fantasy in the telling of the story. We decided to try and blend these two contrasting elements by treating them with absolute realism. (Jack Clayton, *Films and Filming*, February 1956, p. 16)

First published in 1842, Nicolai Gogol's *The Overcoat* is acknow-ledged as one of the first great texts of 'social sympathy' in Russian literature, having an enormous influence on Dostoevsky ('We have all come from under *The Overcoat*,' he is reputed as saying) and on later Soviet artists. It had been famously filmed in 1926 by Grigori Kozintsev and Leonid Trauberg as the first production of the company they had founded, FEKS (Factory of the Eccentric Actor). Curiously, in addition to Clayton's, there were three film versions of the tale in the 1950s: *La Manteau* (1951), co-directed by and starring the great mime artist Marcel Marceau; Alberto Lattuada's *Il Cappotto – The Overcoat* (1952), co-scripted by Cesare Zavattini and modernised as a neo-realist fantasy set in a village in northern Italy; and a version directed by the renowned Soviet actor Alexei Batalov, *Shinel – The Overcoat* (1959), which was a more faithful adaptation of Gogol in terms of setting and period. Never-theless, it would be fair to say that they were all upstaged by Clayton's short film, which won extravagant praise from critics across the world (in the *Brisbane Mail* of 16 June 1957, Joyce Stirling called it 'the best piece of film-making I've seen in a lifetime of going to pictures') and was to win a Hollywood Oscar and British Academy Award as best short film as well as a major prize at the 1956 Venice Film Festival. To this day, *The Bespoke Overcoat* remains one of the finest examples of British short film-making.

It began life as a one-act play by Wolf Mankowitz that was first performed at the Arts Theatre, London in 1953, with David Kossoff and Alfie Bass in the leading roles. It was subsequently broadcast with great success twice on live television. At Clayton's BAFTA memorial service in 1996, Kossoff recalled that when Carol Reed's *A Kid for Two Farthings* (also scripted by Mankowitz and starring Kossoff) was shown at Cannes in 1954, the producer John Woolf got a little tipsy one night and promised Kossoff that if *Kid* showed a profit, he would use it to help finance a film of *Bespoke Overcoat*. It did make a profit and the promise was kept.

Who to direct? Clayton had been associate producer on John and James Woolf's productions for John Huston, *Moulin Rouge* and *Beat the Devil*, and had intimated his desire to direct. This seemed an ideal project on which to cut his teeth. It was a modest financial undertaking (the total budget came to just £5,263), though, as Clayton was later to observe, this could be one of the problems of the short-story film: a director was expected to make a film about one third of the length of an average feature film with about one thirtieth of the budget. Hence the film was shot quickly, for the most part in a converted chapel in Euston Road. After a successful début screening at the 1955 Edinburgh Film Festival (with characteristic courtesy, Clayton was to send thankyou letters to critics Dilys Powell of the *Sunday Times*, Roy Nash of *The Star* and S. Campbell Dixon of the *Sunday Telegraph* for their support of the film), *The Bespoke Overcoat* found a home at the Curzon cinema in the West End supporting Fellini's *La Strada* (1954) and running for over a year. 'A good film at the Curzon, *La Strada*, has been joined by a better one', commented the *New Statesman* (10 December 1955) provocatively. It was later given a general release supporting Vincente Minnelli's *Tea and Sympathy* (1956). It was an auspicious launch to Clayton's career for a modest film that, in retrospect, looks both characteristic and revealing of crucial aspects of Clayton's directing personality.

The film opens as the coffin of an old clerk, Fender (Alfie Bass), is being transported by wheelbarrow to the local cemetery. The only mourner is the Jewish tailor, Morry (David Kossoff), who then returns home to light a candle in memory of his friend. Guiltily, he reproaches himself for not being able to mend his friend's old overcoat and recalls the circumstances in which Fender did not live long enough to wear the new coat Morry had made for him. At the graveside, he has stroked the coat, flicking a feather off the sleeve with a tailor's pride before tossing it on his friend's coffin.

As Morry sips at his brandy, slipping between memory and guilt, pride at his ability as a tailor and sorrow at his friend's death, his monologue is interrupted by a voice from beyond the grave, and he turns to see the ghost of Fender in his room. A real ghost, or a product of his imagination, his guilty conscience even? There are interesting anticipations of *The Innocents* here. To confirm his presence, Fender asks Morry to touch his cold hand: close-up of hands hesitantly touching. This is a characteristic Clayton motif, often given great emphasis in important contexts. The chill of the touch confirms his friend's presence as a 'live' ghost, as it were. (Later, in Ranting's warehouse, when he accidentally touches his friend's hand, the chill will remind him that his companion is really dead. 'You go back to the hotel?' Morry asks him at that stage poignantly, the euphemism gently conveying his adult fear of mortality.)

Fender has come back as an unquiet spirit. A slow dissolve momentarily puts past and present in the same shot and the two are given a view of Fender's relationship with his employer, the ruthless and insensitive Mr Ranting (Alan Tilvern), who is to sack him after forty-three years of service as a clerk. Fender has thus been unable to continue payments on the prized new coat Morry has been making for him, and although Morry has agreed to finish it for him anyway, Fender has died before he can. The ghost has come back to claim a coat from Ranting's warehouse. 'He owes me ...'.

In one sense the tale is, as John Russell Taylor puts it, 'a downtrodden little man's posthumous revenge on authority'.[7] The coat becomes symbolic of a restored, belated self-respect. Mainly, though, the tale relies on mood and atmosphere and is a moving and often funny portrayal of friendship. Much of the humour has to do with Fender's new status as a ghost. When Morry asks, 'You ain't dead?' Fender replies, 'Sure I'm dead. Would I sit here in the freezing cold if I wasn't dead?' (Actually even when alive, Fender had seemed permanently cold.) He adds, 'You know they've got central heating down there?' – an interesting modern reference since elsewhere the piece seems almost timeless. Even in the sadder moments, the resilient Jewish humour asserts itself, as when Morry tells Fender that he will finish the coat even though Fender cannot pay. 'How?' Fender asks, to which Morry replies: 'With a needle, how else?' Later there is a bit of Chaplinesque pantomime when, after dancing and singing in the dark, Morry challenges Fender to confirm his ghostly identity by walking through the wall. After a slight hesitation and some sizing up of the situation, Fender says, 'I feel silly, Morry. The old way's best. Through the door.' Morry sighs: 'I even have to tell him how to be a ghost proper.'

Pauline Kael rightly praised Mankowitz's dialogue, with its 'ear for the poetry of unlikely places':[8] although she does not mention this, it catches something of the lyricism of poverty that one finds in contemporaneous pieces like Beckett's *Waiting for Godot* or early Pinter. Born in 1925 in the East End of London of Russian Jewish parents, Mankowitz clearly knows the idiom and the milieu. A respecter of fine writing, Clayton directs with sympathy, sensitivity and also imagination. When Ranting is bearing down on Fender in the warehouse and putting pressure on him to go ('You got something put by?'), the camera circles the action to convey Fender's sudden feeling of disorientation, entrapment and claustrophobia. The style is echoed in the fine deathbed scene, when Fender on his own berates Ranting for his behaviour but also himself for not saying what was on his mind. 'Why I didn't tell him? I should have told him off, big as he is ...' The mood is similar to that of Morry in his own opening scene, with its anger and self reproach: like Morry, Fender hears voices and gives vent to fantasy. As he speaks the camera describes a hesitant slow circle which as *Films and Filming* critic Peter Baker remarked (January 1956) is 'like a long, penultimate sigh'. At the point of death the camera is positioned behind the bed frame, its bars recalling the opening shot of the film (the coffin in the wheelbarrow glimpsed through the railing that leads to Morry's basement), and indeed anticipating the close (the empty barrow passing, as if part of an unending cycle of poverty and death). Equally fine is a moment near the end when Fender is preparing to depart this life for the last time and talking about his friend Lennie who is also 'down there' and 'selling herrings like hot cakes all day long'. (Alfie Bass's gentle diminuendo on those last three words is a magical thing to hear, the equal of Richard Burton's 'Sunday tomorrow. All day' in *Who's Afraid of Virginia Woolf?*) Watching his friend depart Morry stands in complete darkness at Ranting's warehouse, whereupon Clayton fades up the background to show Morry back in his room – a fade that is a transformation not only of setting but also of night to morning, past to present and perhaps dream to reality. After all, this is where he was standing, with his hand over his face, at the point when Fender's ghost appeared. Has the rest been fantasy, an imaginative reassurance that he has done the best for his friend?

It would be difficult to imagine performances in these roles more perfectly nuanced than those of Kossoff and Bass, neither of whom did anything finer for cinema. For such a low-budget film, it was something of a coup for Clayton to attract a composer of the stature of Georges Auric; certainly Auric's spare, sombre score contributes enormously to the poignant mood. At the time, *The Bespoke Overcoat* was seen as a significant harbinger for new developments in British film that, alas, were not really to bear fruit. In the *Tribune* of 30 December 1955, for example, Richard Findlater had called the film as important an example of the filmed play as Olivier's *Richard III* (1955). Seeing the short story in the context of the rise of television in Britain and the consequent decline of the B-picture from the British cinema, Findlater thought it all the more necessary for British studios to be thinking of the right kind of supporting feature, and *The Bespoke Overcoat* seemed precisely that, coming too at a time when other shorts such as

Dennis Sanders' *A Time Out of War* (1954) and Albert Lamorisse's *The Red Balloon* (1956) were winning great acclaim and achieving wide release. The film seemed to herald a revival of the cinematic short story that was unfortunately to be short-lived.

What is most striking in retrospect is how, even in this short film, Clayton has staked out emotional territory and even certain stylistic signatures that will become his trademarks in later films. Producer Otto Plaschkes mentioned this in his tribute to Clayton in *Direct*:

> That here was a true director became apparent with his short *The Bespoke Overcoat*, a magical essay in Jewish despair and hope. Here also appeared the themes which Jack addressed in all his films: the identification with and love of the underdog, the almost religious importance of background and atmosphere, the relevance of courage and faith and the tricks that destiny plays with us all.[9]

To this I would add the humanity and poignancy of friendship, the sympathy for the insulted and injured, and a compassion for the human situation that will underscore all his later work. The fact that the material is based on a distinguished literary source will also be characteristic. In the case of Gogol at that time, one wonders whether he might have been influenced in his choice of material by his work as associate producer on Thorold Dickinson's superb film of Pushkin, *The Queen of Spades* (1948), another classic Russian ghost story.[10] Indeed, although one notices elements of future characteristics of style and theme (the use of interiors, circling camera movements, dissolves, shots of people's hands, the fluid movement between past and present, dream and reality), it is this ghost-story aspect that lingers in the mind. 'You ain't going to haunt me?' Morry asks anxiously. Fender reassures him that he will not: he is not that important a ghost – 'for haunting, you get a commission'. But from a Clayton character it is a fair question. In his films people do not stay dead in the minds of those who knew them and Clayton will show a predilection for stories of haunting beyond the grave, elements of which will appear in different forms in *Our Mother's House, Something Wicked This Way Comes, The Lonely Passion of Judith Hearne, Memento*

Mori and above all in *The Innocents*, where the dead do not remain buried but walk across the earth by night and day and into the minds of the living.

Notes

1 Brian McFarlane, *An Autobiography of British Cinema* (London, Methuen, 1997), p. 129.
2 Karel Reisz, *The Technique of Film Editing*, introd. Thorold Dickinson (London, Focal Press Limited, 1953), pp. 249–52.
3 'The Way Things Are: Jack Clayton in an Interview with Gordon Gow', *Films and Filming*, April 1974, p. 11.
4 Clayton and Katherine Kath were later divorced. Clayton's first marriage was to the actress Christine Norden, who, according to her publicity, was discovered in a cinema queue by a cameraman who introduced her to Alexander Korda and who was billed as Britain's first post-war sex symbol, appearing in such films as *Mine Own Executioner* (1947) and *An Ideal Husband* (1947).
5 Otto Plaschkes, 'Jack Clayton Remembered', *Direct*, Summer 1995, p. 15.
6 '*Naples is a Battlefield*; Preliminary Report on a Study of Audience Reaction with the Lazarsfeld-Stanton Program Analyzer', p. 17. Report lodged in the Imperial War Museum, London.
7 John Russell Taylor, *Anger and After: A Guide to the New British Drama* (London, Pelican Books, 1963), p. 122.
8 Pauline Kael, *I Lost It at the Movies* (New York, Bantam Books, 1965), p. 58.
9 Plaschkes, 'Clayton Remembered', p. 15.
10 Clayton's career has some curious parallels with that of Thorold Dickinson, both of them intelligent and fastidious film-makers who never took on assignments simply as chores or even entertainments, and whose high artistic standards might have crippled their continuity. Both *The Bespoke Overcoat* and *The Innocents* share some characteristics with *The Queen of Spades*, as well as the same composer. Another curious connection is that Dickinson was to direct one of the first Israeli films, *Hill 24 Doesn't Answer* (1955), starring Haya Harareet – later to become Clayton's partner and wife.

Sex, realism and Yorkshire pudding: *Room at the Top* (1959)

3

I was like an officer fresh from training school, unable for the moment to translate the untidiness of fear and cordite and corpses into the obvious and irresistible method of attack. I was going to take the position, though, I was sure of that. I was moving into the attack, and no one had better try to stop me. General Joe Lampton, you might say, had opened hostilities. (John Braine, *Room at the Top*, London, Penguin, 1959, p. 30)[1]

No finer work has come out of our studios since – oh, since *Brief Encounter*. That's how good I think it is. Take this film's slightest feature, and so barren, timorous and blind have our studios been over a decade that it seems we are in the presence of an innovation. (Alexander Walker, *Birmingham Post and Gazette*, 23 January 1959)

After months when one had begun against all one's instincts to think that the best hope lay in co-production, with directors and players and writers from other countries eking out not so much the talent – there really is plenty of that – as the creative courage of this country, suddenly a film which succeeds by being native. It gives one faith all over again in a renaissance of the British cinema. (Dilys Powell, *Sunday Times*, 25 January 1959)

Jack Clayton's film of *Room at the Top* has been widely credited with launching the 'new wave' in British film, bringing realism, the working class and sex to the national cinema. Made during the year when film production was ceasing at Ealing, it seemed symbolically to displace an Ealing tradition of gentility and restraint and raise the whole emotional temperature of British film. Four years after its première, Penelope Houston could write that 'because of the film's sensational earnings at the box office and because of the ground it covered, the industry is still living in the shadow of this picture'.[2] Its commercial and artistic success eased the way for the others. Its amoral hero, Joe Lampton, ushered in the cinematic era of the Arthur Seatons and Jimmy Porters, of L-shaped rooms and disgruntled long-distance runners. Just around the corner was the decade of permissiveness, the Swinging Sixties, the sexual athleticism of James Bond and the period promiscuity of Tom Jones.

Room at the Top was only part of a tide of change in art and society (from Suez to Kingsley Amis, from *Look Back in Anger* on stage to the British Free Cinema)[3] that was pushing so hard against the British Establishment that something eventually had to give. Nevertheless, in retrospect there is something odd about the breakthrough of *Room at the Top*. For one thing, film critics at the time were looking towards fledgling directors like Lindsay Anderson, Karel Reisz, Tony Richardson and John Schlesinger, who were rehearsing their arguments about the direction of the English cinema and/or society in television, theatre, documentary and even the pages of *Sight and Sound*.[4] Nobody was looking in the direction of an industry veteran like Jack Clayton, who by that time had been in films for over twenty years and whose most recent work included directing a whimsical short, *The Bespoke Overcoat* (1955), and producing such works as *Three Men in a Boat* (1956) and *Sailor Beware* (1956), which were not exactly portents of revolution.

Some aspects of the critical response to *Room at the Top* when it was premièred in January 1959 will be considered later. Its reception reveals a great deal about perceptions of British cinema at the time – perceptions which the film seemed, either consciously or unconsciously, to challenge or subvert. (The comments of Alexander Walker and Dilys Powell in the epigraphs to this chapter are very revealing in this connection.) It seems clear, though, that Clayton had at the time neither the inclination nor the intention of jumping onto any social or cultural bandwagon. He disliked the 'angry young man' label – understandably enough, because he was nearly 40 at the time – and thought the expression 'a silly way of describing people who always existed anyway and have not really anything to do with the current scene'.[5] In other words, young men have always been angry and it was not simply the stagnant social situation of the mid-1950s that was causing them to revolt.

Indeed, it is worth remembering that, although the novel was published in 1957 and thought to be of immediate contemporary relevance, the action takes place a decade earlier. (Like Pip in *Great Expectations*, the hero is looking back not with anger but with sorrow and the benefits of hindsight on a key period of his life.) The fact that it had such resonance in the 1950s is attributable to factors mentioned earlier – its anti-authoritarian hero, its egalitarian message. However, it was the tale's post-war theme, more than its contemporary social theme, that first attracted Clayton. 'The reason I wanted to make *Room at the Top*', he said in an interview with Gordon Gow,

> was that it was indicative of that fascinating period which I personally lived through. It was about what happened to England when everybody came back from the war. Not only to class, because the class thing was always there and is still there. But it changed a great deal ... Joe Lampton was a character who represented, to me, a new feeling that was universal in this country, as a result of people having been put through a very bad five years – and also having had the chance to look around.[6]

John Braine's novel had been published in March 1957 and had been an instant success, augmented by Braine's appearance on *Panorama* in April in an interview with Woodrow Wyatt and by the serialisation of the novel, in an abridged form, in the *Daily Express*. Acquiring the film rights for £5,000, the producers John and James Woolf first offered the project to Peter Glenville, who turned it down. Actors first considered for the leading roles included Stewart Granger, Jean Simmons and Vivien Leigh. (Simmons was to play the part of Joe Lampton's wife Susan in the 1965 sequel, *Life at the Top*, directed by Ted Kotcheff and co-scripted by Mordecai Richler, who had worked uncredited on Clayton's film.) In the event, because they were under contract to the Woolfs, the leading roles went to Laurence Harvey and Heather Sears. Sears, who had just scored a considerable personal success in *The Story of Esther Costello*,[7] seemed ideal casting for the sexually innocent, wholesome Susan, and so she proved, giving a touching perform-ance of a sheltered young woman somewhat at sea in the adult world. However, the casting of the Lithuanian-born Laurence Harvey as a working-class Northerner caused some consternation, notably to the novel's author, John Braine, who only changed his mind after seeing the performance. Clayton, however, who had already worked on four films with Harvey as a producer, was confident that the casting would work. Harvey might not have an authentic Bradford accent,[8] but Clayton knew that he did have another kind of authenticity. Who better to play someone talented, aggressive, ambitious, arrogant, with a huge chip on his shoulder but also bags of charm and self-confidence? As the critic on the *Kent Messenger* (23 January 1959) was bluntly to put it: 'At last the 30-year-old actor is entitled to all the good things he has been saying about himself for the past few years.' Laurence Harvey would in all senses give the performance of his life.

However, the performance that attracted even more praise than Harvey's – and an Oscar – was Simone Signoret's as Alice Aisgill, the married woman who has an affair with Lampton but who will die in a car crash after he has rejected her for the boss's daughter, Susan. Alice is not French in the novel – as Alexander Walker pointed out in his review, she is referred to in the film as 'all woman' and nationality is beside the point – and there has been some speculation about whose suggestion it was to cast Signoret.[9] What is not in dispute is that the casting was inspired and that she gave a performance of an emotional maturity beyond the range of any English film actress one could think of at that time. There may have been a subtler motive too. Given that the film would be unusually frank on sexual matters, the producers may have felt that such scenes would be more acceptable to audiences and censor if played by a foreign actress. As Anthony Aldgate has shown in his excellent study of the relationship between the film industry and the British Board of Film Censors during this period, this instinct proved correct.[10] Taking the unusual step of showing the film in a more or less complete version to the censor rather than following the usual practice of submitting the script for his prior approval, the producers and Clayton were only required to make minor changes for the film to be given an X certificate. It had a disastrous sneak preview at the Brucegrove Theatre in Tottenham in December 1958 with an audience that had expected to be shown *Dracula*; Clayton kept one of the preview cards – which had dismissed the film as 'Tripe' (Fig. 8) – prominently displayed in his office, no doubt partly as a gentle rebuke to potentially inflated directorial ego but mainly as a reminder of the 'accuracy' of the kind of market research and preview testing so beloved even today by film studios and distributors. The gala première at the Plaza cinema, however, was a triumph that, for many critics, marked a turning point for British cinema.

The film opens with Joe Lampton's arrival by train at Warnley station prior to his taking up a new job as a clerk in the borough's Treasury Department. The name of the town has been changed from 'Warley' in the novel (perhaps to avoid any puns on or confusion with 'war' and 'whore'). The opening sound of the train whistle and the early setting of the station evokes a fleeting memory of *Brief Encounter* (1945), to which the film will allude in several subsequent details. Prior to the credits, Lampton (Laurence Harvey) is seen alone in a train compartment with his legs stretched out on the seat opposite, the casual gesture perhaps of a self-confident man. He has a hole in his sock, which betokens the somewhat impoverished background from which he comes, or from which he has escaped, but the hole will in a moment be covered by his new suede shoes, which he strokes lovingly: the new life, and the style of life he covets. Clayton has lost no time in setting up Lampton's character, situation and aspirations. As he travels to a meeting with his employer, Mr Hoylake (Raymond Huntley), Lampton is seen regularly either looking up or moving onwards and upwards: his goal throughout the film. Even Mr Hoylake notices that he has arrived early (he was not expected until Monday). Joe is clearly a man in a hurry. 'You'll meet a different class of people,' Hoylake tells him. An immediate instance of this occurs after he has been introduced to his work colleague and friend, Charles Soames (Donald Houston), and chances to look out of the window. He sees Susan Brown (Heather Sears) for the first time, as she climbs into an Aston Martin with her escort Jack Wales (John Westbrook). His reaction is so pronounced that even Charles notices. 'I can look, can't I?' says Joe, to which Charles retorts: 'Not like that you can't. There's a law against undressing women in the street.'

It is an interesting moment. The line is unusually outspoken for a British film of that time (I can still remember the gasp it caused in the audience of a provincial cinema when I first saw the film in 1962) and it is fair to say that the reputation of the film for sexual frankness owes as much to its dialogue as to any graphic depiction of sex. Visually the film now looks rather chaste: there is no nudity. What still seems unusual is the more open way characters talk about their sexual desires and experiences. It is one way in which the film clearly differentiates the relationship Lampton is to have with Susan from his relationship with Alice. With Alice, he discovers real passion: making love to Susan, by contrast, 'reminds me of a good set of mixed tennis'. Nevertheless, what is striking about Clayton's framing of Lampton's look out of the window at this juncture is that, contrary to his friend's assumption, he is ogling not only the young woman but also the car. (He will tell his friends later that he wants a girl with 'a Riviera tan *and* a Lagonda': sex and status are almost inseparable in Joe's mind.)

Jo's first sight of Susan and the car corresponds to a moment in the novel that has attracted a good deal of comment, largely because of the weight Braine gives it – as a turning point in the action and a key to his hero's motivation. From the window of a café, Lampton notices a posh Aston-Martin parked opposite and a young man and girl coming out of a solicitor's office before climbing into the car:

> The Aston-Martin started with a deep, healthy roar. As it passed the café in the direction of St. Clair Road I noticed the young man's olive linen shirt and bright silk neckerchief. The collar of the shirt was tucked inside the jacket; he wore the rather theatrical ensemble with a matter-of-fact nonchalance. Everything about him was easy and loose but not tired or sloppy. He had an undistinguished face

with a narrow forehead and mousy hair cut short with no oil on it. It was a rich man's face, smooth with assurance and good living.

He hadn't ever had to work for anything he wanted; it had all been given him. The salary, which I'd been so pleased about, an increase from Grade Ten to Grade Nine, would seem a pittance to him. The suit in which I fancied myself so much – my best suit – would seem cheap and nasty to him. He wouldn't have a best suit; all his clothes would be the best.

For a moment I hated him. I saw myself, compared with him, as the Town Hall clerk, the subordinate pen-pusher, half-way to being a zombie, and I tasted the sourness of envy. Then I rejected it. Not on moral grounds; but because I felt then, and still do, that envy's a small and squalid vice – the convict sulking because a fellow-prisoner's been given a bigger helping of skilly. This didn't abate the fierceness of my longing. I wanted an Aston-Martin, I wanted a three guinea linen shirt, I wanted a girl with a Riviera suntan – these were my rights, I felt, a signed and sealed legacy. (pp. 28–9)

Much prominence is given to car imagery in both novel and film of *Room at the Top*, undoubtedly because of the importance attached by the hero to the car as status symbol, as indicator of class superiority. In the novel, when Joe argues with Susan over Jack Wales, he says 'Do you prefer him and his M.G.?' (p. 156); and describing his now prosperous state in the present he will compare himself to 'a brand new Cadillac in a poor industrial area insulated by steel and glass and air conditioning from the people outside' (p. 124). More ominously, the fusion of Joe and Alice in a passionate embrace of love-making is described as 'melting into each other like amoeba but violently, like cars crashing head on' (p. 179) – a portent of where their passion is to lead. 'This is a terribly moral kind of car', Alice has said to Joe ironically in the film, meaning that it is uncomfortable for love-making, but the words will resonate terribly when that very car is the instrument of Alice's death. Coincidentally a destructive car will also play a crucial role in the tragic denouement of *The Great Gatsby*.

Braine's description of Joe's sight of the girl and the car is meant in some way to stand as his hero's epiphany, the vision that will transform his life. David Lodge has done a stylistic comparison between this epiphanic vision and the one of the girl on the beach in James Joyce's *A Portrait of the Artist as a Young Man* – unsurprisingly to Braine's disadvantage (Lodge finds Braine's language flat and clichéd).[11] In literary terms, particularly, with its metaphor for envy as 'the convict sulking', I am less reminded of Joyce and of other obvious descriptions of class and social climbing such as Stendhal's *Scarlet and the Black* and Dreiser's *An American Tragedy* than of Dickens and *Great Expectations*: both share the themes of snobbery and self-realisation, the rise in social class accompanied by the decline in morals; and both share the same point of view, the first-person perspective of a narrator with the benefit of hindsight. In film terms, it might be said that Clayton's *Room at the Top* had the same kind of impact at the end of the 1950s as David Lean's *Great Expectations* in 1946, both debating the promise of class mobility and social change. Much of the critical debate about *Room at the Top* was to centre on Joe Lampton – what drives him, what he represents.

What does motivate Joe Lampton? One of the most perceptive early critics of the film, Alexander Walker, has identified his motivation as class envy,[12] though it seems more complicated than this. As indicated in the passage quoted, the hero dismisses envy as his motive quite explicitly in the novel itself; he may be self-deceived at this point but it does not appear so. Indeed his motivation has more to do with self-perception than self-deception and a feeling that he is entitled to the high life by virtue of skill, intelligence and ambition. Attainment, though, will be at a high moral cost.

Because Joe's aunt and uncle (played by Beatrice Varley and Wilfrid Lawson) 'seem like relics from a past age' and the characterisations of Alice's husband, George Aisgill, and of Susan's mother and boyfriend 'assume a nightmarish awfulness', it has been argued that Joe is given the film's 'implicit approval'.[13] Clayton achieves something more complex than that. 'I wanted you to feel compassion for him but not sympathy,' he said, 'it would have been morally wrong to make him sympathetic'.[14] If the characters surrounding Joe assume a 'nightmarish awfulness', it may be simply that this is how Joe sees them; they are, after all, the principal obstacles to his social and sexual desires. Still, Allan Cuthbertson's forbidding characterisation of George Aisgill seems absolutely truthful to the way Lampton describes him in the novel – '[he] had a watchful coldness about him which almost frightened me: he looked utterly incapable of making a fool of himself' (p. 63). Ambrosine Phillpotts's performance as Mrs Brown is similarly exact: she seems able to say 'Hello' to Joe without moving her lips, her eyes suggesting a disapproval that is belied by the welcoming words. The implication behind this is her fear that Susan might be about to yield to the same temptation that she did: marrying beneath her class. What is undoubtedly different between novel and film is the characterisation of Jack Wales, who in John West-brook's performance is a much more unpleasant character than in the novel. Stuart Laing has argued that the nastiness of Westbrook's Jack Wales is the film's way of compensating for the absence of Lampton's first-person narration.[15] If the film consciously exagger-ates the class difference between Wales and Lampton, emphasising the former's snobbery and the latter's consequent embarrassment and antagonism, the effect is not simply to sharpen Lampton's motivation and to cultivate sympathy for him. It is to highlight the progress whereby Lampton, in fulfilling his social ambition, is to betray himself and become what he hates.

In the film the sharply dramatised antagonism between Lampton and Wales has several causes. They are both rivals for the same young woman, Susan, and Lampton is clearly irritated by Wales's proprietary attitude to her. This is smartly signalled at one stage when an intimate conversation between Lampton and Susan is interrupted by an abrupt shot of Wales's hand on Lampton's shoulder. The gesture seems almost a parody of the poignant tenderness of a famous similar gesture in *Brief Encounter*. It is another example of the way this film plays *against* memories of Lean's masterpiece, whilst in a sense becoming the tragic love story of 1950s British cinema in the way that Lean's was for the previous decade.

As well as in romantic rivalry, the antagonism is rooted in class. When Lampton, in his amateur-dramatics role, mispro-nounces 'brazier' as 'brassière', great visual prominence is given to Wales's derisive laughter. (Mocking laughter is something that happens a lot in Clayton's films: he is an acutely sensitive observer of small moments of individual humiliation in which one almost blushes along with the protagonist.) In the novel Wales is not present at this incident. The film includes him to sharpen the conflict but also for purposes of irony since, in a sense, the laugh will be on him: Joe's gaucheness is one of the things that will charm Susan and even strike a chord with her father, the most powerful businessman in Warnley, Mr Brown (Donald Wolfit). 'Curious names some of these people have,' says Susan's mother when she learns that Susan is seeing a Joe Lampton: the name seems almost aggressively ordinary. (Stuart Laing has noted that the name of the character gave Braine some trouble: in Braine's first rejected synopsis, the hero was called Bob Mayne.) But when Susan later adds that he calls her a 'dear kipper', the mother looks puzzled while Mr Brown laughs (astute characterisation here, as elsewhere, by Donald Wolfit). The laugh seems to imply recognition by Brown of a phrase he has not heard for years, the self-made man having a sudden reminder of his roots. In the novel Lampton comments on Brown's 'overdone' Yorkshire accent and Wolfit's vocal characterisation catches that very well, the self-conscious flat vowel sounds a deliberate reminder to himself and to others of a self-made man who has pulled himself up by his bootstraps. The significance of this is that, for this reason, Brown might ironically be better disposed towards Lampton than he is towards Wales, whose privileges are inherited.

One particular aspect of the antagonism between Susan's suitors has to do with the war. To Lampton's intense irritation, Wales insistently refers to him as 'Sergeant', a reminder of Lampton's subservient place in relation to Wales's 'squadron leader'. We learn that Lampton is very sensitive about his war record: it comes up during his first serious argument with Alice when she taunts him about being a prisoner of war and not trying to escape, as Wales did. Lampton hits back angrily: why should he have escaped back to Dufton, where he felt more of a prisoner than in the war? He was better off where he was, where he could learn from the skills of people around him.

This detail has interesting connotations in the context of late-1950s British cinema, particularly when elsewhere in the film the post-war environment is given little emphasis. Much recent critical commentary on British cinema has noted the popularity of the war film in the 1950s, by far the major genre of the national cinema during that decade.[16] The reason for this has sometimes been identified as a kind of post-imperial nostalgia for Britain's 'finest hour' and even a nostalgia for social status quo and rigid class stratification where everyone knew his or her place. Films like *The Dam Busters* (1955), *Reach for the Sky* (1955) and even *Danger Within* (1958) reflect an instinctive obeisance to authority. But perhaps because of the demoralisation caused by British bungling of the Suez crisis in 1956, war films in the late 1950s are beginning to reflect an air of doubt and unease. Post-Suez disillusionment seeps into a film like J. Lee Thompson's *Ice Cold in Alex* (1958), with its emasculated hero and its complex sympathies, and is unmistakable in David Lean's *The Bridge on the River Kwai* (1957), whose satirical send-up of a wrong-headed British enterprise seemed to be tuning in to a contemporary scepticism about Britain's anachronistic imperialist postures which were not only antagonising its foes but alienating its allies as well. (The British military character is attacked by both East and West in Lean's film in memorable twin tirades from the Japanese Saito and the American Warden.) I think *Room at the Top* (and note Braine's military imagery for Lampton's social strategy as quoted in this chapter's epigraph) belongs obliquely in this cycle. It is not a war film, but it is a film very conscious of the legacy of the war and its associated social regimentation. When Lampton retaliates against Wales's sneering address of him as 'Sergeant' he is signalling a new direction not only for himself but for British film. He refuses to accept deference to an authority based on tradition rather than talent, to genuflect instinctively to the officer class. This adds to the complexity of our response to Lampton as hero, as class avenger as well as sexual predator. It is the moment too when British film signals its attempt to stop being nostalgic about the war, to look to the future and not to the past. As a continuation of this struggle one might recall Harvey's going on to play the role of

Bamforth, the iconoclastic thorn in commander Richard Todd's side in Leslie Norman's film of Willis Hall's anti-heroic *The Long and the Short and the Tall* (1960).

The preparation of theme, style and motifs is brought to a superb culmination in the final part of the film, which is arguably the best-directed section of the whole work. Lampton tells Alice that he is to marry Susan, who is now carrying his child. A distraught Alice gets drunk on her own in the pub, as she leaves confronting her reflection in the large mirror: her age, frustration and misery writ large, and in bitter contrast to the opening of her previous scene with Joe, when she happily checked her appearance in the mirror in anticipation of a joyous evening. The next morning Lampton is seen arriving at the Town Hall. The composition of the shots, the similar chiming of the clock, consciously recall his arrival on the first day of his job at the beginning of the film, but now there is not the same spring in his step. News of his forthcoming marriage has spread around the office but at the moment of triumph and the popping of champagne, Lampton begins to hear three of the office girls gossiping about Alice's suicide. The framing is strikingly distorted, to reflect Lampton's sense of shock but also the twisted nature of his triumph: as Clayton explained, he used 'the widest possible whole angle in order to distort them apart from the different background. I call them the three witches'.[17] The allusion to *Macbeth* is apposite: Shakespeare's play is another study of a man whose ambition twists his character out of recognition. Not for the only time in Clayton's work, it recalls a Huston-style dramatic anti-climax where, at the point of attainment of the hero's dearest goal (such as Gutman's unwrapping of the bronze statue in *The Maltese Falcon* (1941), the discovery of gold in *The Treasure of the Sierra Madre* (1948), the coronation of *The Man Who Would Be King* (1975)), the whole thing blows up in his face. The tension between triumph and tragedy is reflected in an imaginative visual counterpoint between foreground and background, sound and image: the jollity is now in stark, even embarrassing contrast to Lampton's expression and mood. Clayton's soundtracks are always carefully composed, and the sound/image interplay here chimes interestingly with an earlier scene in the film, when the sound noticeably dips as Susan, in her changing room after her amateur dramatic performance as the 'foolish virgin', first notices Joe looking at her. In her dressing-room mirror in the same scene, Alice notices Joe's attraction to Susan, so the emotional triangle is even then being adumbrated: indeed, one could plot Alice's progress through the entire film by the changing significance of mirror shots of her at different points in the narrative. The stylistic similarity of the dressing room and office scenes helps emphasise the feeling that the spirits of Susan and Alice are present at the office celebration. Significantly, at the moment of triumph towards which Lampton has been working for the whole film, the world looks awry – faces distorted, sound unnaturally amplified – as he tastes not the value of his success but its price. And – again like so many of Clayton's characters – he starts being haunted. The ghost of Alice Aisgill will dominate every frame of the film now until the ending.

Revisiting the flat where he and Alice used to meet, Lampton is confronted by Alice's friend Elspeth (Hermione Baddeley), who rages at him, 'How could you do it?' He is driven out by the sheer force of her anger, descending the stairs into the darkness (this from a character who has been obsessively on the way up). In the following scene, where Lampton gets drunk and picks up another man's girl, the continuity of feeling – guilt, conscience, self-hatred – is finely sustained by Clayton and screenwriter, Neil Paterson: even the earlier gesture of smashing the champagne glass at the celebration party is echoed in his threatening gesture with the beer glass towards the pick-up's boyfriend (Darren Nesbitt). When asked his name, Lampton replies 'Jack Wales' – a detail that tellingly clinches his denial of self: he has become what he most despises. Having sacrificed everything for materialism, he now carelessly starts throwing his money around, deliberately antagon-ising the woman's boyfriend with his arrogance. In a sense he is replicating Wales's behaviour in the café scene with Susan and the boyfriend's anger, which he deliberately provokes, is a reminder of his own then. He clicks his fingers rudely for service, in a gesture that recalls one much earlier in the film when Aisgill, in a pub, snapped his fingers impatiently at Alice for the car keys (another image, then, of Lampton having become what he hates). When he staggers outside with the woman and later says good-night, he gives a brief farewell wave with his back to her, recalling a similar gesture of Alice's when, after being humiliated by Aisgill in the pub and refusing Lampton's offer of company, she departs into the night. (Intriguingly, Nick's final gesture to Gatsby in *The Great Gatsby* is a wave with his back turned, when he says goodbye, without realising this is the last time he will see Gatsby alive.) This mosaic of recollected motifs and gestures is a feature of the film's skilful structure but also contributes to the poignancy and irony that add enormous power to these final moments.

Staggering drunkenly across the canal bank, Lampton is stopped by the picked-up woman's boyfriend and his cronies and given a vicious beating, filmed in large close-ups and quite brutal for its time. In the novel he fights back. In the film he is masochistically passive, as if willing his own punishment. As he is being beaten a train whistle is heard in the distance, so shrill that Lampton looks up. This is the sound with which the film opened and is also a ghostly reminder of that painful farewell scene at the station between Lampton and Alice after their idyllic few days together where they both seem to sense their relationship is almost over.[18] 'Even in the flashy beating up episode', says Douglas McVay, who had his reservations about early Clayton, 'Clayton manages to bring off a legitimate and telling – if faintly obvious – touch of pictorial symbolism: the reflection of the Brown factory chimney in the water into which Joe falls.'[19] The symbolism seems to me dense and concentrated rather than 'faintly obvious'. With admirable visual conciseness it expresses Joe's moral descent and the cause of it; as an inverted image and a reflection, it relates both to the film's rise/fall structure and its theme of identity; and like so many other details in this part of the film it rhymes with an earlier moment when Lampton realises he has been set up for the job interview in Dufton by Brown as a strategy to separate him from Susan and we see his reflection in a puddle as he throws his cigarette to the ground in a gesture of defiance. Like the mirror motif which helps to express Alice's development, reflections in water have a lot to say about Lampton's downhill moral journey.

Morning. Shot of a telephone booth, with the phone off the hook. Everything seems disconnected: where are we? Lampton is in both a physical and a moral wasteland and for a moment the setting and the children are a reminder of his return to Dufton in the earlier part of the film (not 'late' as Alexander Walker suggested,[20] but at a pivotal point almost exactly midway through). 'It's my house', a child said to him then, playing on the bomb site, to which he replied, 'It used to be mine too.' (Harvey's vocal inflection of this line is subtle: a softening of tone suggests a gentler, more vulnerable side to his character which he has repressed on his rise to the top.) Where does he now belong? Ironically in the scene in the pub the woman's boyfriend says to him, 'You stick to your own class', confusing the display of money with social origin and acting out precisely the kind of antagonism that was present in the scenes between Lampton and Wales. Lampton's ruthless attempt to rise to the top – to better the Waleses of this world – at this moment finds him literally in the gutter.

A child rolls a toy car towards him. He reaches towards it, almost like Lew Ayres reaching out to stroke the butterfly at the end of *All Quiet on the Western Front*. But the car tips over, a metaphor for Alice's tragic fate perhaps – and here I might agree with McVay's description of forced symbolism. Yet the moment also relates to the upturning of his childhood roots and his loss of innocence – that quality Alice notices in him when she says, 'You look about eighteen sometimes.' It is like the moment in *Brief Encounter* when Celia Johnson says to Trevor Howard, 'You suddenly look much younger ... like a little boy', and when we realise, perhaps even earlier than they themselves, that they are in love.

Found by friends, Lampton is helped into the car. 'Time to come home, Joe', says Charles – but where is home? Joe has gained the world but lost his soul. 'You're a timid soul', Alice tells him, the first intimation in Clayton's work of the theme of souls in danger of damnation (it will recur in *The Innocents*, *Something Wicked This Way Comes* and *The Lonely Passion of Judith Hearne*). After Joe tells Alice he is marrying Susan, Alice says: 'Finally, you've got every-thing you wanted, haven't you?' Simone Signoret delivers the line superbly, spacing it for tempo and rhythm like an expert musician, making every phrase count. It is a key line because of its ironic subtext: it points up what it has cost him to get what he wants, but the question mark at the end also signifies the possibility of self-deception – what if he hasn't got what he wants after all? At one stage in their idyll in the cottage, Joe and Alice quote together Polonius's famous lines in *Hamlet*: 'This above all / To thine own self be true'. John Hill has picked up on the importance of the amateur theatricals in the film and the theatrical imagery: 'The use of a theatrical setting', he says, 'and emphasis on the parallels between theatrical performance and life outside … foregrounds the problem of "authenticity" faced by Joe.'[21] In his courtship of Susan Joe seems quite consciously to be playing the role of the abused and misunderstood lover: at one stage he even goes on his knees to her, and Susan as schoolgirl romantic is a pushover. It is in the scenes with Alice that the tension between identity and ambition become uncomfortable for him. Significantly he cannot quite remember the Polonius line and it is she who has to complete it for him. Not cited in the novel, the line emphasises an insistent theme in the film, and contains the core of Alice's ultimate rebuke of the man she loves: not that he has betrayed her but that he has betrayed himself.

The novel ends with Lampton expressing a remorse that no one understands but him. The film goes one step further, with one of British cinema's most harrowing wedding ceremonies and most ironic happy endings. As the camera descends from the impressive windows of the church, the words of the ceremony itself emerge with great gravity and weight: 'as ye will answer at the dreadful Day of Judgement when the secrets of all hearts will be disclosed'. The secret in Lampton's heart, then, seems to consign him to damnation. Much of the scene is shot from behind Lampton as if afraid to disclose his face. When he is asked if he will take Susan for his wife, there is an agonising, embarrassing pause before he answers, 'I will', as if aware that this is a point of no return. (Because he is a man in a hurry Lampton's pauses are always significant and Harvey always times them to electrifying effect: his long pause before agreeing with Susan that their first sexual experience together was the 'most absolutely wonderful thing' that had ever happened to him; his stunned pause at the celebration party before confirming Mr Hoylake's remark that he had known Alice Aisgill well.) Much of the scene concentrates on the reaction shots of the congregation, mainly the few who have turned out on Lampton's side: his friends, his aunt, and Elspeth at the back of the church, dressed in clothes more suitable for mourning (it is perhaps improbable in realistic terms that she should be there, but her presence contributes to the impression that these shots are a reflection of the state of Lampton's conscience).

As the married couple climb into the limousine – the image of luxury that had triggered Joe's ambition – the tension never lifts: the friends still seem sad and anxious behind the smiles. 'Wasn't it absolutely the most wonderful wedding ...', begins Susan gushingly, echoing the same words she has used after her first sexual intercourse with Joe. Lampton looks abstractedly out of the window. 'Til death us do part', Susan continues, at which point he turns towards her with tears in his eyes. 'Darling, you're crying', she says. 'I do believe you're sentimental after all.' But the tears are not those of sentiment: they are for Alice; for the death sentence that is his marriage; for the death of what was good in him. Mingling in there too, one hopes, is some compassion for sweet, simple Susan. The last shot is of their Bentley disappearing into the distance heading to the Top – Lampton's goal at last achieved – but down what seems an overpoweringly lonely street.

The critical reception afforded *Room at the Top* has attracted some attention over the years. In his book, *Hollywood England*, Alexander Walker suggested that 'contrary to the impression that has since formed, *Room at the Top* did not receive an overwhelming welcome from British critics at the time'.[22] This view was echoed in the 1993 BBC documentary series on 1960s British cinema, *Hollywood UK*, hosted by Richard Lester, who states of the film that it was 'not immediately well received by the critics'. Even a 1999 video magazine, *Movie Mail*, summarised the British critical response to the film as 'sniffy'. This description is quite inaccurate. It is true that an influential minority of critics from papers such as the *Observer*, *The Times*, the *Daily Worker* and the *New Statesman* expressed significant reservations about the film, to the extent that Paddy Whannel felt obliged to query whether British film critics 'would recognise a breakthrough on the screen if they saw one'.[23] The *Times* critic was particularly obtuse, pursuing a bizarrely pointless comparison with Arnold Bennett's *The Card*. Nevertheless the view of critical hostility to the film must be qualified. While it is true that the doyenne of British film critics of that time, C. A. Lejeune of the *Observer*, disliked the film, it is also true – and Walker omits to mention this – that her review provoked a counter-response in the letters pages that ran for three weeks.[24] Although Walker quotes the *Daily Worker*'s attack on Lampton for being a morally repulsive, unfair representative of the working class – John Hill's *Sex, Class and Realism in British Cinema* quotes the same passage – he does not mention (nor does Hill) that the paper's critic, Nina Hibbin, goes on to argue that she judges the film 'streets ahead of the book' – more objective, less biased – and thinks Simone Signoret is wonderful in it (24 January 1959).

These qualifications are important. Walker summarises the British critical response as follows: 'the majority of the British critics to judge from their reviews would have preferred to shut their eyes and deny the relevance to the contemporary scene of what they saw in *Room at the Top*', adding that the majority found the film's rejection of social orthodoxy 'offensive' (unlike the American critics, who found it liberating).[25] Walker is a critic who uses words carefully and if he is suggesting that few critics seemed to relate *Room at the Top* to the contemporary cultural and social scene, then there is a measure of truth in that; but the description seems to suggest an overall critical hostility to the film in England that simply was not the case. Having read well over fifty national and provincial reviews, I have to say that I would be hard pressed to think of any début film by an English director that garnered equal praise. Indeed, Walker's description of the film's reception sits oddly alongside the account in Simone Signoret's autobiography, where she wrote of her shared euphoria with Clayton on reading the reviews.[26] Not only were the majority not simply favourable but rave reviews, they were also remarkably consistent in what they found to comment on and praise. I wish to dwell on this for a moment because it gives an insight into how British cinema was perceived at this time.

One aspect of the film that was discussed in many reviews was its X certificate. The film's classification found its way into many headlines: 'The censor's X marks a spot at the top' (*Star*), 'Mr Harvey puts an X in Yorkshire' (*Evening Standard*), 'Why Bradford gets an X certificate' *Daily Express*). The X certificate was an issue partly because at the time *Room at the Top* was made the Rank Organisation had a policy of not screening X-certificate films, associated in some eyes with sleaziness and horror. In fact, *Room at the Top* was widely congratulated for bringing respectability back to the X certificate by being the kind of film for which that certification had originally been designed: cinema for the mature, intelligent adult. In the *Sunday Express* of 25 January 1959, Derek Monsey spoke for a wide critical constituency when he wrote:

> The way it tells the story of how Joe Lampton, low grade clerk in the town hall, made good has earned it an X certificate. Not for meretricious horror or peep-hole sex, but for sheer blatant honesty. The sex is there, in torrents. The horror is there and the coarse, down to common earth words. This is in no sense a U story. But it is real and straightforward and rings true. In this case at least, and at last, the X-certificate looks very like a badge of honour.

Two subtexts to this debate about the film's certification should be mentioned. *Room at the Top* occasioned comments about the enlightened attitude of the British Board of Film Censors and how superior the system was to that of other countries. In his autobiography *What the Censor Saw*, the BBFC's chairman John Trevelyan recalled that the censorship problems he had with the film – not many and dealt with amicably, which was not Trevelyan's experience with J. Lee Thompson – were more to do with strong language than graphic sex.[27] He did insist that the gruesome description of Alice's death be toned down and less foregrounded, although, set across Lampton's stunned reaction in close-up, we still get Mr Hoylake's description of Alice's prolonged agony after the crash and learn that she had been 'scalped'. (This lends terrible irony to one of Simone Signoret's last gestures as Alice, as she drunkenly examines her reflection in the pub mirror and pulls her hair back very tight on the head, exposing the scalp.) Otherwise the film had Trevelyan's full support. One side effect of this, though, was that *Room at the Top* set a critical standard for what was acceptable X-certificate fare that had a negative as well as a positive effect. Material and style in the vein of social realism were acceptable, but critics were much less tolerant of X-certificate films in the vein of stylised psychological horror, and Michael Powell's *Peeping Tom* (1960) was to take the full brunt of this critical prejudice when it appeared a year later to an almost unprecedented chorus of abuse and condemnation. Powellites have tended to be hostile to the British 'new wave' ever since, holding it in some ways responsible for what happened to Powell and *Peeping Tom*, but it was the critics not the film-makers who set up this polarity. (Ironically Clayton's next film was to be an X-rated horror film, though obviously in a very different vein.)

Room at the Top's depiction of sex, mild as it was, was also widely regarded as a huge breakthrough in honesty and maturity for British film. The headlines again catch some of the excitement and surprise: 'Here's a film that's a real scorcher' (*Woman's Mirror*) or 'Simone sizzles at the Top' (*Daily Sketch*). In her review in *Picturegoer* of 24 January 1959, the invariably astute Margaret Hinxman crystallised much of this critical feeling in her opening paragraph: 'This is it. By far the sexiest film to come out of a British – or almost any other – studio. And, by gum, this scorching analysis of bed and brass in a Yorkshire town rates its X certificate. And it rates a Picturegoer Seal of Merit.' Almost all the key ingredients seized on by other reviewers are there in that paragraph. The film is not only 'sexy', thereby challenging and extending the boundaries of taste and tolerance, but it is British to boot. François Truffaut might opine some years later that 'British' and 'cinema' were incompatible terms, but 'British' and 'sexy'? Clearly something pretty remarkable was going on in *Room at the Top*, offering a whole new perception of the English character on film, in bold contrast to the stereotypical stiff-upper-lip national cinema that had seemed particularly dominant in the 1950s.

Nowadays this view of the film might look rather strange and it would not be difficult to think of British films prior to *Room at the Top* that seemed sexier or even more sexually explicit: to take a few random examples, think of the swirling Technicolor passion of Powell and Pressburger's *Black Narcissus* (1947), or the clinch between Phyllis Calvert and Terence Morgan in the hotel bedroom in Mackendrick's *Mandy* (1952), or Elizabeth Sellars's overt sexual hunger for Dirk Bogarde's villain in Crichton's *Hunted* (1952), or Herbert Lom's sexual advances to a drunken, submissive Sylvia Syms in Lee Thompson's *No Trees in the Street* (1958).

The difference perhaps is that in the case of Powell and Pressburger it is overt melodrama and in the other films the passion is incidental to the main theme. In *Room at the Top*, however, the sexual charisma of the hero is central: notice how Lampton eyes up the office girls (who include Prunella Scales, Wendy Craig and Mary Peach) when he first arrives at the Town Hall. When he first meets Susan backstage, his intentions are at once unmistakable: as one of his women friends says, 'You don't beat about the bush, do you?' Indeed he does not: Lampton's sexual charm is his most important social weapon. Times have changed. Whereas the sexual drives of Thomas Hardy's Jude the Obscure at the end of the Victorian era would obstruct his social and academic ambitions, Joe Lampton's sexuality will work to his career advantage. It is one thing that sets him apart from other literary social climbers with whom he is often compared, such as Julian Sorel in Stendhal's *Scarlet and Black* and Clyde Griffiths in Dreiser's *An American Tragedy* (filmed in 1951 as *A Place in the Sun* by George Stevens, whose stylistic traits – the use of the dissolve, the dramatic counterpoint of sound and image – have much in common with Clayton's). Unlike Sorel, unlike Griffiths, Lampton will 'succeed'.

As Margaret Hinxman's strategic 'by gum' in her review suggested, the film's 'frankness' (a word which recurs time and again in the reviews) is intimately connected with its setting. Unusually a number of critics paid proper tribute to Ralph Brinton's art direction and the way it suggested social status. As Dilys Powell astutely put it, 'The grandiose mansion, the borrowed love nest with its upright piano and its flossy theatrical photographs beautifully stress social barriers' (*Sunday Times*, 25 January 1959). But it was the film's Northernness that caught the imagination, and the relation of the setting to the film's themes and style. 'Now Britain joins the bedroom brigade', was the headline of the *Daily Herald*, but with the crucial subheading 'And adds a slice of Yorkshire pudding'. The reviews contained a lot of references to Yorkshire pudding – sometimes garnished with mustard – as if it were an exotic dish, like Simone Signoret. The *Daily Herald* had an innocuous still of a clothed Laurence Harvey and Simone Signoret kissing on a bed, with the caption 'Whoever heard of such goings on in Yorkshire!' Nevertheless, beneath the occasional condescension, there was a perception that the blunt way of talking by characters in the film was an effective and eloquent correlative to the attitudes expressed about life, sex and relationships. More than that, the reviews collectively implied that the film's setting contributed vitally to its impact precisely because it stood in such sharp relief to a national cinema that had seemed predominantly South of England, middle-class and genteel. The novelty of the setting at that time for a large part of the cinema audience should not be underestimated. In post-austerity Britain, the kind of mobility we now take for granted was only just beginning to happen: in those days, for example, car ownership was a novelty, not the norm. In the 1993 BBC documentary *Hollywood UK*, John Osborne could comment that this new encounter with the North was 'like investigating a different world'. That was the feeling suggested by many of the reviews of *Room at the Top*: it opened up a new world.

Intriguingly, the ghost behind *Room at the Top*, in several reviews, was *Brief Encounter*. Both Alex Walker (as he was then) in the *Birmingham Post* (see epigraph) and Nancy Spain in the *Daily Express* of 21 January 1959 referred to *Room at the Top* as the best British film since *Brief Encounter*. The *Huddersfield Daily Examiner* (24 January 1959) called it 'the most moving and convincing love story of the British cinema since the unforgettable *Brief Encounter*'. I have drawn attention already to certain aspects of the film's imagery, style and themes that bring David Lean's film to mind. In one sense, *Room at the Top* was seen as a continuation and revitalisation of a great British film tradition that had been flagging during the 1950s. In another sense, though, there was recognition that the film was a decisive break from that tradition in its presentation of sexual behaviour. The Home Counties restraint and inhibition of *Brief Encounter* (that 'definitive document of middle class repression' as Gavin Lambert was to call it in the Stephen Frears documentary for Channel 4, *Typically British*) was being displaced by the Northern working-class emotional directness of *Room at the Top*.

Comparison between the two films was to be pinned down further in evaluative terms in Stuart Hall's and Paddy Whannel's book, *The Popular Arts*. 'If we look for British films which take us beyond the almost unbearable inhibitions of *Brief Encounter* and create a fuller and more complex image of love', they wrote,

> we shall have to turn to the group of films which constitute the British 'new wave'. ... *Room at the Top* is particularly interesting in this context. The film seemed at the time to represent a breakthrough in the British cinema – its theme the young man striving to get to 'the top' seemed peculiarly contemporary, and the provincial setting strikingly new. But we find, in retrospect, that the most important advance lay in the quality of the emotional life in the film.

And this was not attributable to anything British, they claimed, but to Simone Signoret creating 'the full and rounded image of an experienced married woman of feeling'.[28] Certainly I think it would be impossible to over-praise the beautiful understatement of her performance, the way she expresses joy with a slight smile, or deep hurt with a quick turn of the head. Even in stills from the film, it is striking how often Lampton is shown looking away, preoccupied, whilst Alice is looking directly at him, her eyes shining: a concentrated study of male self-preoccupation and feminine feeling. *Room at the Top* has been described as a male weepie, but it seems to me to have more in common with some of the great women's novels of the 1930s, such as Rosamond Lehmann's *The Weather in the Streets* (1936), which similarly differentiates male and female attitudes to relationships. The connection is more true of the film version of *Room at the Top* than of the novel, because the film eschews the special pleading of the first-person narrative and gives such prominence to Alice. But this in turn is accentuated by Signoret's heartbreaking performance of 'all woman', of a deeply bruised personality who commits herself too intensely in a new relationship at a crucial point in her life and consequently finds the pain of separation too terrible to bear. Prior to their affair and after a rehearsal as lovers in their amateur dramatics, Alice has suggested to Lampton that he puts more ardour into their embraces. 'I'm not fragile' she says, smiling, 'I won't break.' But she is: she will.

Writing of *Room at the Top* five years after the event, Hall and Whannel had come to a somewhat different conclusion about its significance from that reached by Penelope Houston in *The Contemporary Cinema*, quoted at the beginning of this chapter. With the benefit of hindsight and looking at the film from the perspective of Clayton's subsequent development, I think it is probably the emotional life of the heroine that now seems the most characteristic part of it. The sensitive depiction of Alice Aisgill's character will be matched in future films by Clayton that have similarly generous and tormented women as their protagonists: Deborah Kerr in *The Innocents*, Anne Bancroft in *The Pumpkin Eater*, Maggie Smith in *The Lonely Passion of Judith Hearne*. Certainly, as we have seen, the 'angry young man' dimension of *Room at the Top* did not interest Clayton nor did he intend anything self-consciously provocative in the love scenes. As an indication of his disinclination to be identified with the British new wave, he was to turn down offers to direct *Sons and Lovers*, *Saturday Night and Sunday Morning* and *The L-Shaped Room*; and I think it is fair to say that even Clayton's shooting style veers more towards aestheticism – the conscious deployment of cinema's expressive devices to an artistic end – than an unobtrusive realism where one is hardly conscious of the camera. Interestingly, the only critic at the time who wrote what one might term an 'auteurist' review of the film, in the sense that he gave chief credit for the film's quality to its director, was the critic on the *Daily Mirror*, Dick Richards, always a perceptive, unpretentious reviewer. Elsewhere, although not quite putting it in the terms used by Hall and

Whannel and while wishing to publicise the novelty of the film's hero and setting, most critics did attempt to convey a sense of something original and startling about the quality of emotional life in the film that was quite different from the usual run of British cinema.

The word used to define this quality was 'adult'. 'At long last', said Frank Jackson in *Reynold's News* of 25 January 1959, 'a British film that's truly adult'. In the *Sunday Dispatch* of the same date, Philip Oakes could write that 'this week the British cinema grew up', whilst Harold Conway in *Daily Sketch* of 23 January 1959 declared that 'this is the film that marks the point where the British film industry comes of age – and discovers the double bed'. This adulthood, coming after the state of arrested development that the British cinema had been languishing in for years, was characterised by three particular qualities: 'emotional maturity' (Alexander Walker's phrase), eroticism, and an ability to compete with the best in international and American cinema. It was as 'sexy as the craftiest Continental sex pedlars' (*Daily Herald*, 23 January 1959), and it had the brashness of the better Hollywood films and 'the realism of a Paddy Chayefsky film drama' (*Liverpool Daily Post*, 24 January 1959). This was one of the few reviews to give a contemporary contextualisation to the film; elsewhere there was barely a reference to the way its mood, attitudes and reception might be related to, say, post-Suez disillusionment, post-austerity Britain, Free Cinema, contemporary English drama, *Lucky Jim*, *The Uses of Literacy*. In some ways this seems fair enough: I do not think the film was significantly influenced by any of these things. For most critics – and this would account for its impact – *Room at the Top* seemed to fall unannounced out of a bland blue sky and place an unexpected bomb under the complacency, mediocrity, vapidity and escapism of 1950s British cinema.

It is clear, then, that one of the reasons that Clayton's film was, for the most part, so rapturously received was not simply its quality but its timing: Clayton was never again to make a film whose release so precisely chimed with both the critical and the public mood. *Room at the Top* was the kind of film many critics, wearied from the surfeit of British costume dramas and war thrillers, were waiting for. *Reynold's News* (25 January 1959) is representative of this feeling: 'For the very first time that I recall in a British film', its critic wrote, 'the façade of respectability and the stiff-upper-lip collapse completely. We see how people *really* speak and behave when they are together.' It was a new kind of English cinema, with a dash of exoticism (the North, Signoret) and combining the best of American realism and Continental frankness. It even transcended its literariness, for the critics felt that the adaptation by Neil Paterson (previously best known for his screenplays for Philip Leacock films such as *The Kidnappers* and *Hide Tide at Noon*) was a distinct improvement on the novel: more subtle, more balanced, more poignant. Paterson was to win an Oscar for his screenplay.

Needless to say, the film was soon to be overtaken and upstaged by newer, more strident voices: Karel Reisz's *Saturday Night and Sunday Morning* (1960), Tony Richardson's *A Taste of Honey* (1961), John Schlesinger's *A Kind of Loving* (1962), Lindsay Anderson's *The Sporting Life* (1963), among others. Later still a critical reaction was to set in against the social realist film; it was to be held responsible for the *Peeping Tom* outrage and for the critical hostility to fantasy, horror, stylistic flamboyance, excess and ambition that inhibited the progress of Britain's filmic dreamers and mad poets such as Powell, Roeg, Russell and Reeves. More recently still, that most reviled decade of British cinema, the 1950s, whose style and standards *Room at the Top* was seen as so successfully subverting, has been undergoing substantial revaluation: maybe it is much more interesting than we once thought.

Where does that now leave *Room at the Top*? Hard to say. At the end of the 1950s, for all the reasons indicated, there is no doubt in my mind that it would have topped any critical poll as the most important British film of the decade. But Clayton was no deliberate trendsetter, was resolutely impervious to film fashion, had a horror of jumping on any bandwagon. He simply thought he had made a film with worthwhile things to say about the time and about human relations; about ambition and idealism; about the temptation of materialism and the difficulty and importance of being true to oneself. He might have smiled at the John Lennon lyric 'Working Class Hero' (1969) which, as Stuart Laing has cleverly suggested,[29] seems to catch the theme of the film in a nutshell:

> There is room at the top they are
> telling you still,
> But first you must learn how to
> smile as you kill,
> If you want to be like the folks
> on the hill
> A working class hero is something to be.

But, amidst all the subsequent accolades and British and Hollywood Academy Awards, I think the tribute that would have meant most to Clayton was a telegram he received on Christmas Eve 1958 from his friend and most revered mentor, which simply read:

JUST SAW YOUR WONDERFUL PICTURE AND I CAN'T TELL YOU HOW PROUD I AM OF YOU.

JOHN HUSTON

Notes

1 All subsequent quotes are from this edition but *Room at the Top* was first published, by Eyre & Spottiswoode, in 1957.

2 Penelope Houston, *The Contemporary Cinema* (London, Penguin, 1963), p. 117.

3 John Osborne's play *Look Back in Anger* (1956) is traditionally regarded as an important signpost of an imminent rebellion against the social and cultural traditions of the past. Osborne's hero, Jimmy Porter, became a mouthpiece for a dissatisfied generation whose childhood had been scarred by the Depression and the war. Anger was directed at the Establishment, people with power and privilege who might treat the Porter-protesting generation with contempt but who were still capable of acts of gross destructive folly. This was the year of the Suez crisis, of the Russian invasion of Hungary, and when threats of the Cold War escalating into atomic warfare seemed very real. In Osborne's case, anger was also directed against a middle-aged, middle-class English theatre that bore no relation to contemporary reality, to the common people or to common sense – a theatre addicted to what Kenneth Tynan in his influential 1954 review article, 'West End Apathy' (reprinted in *Curtains*, London, Longmans,

1961, pp. 85–6), characterised as the 'Loamshire' play. Osborne's success was to blaze a trail for young, new, committed or experimental playwrights such as Arnold Wesker, Shelagh Delaney, John Arden and Harold Pinter. This movement in drama was paralleled by similar developments in the novel, from the iconoclasm of Kingsley Amis's *Lucky Jim* (1954) – very tamely filmed by the Boultings in 1957 – to the working-class realism of Braine, Alan Sillitoe, Stan Barstow and David Storey. Richard Hoggart's sensitive, sociological account of working-class life, *The Uses of Literacy* (1957), was also reflective of a shift in social consciousness and awareness.

4 I am thinking of the vigorous argument between Lindsay Anderson and John Russell Taylor in the Autumn 1956 issue of *Sight and Sound* about the role of film criticism: the tension between considerations of commitment and aestheticism, instruction and delight, content and form. Ernest Lindgren's *The Art of the Film* (London, George Allen & Unwin, 2nd edn) 1963), pp. 174–93, has an interesting account of this debate.

5 *New York Post*, 7 April 1959.

6 'The Way Things Are: Jack Clayton in an Interview with Gordon Gow', *Films and Filming*, April 1974, pp. 11–14.

7 Clayton was not only associate producer on *The Story of Esther Costello*, but was also in charge of the second unit which directed some additional scenes with Sears and Rosanno Brazzi after the director David Miller had returned to America.

8 Inevitably a number of critics were to comment on the inauthenticity of Harvey's Northern accent. Alan Dent in the *Illustrated London News* (7 February 1959) set himself up as a sort of Professor Higgins in reverse, criticising Harvey for speaking too correctly and, for example, sounding the 'h' in 'perhaps', which no self-respecting Northerner would do, though Harvey, Dent conceded, did better with the vowels.

9 In her autobiography, *Nostalgia Isn't What It Used To Be* (London, Granada Publishing, 1979), pp. 244–7, Simone Signoret recalls discussing the role with the director, Peter Glenville, who later withdrew from the film. Robert Murphy in *Sixties British Cinema* (London, BFI Publishing, 1992), says it was Glenville's idea to cast Signoret (pp. 304-5). Alexander Walker, how-ever, said that Signoret was Clayton's suggestion (*Hollywood England*, London, Michael Joseph, 1974; repr. Harrap, 1986, p. 52). Clayton's widow, Haya Harareet, told me she thought Signoret was suggested by the film's casting director, Irene Lamb, and that Clayton leapt at the idea.

10 See Anthony Aldgate, *Censorship and the Permissive Society: British Cinema and Theatre 1955–1965* (Oxford, Clarendon Press, 1995), pp. 45–7. Aldgate notes how the censor, John Trevelyan, sent two BBFC examiners to early public screenings to test audience reaction. Both examiners referred to Signoret's presence, one suggesting that she gave the film the appearance of a foreign 'X' film which was unusual for an English audience but not difficult to defend, and the other saying her performance was the most sympathetic in the film and deserved an Oscar – an accurate prediction, as it turned out.

11 David Lodge, *The Language of Fiction* (London, Routledge & Kegan Paul,

1966), pp. 245–8.

12 Walker, *Hollywood England*, p. 45.

13 Murphy, *Sixties British Cinema*, p. 14.

14 *Los Angeles Times*, 7 July 1959.

15 Stuart Laing, '*Room at the Top*: The Morality of Affluence', in *Popular Fiction and Social Change* ed. Christopher Pawling (London, Macmillan, 1984), pp 157–83.

16 See, for example, a very interesting discussion of the treatment of the Second World War in post-1945 British cinema in James Chapman's 'Our Finest Hour Revisited', in *Journal of Popular British Cinema*, ed. Alan Burton and Julian Petley (London, Flicks Books, 1998), pp. 63–75. Chapman makes a persuasive case for regarding the war film in British national cinema as analogous to the Western in American cinema.

17 *Films and Filming*, November/December 1988, p. 11.

18 The scene at the station, incidentally, caused some conflict during filming. Haya Clayton told me that the Woolfs were appalled at the way their star, Simone Signoret, was photographed in this scene, making her look ugly and distraught – precisely why the scene seems so truthful and powerful – and insisting that it be re-shot. If not, the cameraman Freddie Francis would be fired and a replacement found. In response, Clayton declared himself very satisfied with the scene and told the Woolfs that if they fired the cameraman, they would have to find another director as well. The scene remained. The story is confirmed by Freddie Francis in an interview in Brian McFarlane's *An Autobiography of British Cinema* (London, Methuen, 1997), p. 209.

19 'The House that Jack Built', *Films and Filming*, October 1967, p. 5. McVay's is the finest early article on Clayton.

20 Walker, *Hollywood England*, p. 46.

21 John Hill, *Sex, Class and Realism in British Cinema*, 1956–63 (London, BFI Publishing, 1986), p. 158.

22 Walker, *Hollywood England*, p. 47.

23 *Ibid.*, p. 49.

24 Lejeune's hostility to the film provoked a lot of comment and warrants more detailed description. She found the composition of the love scenes gross; felt that Simone Signoret, even though she 'sails away' with it, had no business in the film at all; but in particular judged nearly every aspect of the film – acting, setting, girl's mother, snob RAF suitor – 'phoney'. These characters, she claimed, 'wouldn't last five minutes north of the Trent. They'd either change their tune or be sent packing'. She could say this with conviction, she claimed, because she was writing 'as a north country woman', having been born in Manchester. Her review (25 January 1959) prompted a letter in the following week's issue of the *Observer* from Philip Oakes, who claimed that all she seemed to be saying was that she preferred films about nice people. Having a right to reply, Lejeune responded, 'What I prefer is a film about real people. The fault I have to find in *Room at the Top* is that class distinctions are emphasised but not substantiated. Joe Lampton betrays not class pride but class inferiority. In other words, he is

neither fair to his class nor honest with himself and therefore to me he becomes an artificial character.' At which point the novel's author John Braine felt obliged to intervene in the argument. Courteously praising Lejeune's work in the past and generously forgiving her for confusing Bradford with Sheffield, he nevertheless criticised as inadequate her reasons for dismissing the Lampton character. 'We should all be honest with ourselves, many of us aren't. That doesn't make us artificial or unreal; we remain human beings, good or bad. Because we can't live up to Miss Lejeune's standards, it doesn't follow we're non-existent' (*Observer*, 8 February 1959). Derek Monsey brought the debate to a conclusion the following week by expressing disagreement with Lejeune's judgement on *Room at the Top* but praising the standards and precepts she had 'so brilliantly maintained over the years'.

25 Walker, *Hollywood England*, pp. 49–50.
26 Signoret, *Nostalgia Isn't What It Used To Be*, pp. 254–5.
27 John Trevelyan, *What the Censor Saw* (London, Michael Joseph, 1973), pp. 106–7.
28 Stuart Hall and Paddy Whannel, *The Popular Arts* (London, Hutchinson, 1964), p. 220.
29 Stuart Laing, '*Room at the Top*', p. 182.

1 A thoughtful Jack Clayton on the set of *The Great Gatsby*

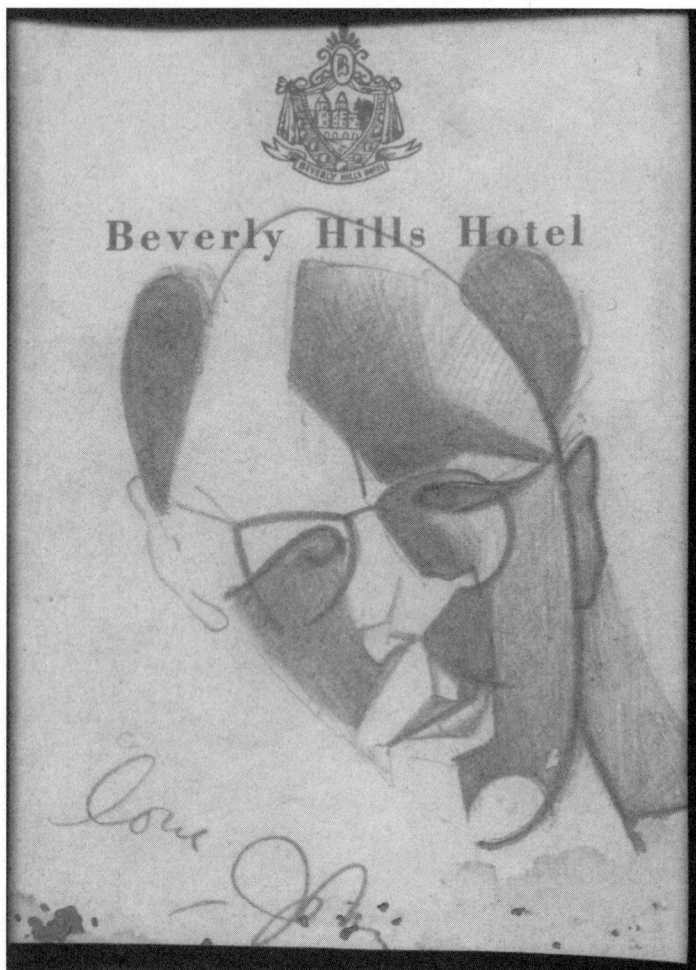

2 Jack Clayton as sketched by John Huston at the Beverly Hills Hotel, 1953

3 Clayton as a child actor with Peggy Ashcroft in Carl Zuckmayer's *The Golden Toy*, London Coliseum, 1934

facing 4 Clayton as a bespectacled young third assistant director on the set of *Wings of the Morning* (1937), the first British Technicolor film. The stars in the centre of the photograph are Henry Fonda and Annabella, in her role as a heroine dressed as a boy

5 Sex comes to British cinema: Laurence Harvey and Simone Signoret in *Room at the Top*

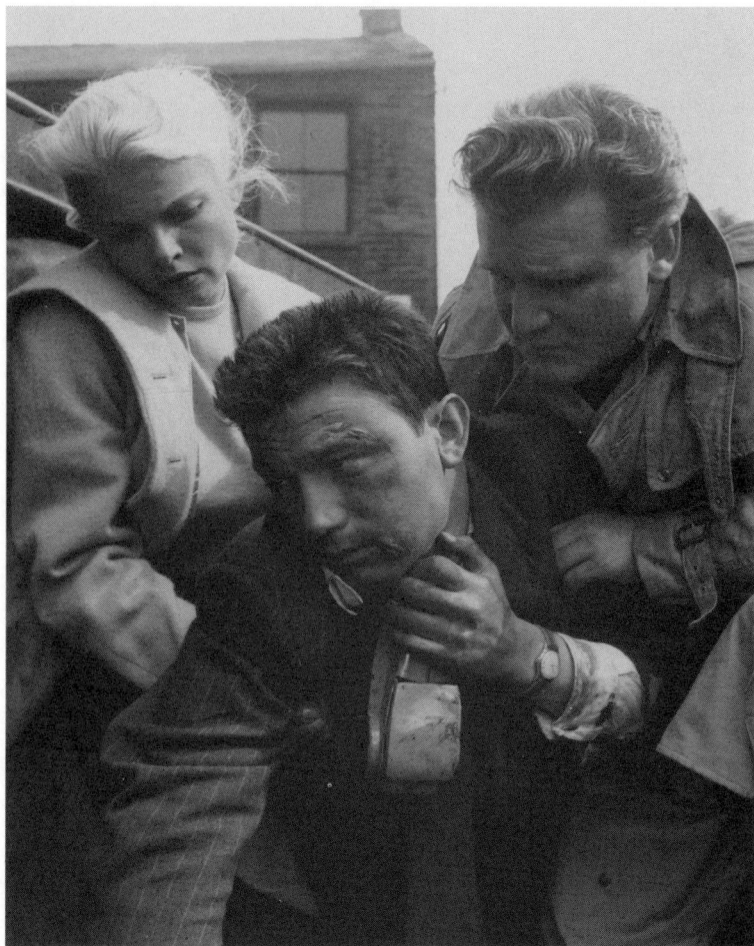

6 The price of wealth: Mary Peach, Laurence Harvey and Donald Houston in *Room at the Top*

7 Unhappy is the groom: Laurence Harvey and Heather Sears in *Room at the Top*

8 The famous preview card of *Room at the Top* that Clayton displayed in his office

ROMULUS *presents*
SIMONE SIGNORET · LAURENCE HARVEY and HEATHER SEARS in "ROOM AT THE TOP" A REMUS Film

THE PRODUCERS of this new film would be grateful if you would answer the following questions :—

1. Did you enjoy " ROOM AT THE TOP " ? .... NO ! ! ! ! !

2. Are there any scenes you particularly liked or disliked ? :—

(a) Liked ....

....

....

(b) Disliked ....

.... ALL OF THEM

3. Any other comments ....

.... TRIPE

9 Deborah Kerr and Jack Clayton on the set of *The Innocents*

10 Clayton's sketch of the last scene of *The Innocents*

11 Clayton, Haya Harareet and James Mason arrive for the screening of *The Pumpkin Eater* at the Cannes Film Festival, 1964

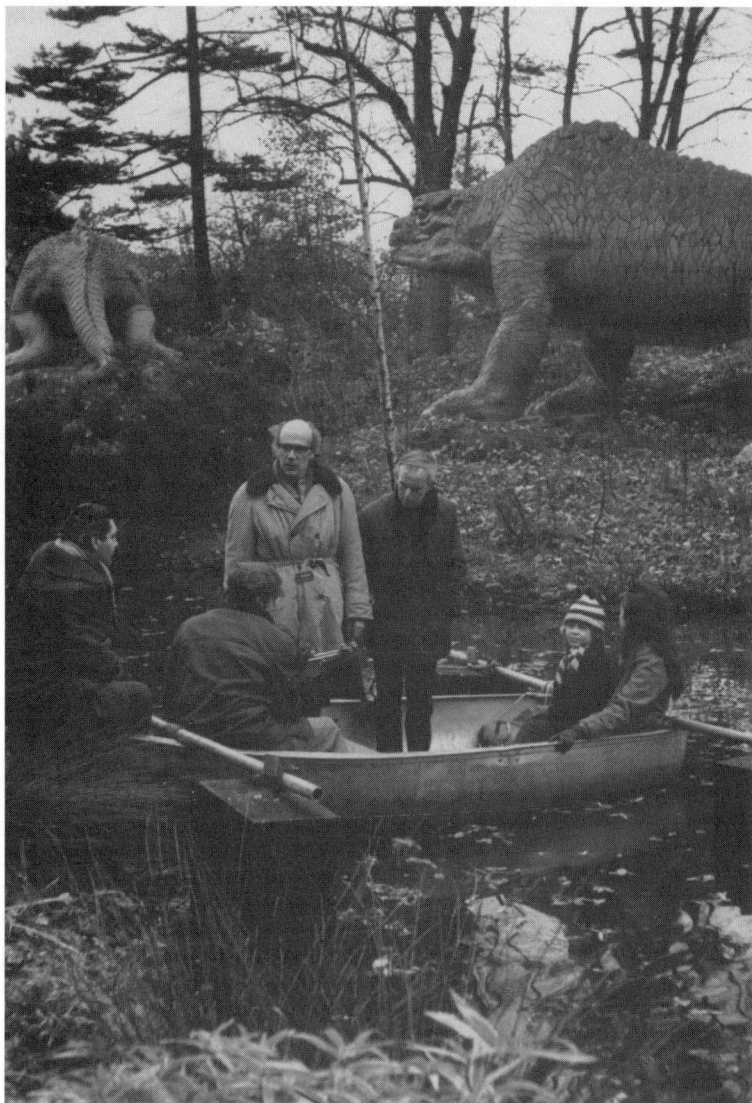

12 Clayton at Jurassic Park: directing the scene on the boating lake in *Our Mother's House*. Photography by Eve Arnold. Reproduced by courtesy of Eve Arnold and Magnum Photos, to whom grateful thanks

13 Dirk Bogarde and Pamela Franklin in *Our Mother's House*

14 Clayton directs Robert Redford and Mia Farrow in *The Great Gatsby*

15 Mr Dark in Disneyland: Jonathan Pryce and Jack Clayton on the set of *Something Wicked This Way Comes*   **16** Clayton (*right*) shares a joke with his favourite film composer, Georges Delerue, 1987

17 Maggie Smith in *The Lonely Passion of Judith Hearne*

18 Clayton at home, with his pigeons. Photograph by Haya Clayton

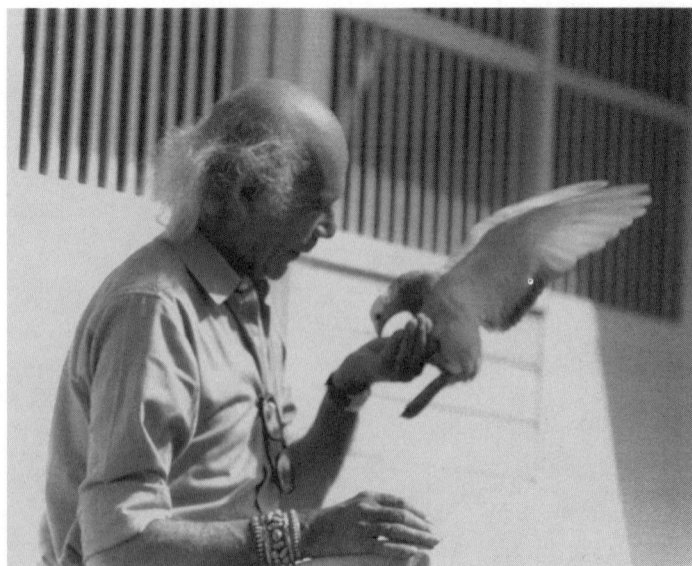

Pearl of ambiguity: *The Innocents* (1961)

4

Twenty years after it was made, a waiter in a restaurant brought a message to Jack's table from an unknown guest. The note was addressed to him and read: '*The Innocents* is the best English film after Hitchcock goes to America.' It was signed François Truffaut.
(Karel Reisz, *Guardian*, 25 March 1995)

Only make the reader's general vision of evil intense enough ... and his own experience, his own imagination, his own sympathy (with the children) and horror (of their false friends) will supply him with all the particulars. Make him think the evil, make him *think* it for himself, and you are released from weak specifications.
(Henry James, *The Art of the Novel: Critical Prefaces*, New York: Charles Scribner & Sons, 1962, p. 176)

In its Spring issue of 1959, *Sight and Sound* invited nine British film-makers for their response to the following question: What particular subject would they personally choose to film at this moment, assuming that they enjoyed a completely free hand?[1] Recognising the idealistic nature of the question, Clayton gave an idealistic reply:

It must be a subject that has at least some aspect one can believe in, love and actually feel. It should, even if only partially, give the opportunity of expressing some facet of man to his inner self and of that same man to the outside world. It must be valid for today: not the today of the newspaper stop press, which is usually dead by the time it is read, but the real today which, with different clothes, is true of yesterday and tomorrow. Finally the subject must try

above all else to prise open the doors of convention and snap
through as many archaic rules as possible.[2]

In the long term it would be fair to say that Clayton never lost that
idealistic perspective: it accounts for why he made so few films,
and why he was so obsessive with the films that he did make. In
the short term, though, his answer to the question would have
been very simple. What he was looking for in a subject at that time
was something as unlike *Room at the Top* as possible. He had no
desire to be typecast as the leader of the British cinema's 'new
wave', a danger he espied particularly when *Room at the Top* was
shown at the Cannes Festival of 1959 at the same time as a
number of films such as François Truffaut's *Les Quatre Cents
Coups* (1959) and Alain Resnais's *Hiroshima Mon Amour* (1959)
which became important harbingers of the French *Nouvelle Vague*.

Nevertheless, given the intense interest in the choice of Clayton's next assignment following the international success of *Room
at the Top*, some eyebrows were raised when it was announced that
he was to film *The Innocents*, an adaptation of the classic Victorian
ghost story *The Turn of the Screw* (1898) by Henry James, which
Clayton had read when he was 10. Part of the attraction was the
difficulty of the material. The cast basically consisted of two
adults, two children, and two ghosts who were trying to possess
the souls of the children; and the key to the telling of this most
haunting of tales was uncertainty and ambiguity. This in turn set
Clayton a formidable technical challenge in that it was a tale in
which mood and mystery were all-important. Were the ghosts real
or figments of the governess's imagination? To this end, Clayton
was to experiment with multiple dissolves, 'images which hang
there', as he put it, 'and have a meaning which applies both to the
end of the last scene and the beginning of the next'.[3] In a visit to
the set at Pinewood, Penelope Houston reported that Clayton and
his editor Jim Clark were working out a technical effect whereby
the film would be using dissolves that burn out into white instead
of fading into the usual black.[4] Because the rights to the property
were owned by Twentieth Century-Fox, another technical problem
was Cinemascope, which Clayton disliked but which, in the event,
he and his photographer Freddie Francis exploited brilliantly,

diffusing and softening the edges of the frame to give the impression of something unnervingly not quite discernible at the fringes of vision.

A technical exercise, then? This was, after all, what Henry James had claimed for *The Turn of the Screw*: 'it is a piece of ingenuity pure and simple, of cold artistic calculation, an *amusette* to catch those not easily caught (the "fun" of the capture of the merely witless being ever but small), the jaded, the disillusioned, the fastidious'.[5] Ironically, it has become one of the most deeply analysed of all James's fictions and perceived as one of his most deeply ambiguous and indeed personal works (no work of his more powerfully dramatises his recurrent theme of innocence lost, or violated, or under siege). Similarly, although it might seem a calculated fairy-tale contrast to Clayton's gritty début feature and thereby probably chosen simply for its novelty, it is possible to argue it as a deeply considered project with a lot of personal resonance for Clayton. Haya Clayton recounted that the atmosphere evoked by the film seemed to have parallels with the childhood Clayton had described to her: being brought up in a house full of secrets and whispers (particularly to do with the identity of his father), and where to reveal the secret would produce horror. In his obituary notice in the *Guardian* (25 March 1995), Clayton's fellow director and close friend Karel Reisz – who thought *The Innocents* the greatest of Clayton's films – also relates the power of the film to the chord the material struck in Clayton's memory of childhood. 'It was the perfect subject for him', said Reisz.

> Jack himself had never been to school. He grew up not knowing his father, never settled in one place for long, in the company of pets and nannies. In his variation of the Henry James story, the exclusion of the boy (Miles) from the secret world of grown-ups is seen as a condition of life, something to be expected. The evil things that happen there are no more than Miles has imagined. And the ghostly intimations of evil which might have tempted another director into 'horror', come to us in brief, almost subliminal flashes of recognition – Miles' recognition ... *The Innocents* is in black and white, beautiful and unexpectedly lyrical. And it chills you to the bone.

As a postscript, it might be worth mentioning that Clayton told at least two interviewers (Gordon Gow and Andrew Higson) that he saw the ghost of Miss Jessel standing at the end of his garden when he was working on the film. According to his widow, Clayton believed in ghosts: in this film above all others, it shows.

The film is based both on James's novella and, by necessity (because of the rights being owned by Fox), on the William Archibald stage adaptation entitled *The Innocents* which had been premièred at the Playhouse Theatre, New York on 1 February 1950, with Beatrice Straight as the governess, music by Alex North and direction by Peter Glenville.[6] The play is a reasonably effective theatrical transposition of James, though not as powerful and impressive as the Ruth and August Goetz dramatic rendering of James's *Washington Square* under the title *The Heiress*. (It might be worth remembering that one of the stars of Clayton's film, Michael Redgrave, also did a fine adaptation of James for the stage, *The Aspern Papers* – all the more remarkable because James himself, who longed for success as a London playwright, wrote disastrous plays.) It contains some of the ingredients and incidents of the novella and/or the subsequent film: an opening song (though much eerier in the film – it even silences the Twentieth Century Fox fanfare); the game of hide and seek; Miles's sinister recitation that seems to invite Quint's ghost to enter the house; the broad thrust of the narrative. What it palpably does not have is the novel's and the film's sense of suggestiveness and ambiguity. This is particularly true of the play's final scene, where Miles is overtly sinister and where it is made quite explicit in the stage direction ('Ghost of Quint appears. Miles stiffens in his chair, fully aware of Quint')[7] that the boy sees the ghost.

Archibald did a first draft script for the film. In his preparatory notes, Clayton wrote that 'while I am a great admirer of the play and I feel that certain elements of it should be incorporated, I think the script follows the play too closely'.[8] What particularly worried him was that, given the limited number of characters and setting, and the 'normal opportunities in a film for constantly varying tempo, atmosphere and tension', the onus was on the script to provide a different kind of impetus and variety, which he thought Archibald's failed to do. 'Perhaps our only chance is through constant change – change within the scene itself – of tempo and atmosphere – going from something sinister to laughter, or the other way round. In other words we have at all times to keep the audience guessing – and I don't mean plot only.' Certainly in the finished film one notices how well Clayton accomplishes this: how each scene has a disquieting aspect and how each moment of significant silence, or secret looks, or double meaning, is made to tell through a precise line inflection or camera angle (for example, the quick look exchanged between Miles and Flora when the former has asked Miss Giddens if her home had been 'too small for you to have secrets'). For the ability to locate the precise moment of maximum tension in a scene, Clayton's direction has a mastery comparable to that of another great director of domestic tension, William Wyler. And it is an ability that is profoundly Jamesian – the capacity to convey 'the maximum of intensity with the minimum of strain'.[9]

Another difficulty with Archibald's script, Clayton felt, was the abundance of dialogue given to the children. 'We have to try to maintain tension with every scene', he wrote. 'Children can rarely maintain tension during a long scene or keep variety in their voices – or even time their lines correctly. I do not propose to shoot this picture in little short sections just to keep the performances for the children.' The dialogue was later modified accordingly, though it must be said that Clayton did obtain remarkable performances from Martin Stephens (as Miles) and Pamela Franklin (as Flora). In an interview with Joe Hyams in the *New York Herald Tribune* (29 January 1962) he revealed something of his method, which sounded rather like the way Carol Reed had directed the boy in *The Fallen Idol* (1948): 'All they knew was that they were playing in a ghost story and they adored that. I never allowed them to read the entire script and they were given their lines only a day or two before the scenes they were supposed to play.'

Then there was the filming of the ghosts. 'There is the tremendously important point that does not emerge clearly [in Archibald's draft] – and that is that Quint and Miss Jessel to a lesser extent are not just ghosts that haunt the premises, but they are there for a very definite purpose – to obtain Miles and Flora.' This is managed perfectly in the film in the appearance of Quint (Peter Wyngarde) at the window staring past Miss Giddens into the house, a moment prefaced by an unnerving jump cut that catches the governess as she is in the act of concealing herself behind a curtain during a game of hide and seek. (It is another tangential reference to *The Fallen Idol*, where a game of hide and seek in a huge house also brings forth horrors.)

There were two other fundamental problems in filming the ghosts, both of which Clayton solved brilliantly. How do you photograph ghosts in daylight, and still make them palpably ghosts and sinister? And how do you show or imply that the ghosts may be figments of the governess's imagination? The ghosts have to be shown if the governess's state of mind is to be understood at all; but once seen they will surely convince an audience of the validity and reality of her visions, thus undermining the material's all-important ambiguity.[10] Clayton's major visual solution – probably worked out with his superb editor, James Clark – is disarmingly simple. He reverses the usual cause and effect by always showing the governess's reaction to what she sees before we see the thing itself. Deborah Kerr is magnificent at these moments. As Penelope Gilliat graphically puts it, 'her lips draw back like a horse that smells fire'.[11] Close-ups of the governess before the visions appear give the impression that it is her own sense of horror that is *producing* the visions.

The effect of the ghosts too is enhanced by Clayton's camera placement and the quality of Freddie Francis's cinematography (it was surely this film that should have won him the Oscar rather than *Sons and Lovers*). I could not disagree more with the critic of *The Times* (24 November 1961) who pronounced that 'the camera, for instance, comes off a very second best to the exquisite prose passage, wonderfully ominous yet never ostentatiously seeming so, which describes the appearance of Quint on the battlements'. Clayton's visual imagination and Francis's technical capability are fully equal to this moment, showing us a visually insubstantial yet somehow tangible figure as if seen through a sultry haze. The governess has been clipping a huge rose to a background of

Flora's humming 'O Willow Waly'. Chancing to peep through some undergrowth in the garden, the governess sees a small statue of a child, but is disconcerted when a black beetle falls dangling from its mouth, like, to use the description in the screenplay, 'a small black tongue'. At this point the sound suddenly dips: Flora is no longer singing; Miss Giddens has dropped her scissors in the fountain in the shock of feeling another presence near; and in this haze of sunlight and silence, something sinister stirs. As Miss Giddens goes to investigate further, there is an extraordinary shot of the battlement with Quint not now visible but where a pigeon flies across the tower in eerie slow motion: it must have been that shot that caused William Wyler to remark at a preview screening that if Clayton could get performances like that from pigeons, heaven knows what he might achieve with actors.

The photographing of Miss Jessel's ghost is no less noteworthy. When she appears in black in long shot across the lake (again an appearance prompted by Flora's humming of that tune) she is the visual epitome of the lovelorn Victorian heroine, like Tennyson's Mariana.[12] The scene where she appears in the schoolroom, at a point when Miss Giddens is planning to leave, is one of the finest of the film. Again the governess reacts before we see the ghost sitting sobbing at the teacher's desk. Miss Giddens slides along the wall towards her but the vision has gone by the time she reaches the desk, the only evidence of her presence being a teardrop on the slate. Clayton arrived at this image through a rationalisation. What would most terrify him in a situation of that kind, making it impossible to explain the vision away as a hallucination? 'A tear mark on a piece of paper would really frighten me very much', he told Gordon Gow,[13] 'as well as being very sad'. The image sustains uncertainty, for it is evidence so evanescent as to be no evidence at all. (In this respect there is a similarity to Orson Welles's Rosebud: the moment of revelation and proof is almost simultaneous with the moment at which the evidence will evaporate and perish for ever.) In another striking visual moment, when Mrs Grose comes into the schoolroom in search of Miss Giddens, the governess is sitting at the desk in the precise position where the ghost of Miss Jessel (Clytie Jessop) sat, and is wearing similarly funereal shades of black. As the tale unfolds, the governess will become more and more like Miss Jessel. In her final scene with Miles, she will inadvertently act out a version of the Quint–Jessel relationship – he bullying, she supplicating; and at Miles's death she will howl like a wild beast in the way Jessel is said to have howled at Quint's death, just as Miles himself will lie dead with his eyes open, like Quint.

The casting of Deborah Kerr in the role of the governess was settled on by Twentieth Century Fox: it was part of the package that was sold to Clayton in return for the chance to direct. In one sense, the casting is curious as, in James's story, the governess is only 20 years old (Kerr at that time was nearly 40). However, it has become something of a convention to have an older actress in the role. A 44-year-old Ingrid Bergman had played the part on American television only a year before, and Claire Bloom was to star in a theatrical revival at the age of 45. The reason for this is perhaps that in James's novella the story is told in retrospect and the quality of the narration comes over as mature and experienced. Moreover, it adds a mystery to the character of the governess, whose first post this is, which connects to the other characters: what were they doing before the story proper began? Whatever the critical controversy over the casting, Clayton could not have been happier with the performance: twenty years later he said he still could not imagine anyone playing the part better.[14] Clayton and his actress were in perfect agreement throughout the film. 'I remember asking Jack (Clayton) what he wanted me to stress in playing the part', Kerr wrote, 'and he replied: "You play it the way you feel, but don't forget the ambiguity!" So I tried the very nervous tight-rope between sanity and insanity, and left the audience to exercise its intelligence.'[15]

If Clayton was blessed in the casting of his leading actress, he had greater difficulty in finding a script that entirely satisfied him. His working notes reveal that, dissatisfied with William Archibald's first draft screenplay which too closely followed the play, he consulted several writers for ideas and, in some cases, sample scenes. Talking with Peter Viertel (Deborah Kerr's husband) clarified for Clayton what he most loved about the story – the fact that this is the 'most perfect example of real horror which is, in other words, leave it to the person's imagination to ... make for himself his conception of the horror'. Probably unconsciously he is almost directly quoting Henry James's aesthetic precepts and his recognition of 'that odd law which somehow always makes the minimum of valid suggestion serve the man of imagination better than the maximum'.[16] At this stage he was being tempted by the idea of tackling the film as 'a rather strange detective story and rather as though one accepts in principle the fact that all the important incidents have ... occurred before we arrived on the scene'. He was also tempted by the idea of using flashbacks to elaborate what went on between Quint, Jessel and the children before the governess arrived. (This was to be the subject of Michael Winner's 1971 film, *The Nightcomers*.)

Talking over the subject with the writer Nigel Neill, Clayton particularly focused on the disguised and indirect way James's tale dealt with a number of forbidden subjects of that time, one being the possibility of the boy's being in love with the governess and vice versa. This in turn might have been the inspiration behind the two passionate kisses shared between boy and governess which were to become perhaps the most controversial aspect of the film and which Clayton, despite pressure from Twentieth Century Fox, refused to remove. It was through talking to Harold Pinter, Clayton said – he was not at this time thinking of Pinter as a writer for the screenplay but certainly thinking of him as a writer with whom he would like to work in the future – that he realised flashbacks would not work. 'If one shows Quint and the first governess in the flashbacks, any suggestion of them as ghosts is enormously watered down.'

Rhys Adrian did a draft of some of the early scenes, including the interview with the uncle which, on the page at least, does not quite get across the crucial spell his charm casts over the governess. Clayton originally asked Cary Grant to play the role, and Grant was interested, except that he wanted the uncle to return for the end of the film and Clayton felt that to be impossible. In the event the part was played in a one-scene cameo by Michael Redgrave, who achieves exactly the mix of calculated insensitivity with insidious seductiveness the part requires. There was to be some comment about so small a part being given to such a major actor. 'Michael Redgrave, in a guest spot as the children's uncle,' said *Variety* (6 December 1961) 'is suavely effective. Since he disappears after the first few minutes, it might have been wiser to use a lesser figure. As it is, audiences may be expecting Redgrave to play an important role in the plot, which doesn't happen. It is a let down.' But Clayton recognised that the part was crucial; reference to the uncle throughout the film requires that his only appearance be given great weight. (Possibly, too, the figure of the male relation who wanted nothing to do with his own family, particularly the children, had personal meaning for Clayton.) Redgrave's appearance as the uncle, a crucial figure outside the main narrative, is an interesting anticipation of his role in Joseph Losey's *The Go-Between* (1971) and a reminder of the similarity between both the Clayton and Losey films and the James and Hartley novels: opening journeys to a large house; games of hide and seek; a sinister relationship between the mistress of the house and a servant; the disturbing equation of sexuality and evil, which has a traumatic impact on the minds of the children; and symbolic use of weather, where heat correlates to repressed passion and the outbreak of thunder and rain unleashes a torrent of emotion.

When Archibald was disengaged from the script, Clayton turned to John Mortimer, having been impressed by the ghostly feeling the writer had got into his script for *Dock Brief* (originally a radio drama that became a one-act play which in turn became a film). Unfortunately Mortimer was committed to something else at the time, and was only able to work on the film for three weeks. He did have a crack at writing a scene which reintroduces the uncle, visiting the children at Bly with a lady friend, Miss Fawcett. It occurs during the schoolroom scene, when the children are clearly bored and squeaking their pencils on their school slates. After he has taken them into the country – to a village pub and to a cricket match at the village green – he departs with Miss Fawcett, the governess trying and failing to engage his interest in Miles's expulsion from school and her first sight of Quint. It is an interesting addition but was eventually to be cut, probably because it distracted from the narrative, diluted the claustrophobic atmosphere, and did not tell us anything about the uncle that had not been established in the first scene. Mortimer did polish the dialogue, though, and Haya Clayton credits him with one of the finest lines in the whole film, when Miss Giddens insists that the housekeeper Mrs Grose (a career best performance from Megs Jenkins) tells her exactly what went on in the house between Quint and Jessel. Mrs Grose says: 'Rooms ... used by daylight as though they were dark woods'. It is a wonderful evocation of Victorian evasiveness on the matter of sex, which goes to the heart of the film's meaning.

The screenplay was finally taken in hand by Clayton's friend Truman Capote, with whom he had worked on *Beat the Devil* (1954). Capote did a superb job of catching the period flavour, and despite the credit decreed by the Screen Writers' Guild which suggests co-authorship with Archibald, Clayton always insisted that the script was 90 per cent Capote. 'The result on the screen is Truman's version, totally, with a few changes, which I always do on the set', Clayton wrote in answer to a query from a film student. 'The reason why Archibald is coupled with Truman Capote on the credits is because the Writers' Guild in America have a silly rule that the first writer automatically shares the credit if it is based on a book. Very unfair, I think'.[17]

After his collaboration with Clayton on *Room at the Top*, Freddie Francis was the natural choice for cameraman. It turned out to be one of the most creative experiences of his career: on the basis of his work on the film, Clayton was to call him 'quite brilliant' and 'a genius'. The casting of Miles and Flora, too, could not have been bettered. In his script notes for Flora, Clayton wrote of 'simple, beautiful charm – underplayed simplicity', and he found that in Pamela Franklin, who was making her screen début. 'Pamela stood right out', said Clayton about the tests for the part. As for Miles, 'he must look beautiful and angelic and behave with dignity without being priggish'. Clayton found his ideal Miles in the 11-year-old Martin Stephens, who by that time was an experienced child screen actor, having appeared in *The Divided Heart* (1954), *The Hellfire Club* (1960), *Count Your Blessings* (1959) and, perhaps most significantly, *Village of the Damned* (1960) as a preternaturally intelligent child with a sinister disposition.

According to Stephen Rebello,[18] one of the few instances of discord during the making of *The Innocents* occurred between Clayton and his composer Georges Auric. Auric seemed a perfect choice for the film, having worked with Clayton to great effect on *Moulin Rouge* and *The Bespoke Overcoat* and having written scores for Cocteau's *Beauty and the Beast* (1946) and Thorold Dickinson's *The Queen of Spades* that suggested a facility for this kind of fantastic subject. But Clayton was dissatisfied with the finished score and wanted revisions which Auric, because of ill-health, was unable to provide. The re-orchestration was put into the hands of W. Lambert Williamson, who did such a fine job that many critics singled out the score for special praise.

I want now to comment on some key scenes in *The Innocents*, particularly with regard to how well Clayton's stated intentions in them have been realised. It is worth beginning with Clayton's own notes on what attracted him to the subject.

> My original interest in the story was in the fact that one could tell it from a completely different point of view – in other words – evil was alive in the mind of the governess and in fact she more or less creates the situation. Now this was long before I read the notes on Henry James and found that somebody else also imagines that Henry James wrote it in this way – sort of almost Freudian hallucinations the governess had.

Although *The Turn of the Screw* has never lacked for critical inter-pretation and is now regarded as an archetype of literary ambiguity, the main interpretations can basically be grouped, with variations and refinements, under one of two headings. On the one side it is an allegory of Good versus Evil, with the virtuous governess fighting to save the children in her charge from being possessed by the demonic ghostly spirits of the former governess, Miss Jessel, and the vicious valet Quint. On the other side, it is a pre-Freudian study of sexual neurosis, in which a repressed Victorian spinster with a colourful imagination and a tendency to insomnia starts seeing things, believes that these ghostly visions are connected with the children and starts behaving in such a manic way that ultimately she terrifies them to the point of nervous breakdown and heart failure. The most famous proponent of this latter interpretation was Edmund Wilson in his 1938 essay 'The Ambiguity of Henry James'.[19] Among Clayton's papers there is a copy of this essay, typed up and included with the First Master Script (December 1960). However, Clayton was adamant that he did not want to come down categorically on one side or the other. It was more interesting, he felt, if you thought that all of the four main characters were innocents – which does not preclude their feeling passion – who were telling the truth as they saw it. 'One should really try and give it a dual life,' he wrote, 'one on the level of the governess and one on the ordinary obvious level of there are the ghosts and they are after the children.' It is the duality that gives the tale its horror.

In some hand-written notes, Clayton wrote that he wanted a 'completely new opening', one that was different both from the novella's rather laboured prologue and the introduction of the governess's narration. 'Its purpose', he went on, 'to arrest and intrigue the audience before and after the titles. Perhaps to plant Miss Giddens' state of mind – her doubts as to whether she is guilty or not – possibly to show the world's attitude to her now and in the future.' Clayton was later to confess that the opening of the film gave him more trouble than the rest of it put together, and that the original opening was altered in post-production.[20] In the earlier script versions the film was to begin in a churchyard on a rainy day with a burial in progress (that of Miles). Present would be a distraught Miss Giddens; the housekeeper Mrs Grose, who turns away when she sees the governess; and the uncle, who deliberately turns his back and enters the carriage with, as the screenplay indicated, 'his face set and disapproving'. The intention: 'establish Miss G being shunned by all. No dialogue. She is left alone'. She would then enter the silent house at Bly.

> We establish dust sheets etc. – the house closed up. She goes to her room – starts writing letter to the uncle – we hear her voice over reading the lines: 'Dear Sir, ... if you blame me – as you must – for the terrible happenings at Bly – it can be no more than I blame myself. And yet, if you knew it all, how else could I have acted? I

shall ask that of myself for the rest of my life. If you remember, when I first came to see you in answer to your advertisement, you said to me ...'.

The film would then fade into the interview scene with the uncle.

Clayton did not record why this opening no longer satisfied him, but it does seem less atmospheric than the film's actual opening (there are enough funeral scenes elsewhere in Clayton). Also it takes a little longer to get into the central narrative, and length of scenes was something about which Clayton was enormously concerned on *The Innocents*. 'We daren't have any scene go one fraction too long', he wrote, 'because if it sags we've got no other characters to go to.' What we have instead is more focused but also more mysterious. Before the films opens – before we even see the Fox logo – we hear the song 'O Willow Waly' sung by a solo child's voice that we later identify as Flora's. In the play there was also a song associated with Flora, 'O bring me a bonnet', which she is singing as the curtain opens. In the film, the song seems haunting, melancholy. The lyric is by Paul Dehn, a former film critic who was to develop into a successful screenwriter on such films as *Goldfinger* (1964) and *The Spy Who Came in from the Cold* (1965). He was also lyricist on a sub Kurt Weill song, 'I Only Saw Him in a Café in Berlin', composed for *I Am A Camera* which Clayton had produced. (The melody is a traditional folk tune that has been arranged by Benjamin Britten who, coincidentally, wrote an opera based on *The Turn of the Screw*, with the part of Miles being sung in its début recording by the young David Hemmings.) The song will become an important leitmotif in the film. It will feature on the music-box which Miss Giddens discovers in the attic during the game of hide and seek, and where she also discovers the miniature of Peter Quint. Flora will hum it on two occasions immediately prior to the appearance of the ghosts – implying that it was Miss Jessel who taught her the tune, but the tune itself being a useful portent, or warning, of imminent supernatural visitation.

As the credits come up, we see two hands clasped together at the side of the screen against a completely dark background. It is a moment before the hands are identified as those of the governess;

and it is not until the end of the film that we realise that the credits are taking place *after* the main events of the film are over. Clayton's intention was immediately to create mystery. Where is Miss Giddens? The darkness prevents identification. One might guess a church, for the hands are clasped as if in prayer, but the sound of birds suggests that she is out in the open air and, moreover, the clasped hands suggest tension as much as supplication. The face of the governess comes into close-up, perspiring, distressed, and we hear her whispered thoughts over the soundtrack: 'All I want to do is save the children, not destroy them. More than anything, I love the children. They need affection, love. Someone who will belong to them and to whom they belong.' The tenderness of the sentiments is belied by the tormented face we see and, in retrospect, the lines are full of tragic irony. She speaks of the children in the present tense, but the dead body of one of them is at that moment lying at her feet. She speaks of 'belonging' but 'belonging' in the film will gather terrifying connotations of 'possession'. At which point Clayton dissolves into flashback and the interview scene with the uncle, and we have just time to register the contrast between the traumatised face seen in the opening to how the same woman looks at the interview – what has changed her from that to *that?* – when we, as she is, are brought up short by a leading, loaded question: 'Have you an imagination?' It is a question that reverberates as the film develops.

The interview scene has already been alluded to in the context of scripting difficulties, its narrative importance, the personal resonance it would have for Clayton and Redgrave's perfectly judged performance. It is worth adding that the scene is also important for its early suggestion of a mystery surrounding the death of the previous governess. But this is also shrewdly entwined with a sense of the uncle's heartlessness ('it did come as an appalling shock ... the *confounded* woman died') which he then subtly elides into his helplessness, all of which the governess romantically construes as honesty. His entreaty 'Give me your hand ... give me your promise' – a promise essentially to leave him alone to his gentlemanly pursuits – sounds like a proposal of marriage and seals her devotion. The big opening close-up of her gives the key: the uncle seems like a god to her and, as Clayton said in an interview with Gordon Gow, she falls for him in a kind of 'enormously Victorian romantic way'.[21] The key word there may be 'enormously': the governess's feelings will lead her, as Clayton said, to magnify everything. One aspect of this will be a consciously hypersensitive soundtrack that will capture the governess's heightened perception but also her nervousness, the impression of a mind stretched taut. Such sound effects as the sash hitting the window pane, the creaking of the puppet's head as it rocks, natural sounds, echoes, are all to pass – filtered, charged, amplified – into the private chamber of Miss Giddens's mind.

There follows the coach drive and the first sight of the house and grounds at Bly (scenes shot, incidentally, at Sheffield Park in Brighton; Clayton chose this location after the location scouts came up with nothing and he happened to see photographs of the park in a magazine – did they trigger memories of his own childhood in Brighton?). The key thing here is that the setting seems the very reverse of your clichéd Gothic house: it is described as beautiful and the child Flora as 'angelic'. Indeed, everything seems almost too perfect – something that James himself comments on in the novella. The dramatic problem for Clayton, then, is to punctuate this idyll with hints of tension beneath the surface, like the tracking shot behind the trees as Miss Giddens is walking through the grounds, as if someone is watching her; like the fact that Mrs Grose seems so relieved to see Miss Giddens as, to use James's own expression, to be 'positively on her guard against showing it too much'. Uneasiness is made palpable in other ways. For instance, there is the moment when Miss Giddens is being shown the house and notices a vase of roses.

> MISS GIDDENS (*looking around*) I had no idea! I never imagined ...
> *Her eye is caught by a vase of beautiful roses. She puts out a hand to touch them – and at her slight touch the petals seem to shiver off every bloom.*
> MISS GIDDENS Oh, I'm so sorry!
> MRS GROSE (*a little laugh, reassuringly*) Oh, that's all right, Miss. It's always happening.

Later in the film the governess's presence throws all nature into disarray: winds howl, thunder crackles and all animal life in the film is disturbed. But at this stage her effect on the roses causes a sliver of unease because it is unexpected. She makes a gesture of enthusiasm and the very thing she wishes to celebrate seems to die at her touch – perhaps a premonition of the effect she may have on the children. A little later in the same scene, Miss Giddens is asking Mrs Grose about the uncle with, as the script says, 'studied casualness', and the conversation moves on to the previous governess:

MISS GIDDENS (*studied casualness – not looking at her*) He doesn't come down here very often?

MRS GROSE Oh well, he likes the town life. He always was a very popular gentleman. And what's the good of being popular down here – with only the children and the pigeons and me.

Miss Giddens has moved across the room and now stands gazing abstractedly into a small ornate mirror on the wall – she puts out a hand to a vase of roses on the table before it.

MISS GIDDENS Mrs Grose ...

MRS GROSE (*busying herself with tea things in b.g.*) Yes, Miss?

MISS GIDDENS What was she like?

MRS GROSE Who, Miss?

MISS GIDDENS The other governess – the one who died?

MRS GROSE Miss Jessel? She was a young woman. Some thought her pretty, and – well I suppose she was. But not as pretty as you, Miss – not by half.

MISS GIDDENS (*moving towards her – smiling, somewhat embarrassed*) He seems to prefer them young and pretty.

As Miss Giddens reaches Mrs Grose, Camera moves in slowly.

MRS GROSE (vehemently) Oh, he did – he had the devil's own eye.

Miss Giddens turns to look at her in surprise. Mrs Grose catches herself – then, hurriedly:

MRS GROSE I mean – that's his way, the master's.

MISS GIDDENS But of whom did you speak first?

MRS GROSE Why, the master of course. There's nobody else, miss. Nobody at all.

And she moves off. Camera holds a moment on Miss Giddens' puzzled face.

Again Miss Giddens's romantic effusiveness, this time prompted by thoughts of the uncle ('He seems to prefer them young and pretty') is abruptly checked by Mrs Grose's unexpectedly vehement response ('Oh he did – he had the devil's own eye') – an unguarded slip underscored by Auric's music. Miss Giddens picks up that the housekeeper is referring to someone other than the master but the mystery for the moment remains unsolved. Mrs Grose's line is a particularly good one. In the novella she unwittingly says, 'it was the way he liked everyone'. This has nothing like the stabbing intensity of the film's line, which also has the advantage of bringing in the demonic theme. This in turn carries on into the scene between Flora and Miss Giddens in their bedroom where Flora, having completed her prayers ('If I should die before I wake, I pray the Lord my soul to take'), asks where the Lord would take her soul to. There is no problem if she is a very good girl, but what if she is not? *The Innocents* is to develop into another Clayton film about souls in danger. Flora may look angelic but the suggestion of something darker is hinted at in a number of minor details, such as the way she stands at the end of the sleeping governess's bed like an incubus; or the way she moves to the open window humming that tune and seems to see something in the garden; or her presentiment about Miles's early return home from school. When the governess questions Flora about this latter point, she is too engrossed in the sight of a butterfly trapped in a spider's web to give a straight answer. Is this casual childish cruelty or demonic possession?

For the scene when Miles meets the governess for the first time and is being brought home by carriage, Clayton wrote in a personal note to himself on the screenplay: 'Miss Giddens must show great relief during this scene and it must become the start of the enchantment with Miles.' She tries to broach the subject of his dismissal from school, but he puts her off the scent with flattery, much as the uncle has done. (At this stage, Miles is calling her 'pretty': part of his terror in the latter stage of the film is the fact that the prettiness has been transformed by fear into something else entirely.) Miles is a strange-looking boy, a little adult who has the capacity to be a 'deceitful flatterer'. He is sensitive to the absence of parents or relatives who do not have time for their children. Like Flora, he seems blessed with second sight and magical powers that may also have a rational explanation. He can tell when the governess is outside his room. When she exhorts him to 'trust me' his eyes flash and, as if at his bidding, the wind gusts and the candle blows out. But then again, it may be just the wind, and Miles's behaviour may be dictated by an understandable scepticism about the trustworthiness of adults – he has been talking of his uncle 'not having time' for them and a tear has run down his cheek. He may also be picking up the governess's tension under the tenderness. As Clayton noted about the mood he wanted from the scene: 'Miles adorable. Miss Giddens stands by the door, then moves near the bed. Then picks up the clothes or tidies the room – shy and a little anxious to cover her asking about the school.' At this stage everything seems in a perfect balance of uncertainty. The punning dialogue matches this. 'I like a boy *with spirit*', Miss Giddens has said, but Miles's 'spirit' is ultimately to cause her the greatest anxiety.

The first appearance of Quint's ghost on the battlements has already been mentioned. It is worth adding that in earlier versions of the script, Quint's ghost appeared before Miles's dismissal and return from school: at that stage the adaptation seemed to be following the structure of the play more than that of the novella. It seems dramatically more sensible to save Quint's appearance until after Miles's return, to imply that the two events are inextricably linked. It is also worth elaborating on the visual and soundtrack preparation for this 'vision'. Immediately before it, Miss Giddens has caught sight in the garden of a spoiled statue of a stone Cupid – described in the script as 'head tilted back, infantile, toothless, mouth smiling – the figures to which its hands were joined lie broken on either side'. The image, with the cherub's face, is a momentary recollection of Miles, but the eroticism of the statue is disconcerting to Miss Giddens, and the smiling mouth suddenly reveals a black beetle crawling from it, causing Miss Giddens to recoil. (A recollection of this tiny moment is to recur in the disturbing later scene when Miles, to borrow Alexander Walker's evocative description, 'suddenly presses his Cupid's mouth to hers and makes her feel the devouring passion of the dead man and notorious womaniser',[22] causing Miss Giddens once again to recoil in revulsion.) It is in this confused emotional state, heightened by the oppressive heat, that Miss Giddens will see a hazy figure on the battlements, a vision preceded by an 'electronic warning', as Gordon Gow puts it, over the soundtrack, which invariably accompanies these apparitions. We notice the dip in Flora's song in the background, the splash of the scissors in the fountain, the flutter and cooing of the pigeons. 'Natural sounds', as Gow says, 'have been magnified by supernatural influence'.[23]

Another example of this occurs shortly afterwards. Miles is riding his pony and showing off his powers before Flora and Miss Giddens. He is either a precociously gifted young horseman, or he is possessed by the spirit of someone else, as it were, who is riding the horse for him. The display terrifies Miss Giddens, whose fear then seems to be taken up by an agitated cacophony of natural sound that blows through and seems to rock the poplar trees. Is it the sound of the wind? Or the wings of birds? Or, as the script suggests, the sound of ghosts applauding? It could be all of those things, as well as being most certainly a powerful aural correlative to Miss Giddens's psychological turbulence. It should be said that the sound recording by John Cox and A. G. Ambler is a masterpiece of atmosphere and tension throughout.

It is during the hide-and-seek scene that Miss Giddens discovers in the attic room the music-box with the tune that Flora sings and the miniature with Quint's face on it. This serves a number of purposes for Clayton. It enables him to add some visual variety by exploring further into the house; it also allows him to develop his material's emotional impact. There is a brief heart-stopping moment when, searching for the children, Miss Giddens sees a ghostly figure float soundlessly across the landing. 'Anna?' she enquires, thinking it might be one of the maids, but there is no reply. When she finds the attic the moment is banished from her mind, but we may at that point have had our first glimpse of Miss Jessel. Discovered in the attic by Miles, Miss Giddens struggles to get free from his grip in a tussle that momentarily becomes disturbing. Miles seems to have a man's strength and the struggle appears to be developing into a violent embrace. When Miss Giddens asks Miles to stop, and he says 'Why?', she replies, 'Because you're hurting me.' Later in the film, when she thinks she hears voices and explores the house, she 'hears' a voice that she must assume to be Miss Jessel's saying 'You're hurting me' from behind a locked door. This scene in the attic, then, is the first hint of something that will occur very disturbingly later: the way the relationship between Miles and Miss Giddens will follow the pattern of that between Quint and Miss Jessel.

It is at the point when Miss Giddens is hiding behind the curtains from the children that she becomes aware again of the ghost of Quint (Peter Wyngarde), but this time at close quarters. Visually it is a wonderful moment: she has caught sight of her own reflection in the window; almost instantaneously it is terrifyingly displaced by the face of Quint, at the window and staring in, his breathing audible on the soundtrack. Interestingly, Clayton was less happy with Quint's ghost than with Miss Jessel's: it was altogether cruder, he thought, more obviously melodramatic and Gothic, less atmospheric. But the film probably needs this extra frisson. Miss Jessel can provide the dimension of supernatural sadness, but Quint is necessary to give the weight of diabolical threat. As Henry James said in his preface to the tale: 'There would be laid on them [i.e. the ghosts] the dire duty of causing the situation to reek with the air of Evil.'[24] If in the film Miss Jessel's ghost does not do that – she seems to stir other feelings in Clayton – Quint's ghost certainly does.

There are some interesting points of interpretation here. It has often been said that one of the weaknesses of the Edmund Wilson reading of the tale is that if the ghosts are the product of the governess's imagination, how can she describe Quint in a way that enables Mrs Grose to identify him? (Wilson attempts to deal with this but it is the least convincing part of his argument.) The film sustains the ambiguity quite well. As Mrs Grose says later when this point comes up, 'Well you *had* seen his picture', as if Miss Giddens, in her undeniably agitated state, might have projected her disturbance into that image of the face at the window. The children's mocking laughter, with its echo amplification, heightens the governess's sense of disorientation. Also, how can you convey visually that the ghosts are after the children? The shot of Quint at the window achieves this, I think, but it is reinforced by the fancy dress scene that follows, where Miles's recitation, both in terms of thematic material and actual delivery, seems unequivocally directed towards the departed spirit of the dead valet who befriended him:

> What shall I sing
> To my Lord from my window?
> What shall I sing?
> For my Lord will not stay –
> What shall I sing?
> For my Lord will not listen –
> Where shall I go?
> For my Lord is away.
>
> Whom shall I love
> When the moon is arisen?
> Gone is my Lord
> And the grave is his prison –
> What shall I say
> When my Lord comes a-calling?
> What shall I say
> When He knocks on my door?
> What shall I say
> When his feet enter softly
> Leaving the marks
> Of his grave on my floor?
>
> Enter, my Lord! Come from your prison!
> Come from your grave!
> For the moon is arisen!

In the play Miles is instructed to sing the last line and throw open the window. In the film, Miles delivers it in a whisper and then casts a meaningful look over at the governess – much subtler and more sinister. Miss Giddens is shocked, and turns to Mrs Grose to say, 'What if Miles *knows*?' At which point Flora leans forward into the middle of the frame, puzzled but with a sweet half-smile on her face, to say, 'Knows *what*, Miss Giddens, dear?'

There follows a slow dissolve as Miss Giddens and Mrs Grose converse from either side of the Cinemascope frame whilst, in the centre of the shot, Flora's picture-of-innocence face slowly fades from our vision. It is a superb composition as it not only cues in the subject of the animated conversation but gives the impression of the subject's still watching: Flora's spirit is still in the air. This in turn will lead to the first scene at the folly by the lake where the ghost of Miss Jessel appears. In the screenplay, Clayton describes the setting thus: 'The folly is a small circular building, like a small temple, its arched roof supported by slim white columns. It is open to the air on all sides.' The setting is empty and idyllic prior to the appearance of the ghost. Signs of how the atmosphere changes are indicated by the corresponding later scene which takes place in a thunderstorm, with Miss Giddens now dressed in black, harrying a child whom she thinks is lying but is also in spiritual danger, and the child terrified by a governess whom she now thinks is mad. Clayton's tight framing here adds enormously to the sense of the child's entrapment and two other visual details are equally compelling: the way the black-clad Miss Giddens comes up behind Flora, for all the world like Quint sneaking up on her; and a final shot of the governess alone in the folly, without a hat in the rain, shattered by Flora's outburst, and suddenly looking every bit as unutterably forlorn as the ghost.

'Have you an imagination?' Is the answer now that Miss Giddens has an over-active one? In an early scene, when she is tucking Flora into bed, she hears what sounds like an animal crying in pain. Flora pays little attention and says that Mrs Grose always tells them that they are imagining things. 'Sometimes one can't help imagining things,' says Miss Giddens. That this is true in her case is particularly well illustrated in a scene in which she is sitting by the fire reading the Bible, which she puts down on a table: a petal drops quietly on it, as if from nowhere. She starts poking the fire, seeming to hear in the flames sounds of whispering. She looks across at the piano, which she hears playing although the keys are still. Now exploring the house with her candle she hears voices, sounds of laughter, crying, but sees nothing. Even the soft swish of her skirt as she moves sounds like whispering. A female voice whispers, 'Love me, love me' and 'You're hurting me'; a man's voice shouts 'Knock before you enter' as a door slams shut; we hear children's laughter and sobbing. She tugs at the doors only to find them locked and she on the outside, and we think quickly of Mrs Grose's evasive description: 'Rooms used by daylight as though they were dark woods'. Clayton caps the governess's torment with an overhead shot of her turning back and forth in the corridor, assailed by sound from all sides but unable to find an unlocked door, and twisting, turning – like a screw. As an evocation of a haunted house, the scene is a *tour de force*, a visual and aural assault that is tremendously exciting and spooky. (Clayton's inspiration may have been that wonderful sequence in Dickinson's *The Queen of Spades* where Anton Walbrook's gambler is haunted by the ghost of the old Countess whose death he has caused.) At the same time it can be read as a powerfully heightened vignette of sexual imagining and frustration.

'They must be made to admit what is happening.' Miss Giddens's attempt to do that with Flora has led to the girl's nervous breakdown ('to hear such filth from a child', says Mrs Grose). She must now confront Miles. The servants are dismissed and Mrs Grose packed off with Flora to see the uncle. 'Wait until you see Miles again before you judge me', the governess has said in parting. Mrs Grose will never see Miles again. As the door of the huge house closes with a shudder, the governess is left alone, awaiting Miles. A montage of the ornate clocks, of her restlessly walking the grounds, builds up the suspense, but there is an ache and an apprehension too in the way she clasps Flora's doll to her, a reminder of what her actions have done to the girl, an omen of they may do to the boy.

Clayton's notes on the screenplay for the last scene say: 'This scene should be claustrophobic and played very close – developing into violence and savagery. It is bad and heavy and both are frightened.' Miles does attempt to tell Miss Giddens why he was expelled. 'I said things ... I frightened the other boys ...'. If he and Flora were privy to the passionate affair between Quint and Jessel, it is quite possible that in his sleep Miles might have said things that disturbed his school friends. Indeed, one could offer the interpretation that if the children are not 'innocent' – if they are precocious, if they play wicked games – maybe it is not they whose innocence has been corrupted but the governess whose apparent innocence is corrupt. According to this reading, evil in *The Innocents* does not come in the form of sexual demons but in a set of attitudes that sees sexual knowledge as evil, the villains therefore being Miles's unseen headmaster, who has expelled him without explanation, and a governess driven to the point of hysteria by her horror of sexuality. The monsters in this reading are not Quint and Jessel but the values and repressions of Victorianism.

In the novella, as Miles is telling the governess her story, which seems consistent with his being the victim of childish confusion rather than demonic possession, James inserts one of the most disturbing passages in the whole text: 'I seemed to float not into clearness, but into a darker obscure, and within a minute there had come to me out of my very pity the appalling alarm of his being perhaps innocent. It was for the instant confounding and bottomless, for if he *were* innocent what then on earth was I?'[25] The phrase 'the appalling alarm of his being perhaps innocent' is shocking but it gives the final part of the story an extra dimension of suspense, an extra edge to the governess's behaviour, which is now propelled not only by a search for the truth but by a frenzied self-justification. If she does not demonstrate Miles's demonic possession, what then on earth is she?

About the end of the film, Clayton said: 'I don't want to leave it in the room, as in the play. It will go dead there. Possibly it's all played, or part of it is played, on the run in the grounds ... There should obviously be, in the last scene, created the most tremendous amount of movement.' One early idea he had, which comes into its own in this final part, was to have as part of the set 'an enormous greenhouse – I mean really a kind of Victorian heated conservatory ... literally, like walking into a tropical climate'. The scene moves to the greenhouse as the exchanges become more heated and intense. What is marvellous about the setting is that it is a visualisation of an image of a human soul that James dropped into the tale at this point as governess and boy are locked in psychological struggle: 'It was like fighting with a demon for a human soul, and when I had fairly so appraised it I saw how the human soul – held out, in the tremor of my hands, at arm's length – had a perfect dew of sweat on a lovely childish forehead.'[26]

As was Flora, Miles is petrified by Miss Giddens and retaliates by lashing out at her with vile language. As he does so and behind his back, Quint appears at the window, laughing ('such a savage laugh he had', Miss Grose has said of him). As Miles's outburst culminates in mocking laughter, the sound of both child and ghostly adult laughter amplify the governess's terror and humiliation; and Flora's hapless tortoise, Rupert (who has a hard time throughout the film), is thrown through the conservatory window as Miles rushes out into the garden and then stumbles to the ground.

The drama is not yet played out. Miles is contrite, tearful, begging forgiveness; the governess comforting, clutching the boy to her, but still insisting that the demon be exorcised. 'Say his name!' she insists. 'Who?' he asks and the pattern begins again. Is Miles really possessed by Quint or is he now spinning in total bewilderment and terror at the governess's hysteria? The camera whirls round the statues in the garden – a spiralling correlative to the governess's state of mind – and Quint seems to be amongst them, like a statue come to life. Miles finally gets her drift and shouts Quint's name but again, in keeping with the Jamesian ambiguity, when he says, 'There – you devil', the eyeline match suggests that he is looking at the governess, as if she is the devil; as if it is her face that truly terrifies him. The last word on his lips, before he collapses and dies of heart failure, is: 'Where?' He falls at Miss Giddens's feet, who cradles him, saying, 'You're safe – you're free – I have you – he's lost you for ever!' before the body goes limp and, in James's phrase, she 'begins to feel what it truly was I held'. Her cry 'Miles!' into the black night is chilling, and there follows the moment that caused such concern: in Clayton's screenplay notes, 'she kisses this cold, beautiful dead little face. She kisses it fully, completely on the lips as one would with one's lover'. It is as if she is returning at last the disconcerting kiss that Miles had planted on her mouth in the garden earlier, his Cupid's lips now as cold as the statue. We then see her hands and we are back where we started in an almost exact duplicate of the film's opening where, as Clayton has said, 'You're not certain if she is lost in her thoughts or is in reality.'[27] The whole film could be read as a subjective flashback, casting very Jamesian doubt on the trustworthiness of the narration. Clayton's phrase for the flashback structure was 'it's almost like a fly caught in a spider's web'.[28] The ending of *The Innocents* is pure Clayton: a question mark rather than a full stop. It also has that sense of Hustonian irony: the momentary triumph – when Miss Giddens thinks the ghost of Quint has been exorcised – that then goes limp in her arms. Pauline Kael had a fine phrase for Miss Jessel's tear on the blotter: she called it 'that little pearl of ambiguity'.[29] That is what this film is: a pearl of ambiguity. The best ghost story in fiction has been turned into the best ghost story on film.

References

1 For the record, the nine film-makers were Jack Clayton, Clive Donner, Robert Hamer, Seth Holt, Pat Jackson, John Krish, Jack Lee, Tony Richardson and Paul Rotha.

2 *Sight and Sound*, Spring 1959, p. 9.

3 'The Way Things Are: Interview with Gordon Gow', *Films and Filming*, April 1974, p. 12.

4 '*The Innocents*', *Sight and Sound*, Summer 1961, pp. 14–15.

5 James, *The Art of the Novel*, p. 172.

6 Peter Glenville's career intersects with Clayton's quite interestingly at certain stages. At one time, Glenville was set to direct *Room at the Top*. In 1962, when Clayton turned down the chance to direct *Term of Trial*, which had a strong role for Simone Signoret, Glenville took over.

7 William Archibald, *The Innocents* (New York, Samuel French, 1950), p. 73.

8 All subsequent Clayton quotes, unless otherwise indicated, are taken from his personal notes.

9 The phrase is from his Preface to *Portrait of a Lady* – see *The Art of the Novel*, p. 56.

10 Andrew Higson provides a detailed and persuasive study of the film's variety of visual presentation which makes up its 'numerous more or less ambiguous signs and semiotic relationships' in his chapter 'Gothic Fantasy as Art Cinema: the Secret of Female Desire in *The Innocents*', in *Gothic Origins and Innovation*, ed. by Allan Lloyd Smith and Victor Sage (Amsterdam, Rodopi, 1994), pp. 204–17.

11 *Observer*, 26 November 1961.

12 The poem is quoted in the play by Flora: 'She said, I am aweary, aweary / I would that I were dead/'

13 *Films and Filming*, April 1974, p. 14.

14 In an interview with Andrew Higson, 2 August 1985.

15 Letter to Tina Snider and James Palmer, 26 June 1986.

16 James, *The Art of the Novel*, p. 161.

17 Letter to Marcella Farina, 17 May 1994.

18 Stephen Rebello, 'Jack Clayton's *The Innocents*', *Cinefantastique*, Vol. 13, No 5, June/July 1983, pp. 51–5.

19 In *The Triple Thinkers* (London, John Lehmann, 1952).

20 Rebello, 'Clayton's *The Innocents*', pp. 54–5.

21 Gow, 'The Way Things Are', p. 14.

22 Alexander Walker, *Hot Tickets*, 30 April 1998, p. 12.

23 Gordon Gow, 'Sound in *The Innocents*', broadcast on 7 January 1962, BBC Home Service.

24 James, *The Art of the Novel*, p. 175.

25 Henry James, *The Turn of the Screw and Other Stories* (London, Penguin, 1969), p. 119.

26 *Ibid.*, p. 117.

27 Rebello, 'Clayton's *The Innocents*', p. 55.

28 Higson interview, 2 August 1985.

29 Pauline Kael, *I Lost it at the Movies* (New York, Bantam Books, 1966), p. 150.

Woman on the verge
of a nervous breakdown:
The Pumpkin Eater (1964)

5

Some of these things happened, and some were dreams. They are all true, as I understood truth. They are all real, as I understood reality. (Penelope Mortimer, *The Pumpkin Eater*, London, Penguin, 1964, p. 158)[1]

Jack Clayton's films are marked by a deeply felt personal vision. He never copied anyone, and never repeated himself as so many film makers are inclined to do. His films were very much his own – permeated with the multitude of unique details which, one by one, accumulated to give them their unusual perspective. Unlike most commercial Hollywood film makers, he didn't tell stories about heroes. Instead, he looked for the heroism in unconventional people – a tougher, but higher aspiration. (Anne Bancroft, quoted in memorial booklet accompanying Clayton retrospective at National Gallery of Art, Washington DC, 9–23 September 1995)

The critical controversy concerning the status of Clayton as director and artist is probably at its most intense over *The Pumpkin Eater*. In my view, it is one of the ten best films of post-war British cinema. (I would also include *The Innocents* in that list.) As a portrait of the commitment, the crises and the compensations of married life, I do not think there is a British film that comes near it in terms of maturity and insight. I agree with Otto Plaschkes when he says that Anne Bancroft, Peter Finch and James Mason give the very best of themselves in this film, thanks to Clayton's 'ability to shape performances that were God-like'.[2] I would add that the cameos by Maggie Smith and Yootha Joyce are two of the best screen-acting miniatures one could hope to see; that Harold Pinter's screenplay is on the level of his screen writing for Joseph Losey and Karel Reisz and, while radically reshaping the form and sharpening the dialogue of the novel, provides additional scenes of glittering wit and perception;[3] and that Georges Delerue's score surpasses even his work for Truffaut, and notably *Jules et Jim* (1961), in its ability to get straight to the heart of a dramatic situation.

At the time of the film's first appearance, this praise would have been shared by a number of critics. In the film's publicity, Alexander Walker's view of it as 'a masterpiece' was highlighted; Philip Oakes felt the same and thought the film superior to Ingmar Bergman's *The Silence* (1963), which had provoked much controversy but had also received great acclaim some months before.[4] The critic of the *Middlesex County Times* went one better, to declare it 'the best British film ever';[5] whilst Douglas McVay, in his fine *Films and Filming* survey of Clayton's career up to *Our Mother's House*, called it 'the best film from an English studio that I'd ever seen'.[6] Running counter to these high opinions, however, was a negative view. The film critic on *The Times* found the film 'arty' but not art;[7] Penelope Houston in *Sight and Sound* thought the film detrimentally influenced by Antonioni and a pretentious attempt to ape the style of the European art movie;[8] and Peter Graham in *The International Film Guide* criticised Clayton for attempting 'over self-consciously, to be cinematic', though feeling that 'Anne Bancroft's splendid performance would have been ideal in a film by Antonioni'.[9] The battle lines over the film were drawn: artistry or artiness, profound or pretentious.

Never a great Clayton fan, Andrew Sarris was to re-open the critical debate in a review of Richard Lester's *Petulia* (1968), another stylistically adventurous and incisive interrogation of marriage. 'Unfortunately', Sarris wrote,

> Lester is no closer to Resnais than Jack Clayton was to Antonioni in the poetically pregnant pauses of *The Pumpkin Eater* ... Whereas the styles of Antonioni and Resnais are related to the way these two directors see reality, the styles of Clayton and Lester are related more to the manipulation of dramatic conventions to beguile the audience with the surface if not the substance of modernity.[10]

This opinion is never substantiated by any thematic or stylistic discussion or evidence. One could easily turn the names round and say that it was Resnais and Antonioni who were beguiling audiences with 'the surface if not the substance of modernity'. Certainly if one compares, say, *The Red Desert* with *The Pumpkin Eater*, it is the Antonioni film rather than the Clayton one that seems to me more surface than substance. A far more acute assessment of *The Pumpkin Eater* seems to me to be Viveca Lindfors's postcard to Clayton in February 1965: 'I loved *The Pumpkin Eater* – what superb work'. What superb work indeed.

There is something very familiar about the mixed response to *The Pumpkin Eater*: it says something about the state of film culture in this country that still persists. When British film-makers are not being attacked for lack of ambition – as in a Jonathan Romney piece for the *Guardian* entitled 'British Film is Sick'[11] – they are berated for pretentiousness and artiness when striving to be more experimental and difficult. 'There are three lovely critical expressions: pretentious, gratuitous and profound', said Nicolas Roeg, adding, 'none of which I truly understand'.[12] Roeg is another director whose ambitious and challenging visions have met hostile and sometimes vicious resistance in this country. Interestingly, Roeg quoted a scene from *The Pumpkin Eater* in his film *Castaway* (1987) when his heroine has her first telephone conversation with the man who is proposing to whisk her away to a desert island. It is one of the densest, most allusive quotations in all of Roeg's movies, and I have discussed it in detail elsewhere.[13] It ends with the moment when Jo (Anne Bancroft) says to her husband Jake (Peter Finch) after a ferocious row at their home: 'I could die here'. That must be the feeling of British film-makers with artistic aspirations who come up against a wall of critical indifference and hostility to their efforts. Clayton was deeply upset by some of the reviews: he was convinced in his own mind that he had made a much better film than the extravagantly praised *Room at the Top*.

In a personal note dated 31 December 1962, Clayton defined the appeal of *The Pumpkin Eater* as follows: 'I am attracted by the infinitely simple idea of the difficulties in any married relationship while at the same time showing the tremendously strong relationship that grows almost inevitably.' He added: 'I am not sure what it is trying to say is not very prejudiced and one-sided.' Actually *The Pumpkin Eater* was the third consecutive Clayton piece to be based on material narrated in the first person; and in each case, although the main character appears in just about every scene, the presentation is more objective. A lot of his discussion with Harold Pinter would centre on the question of whether they had the balance right. In his notes prior to a script meeting with Pinter on 3 July 1963, Clayton wrote: 'I think in our endeavour to present a more equal picture of the relationship, we have slightly over-balanced and treated Jo too harshly. However fairly we show both sides of the relationship, we must absolutely be sure that we can retain a definite sympathy throughout for Jo.' For some audiences and critics this proved difficult, but perhaps that was partly because the film was ahead of its time in dealing so directly with feminine issues. As Michael Billington put it, '*The Pumpkin Eater* was one of the first post-war British movies to treat a specifically feminine problem with any degree of seriousness'. Linking it thematically with Pinter's contemporaneous work for the stage, *The Homecoming,* Billington suggested that it was a work 'filled with dismay at men's abysmal failure to understand women's needs and desires'.[14]

When Clayton asked the author Penelope Mortimer what the novel was about, he received a very confused but honest (undated) letter in reply that suggests a lot of ideas without coming to any definitive conclusion. 'When you first asked me what the book was about', she wrote, 'I said money'. This is not the theme that immediately jumps out at one but it does prompt a reassessment of the role and importance of money in the film. It is money that has alienated Jo from two of her sons, when her father has insisted on sending them to boarding school to ease the strain on Jake when he marries Jo. Although she denies Jake's accusations that she 'resents the money' after he has become a successful screen-writer, we rarely then see the happy Jo or the rapport between her and Jake that we saw in the earlier scene in the barn when she met Jake for the first time. Attempting to define the money theme more clearly, Penelope Mortimer went on: 'It boils down to the conflict between and the fusion of reality and fantasy; and perhaps what results from some kind of uneasy balance between the two. It's also about money (and success); love (and sex and hate); and the creation of children.' The balance between reality and fantasy, and the situation of characters who up to a point live in a dream world, is something that recurs in Clayton's work: many of his major characters (Jo, Gatsby, Judith Hearne) are dreamers and romantics who are compelled to confront a real world. Yet Clayton has great sympathy with their dreams – the imaginative fantasy side of human nature is always very alive in his films. This is perhaps one of the reasons that he directs children so well. The ensemble performances of the children in *The Pumpkin Eater* seem a miracle of spontaneity and naturalness. Their constant babble in the background and foreground is a crucial source of the film's meaning and atmosphere – signifying at different stages, life, the future, an irritation, a distraction, and a battleground for attention which parents either fight, participate in or retreat from.

Another point of earnest discussion between Clayton and Pinter was when, and how, the film should start. The novel begins with Jo in one of her meetings with her psychiatrist (played in the film by Eric Porter). The film clearly needs something more dramatic, though the idea of opening with the Harrods scene was discussed and rejected: as Pinter said, 'It might blow too many fuses at the beginning'.[15] Clayton stressed the importance of an opening that established right away the situation of 'a woman in crisis' but wanted to delay the Harrods scene so as to build up an atmosphere of suspense. Like Hitchcock with the Bates motel in *Psycho*, Clayton needs to get his heroine and his audience to Harrods in a particular frame of mind – so that what follows will be shocking but will seem inevitable.

Is the actual opening scene a precise evocation of mood or a miscalculation of audience sympathy? A downbeat tone is immediately established through Delerue's sombre, sparely orchestrated theme and a shot of Jo's haggard face at the window. She is wearing an outdoor coat and hat but seems to have no inclination or impetus to leave the house. Only the sound of Jake's coming downstairs motivates her to move outdoors, and when he is about to get into his car he notices her standing listlessly in the garage. 'What are you doing?' he asks. 'Do you think you're going to get over this period in your life because ...' (he leans over and kisses her on the cheek) 'I find it very depressing'. The light irony fails; he departs; Jo returns to the house. The phone is left to ring unanswered. It is only in this opening sequence that I am reminded of Antonioni: the use of silence, pauses and space concisely suggests alienation and non-communication in the manner of the opening sequence of Antonioni's *The Eclipse* (1962). The rest of the film – in what Pauline Kael described as a 'remarkable study of modern sexual tensions'[16] – seems to me more akin to Bergman or the marital dramas of Strindberg.

Although full of praise for Clayton ('a very tasteful director, good technical man'), James Mason, who gives a magnificently malevolent performance as the most unpleasant character in the film, Bob Conway, felt that the opening drew sympathy towards the husband and away from the female protagonist. 'They showed her in such a way that you immediately took sides with the husband and thought, "Jesus! This poor man married to a nut"!'[17] A different spectator, however, might find it equally possible to sympathise with Jo, and might feel the husband's response, however well-intentioned – that little joke about her depression, to try to lift her mood – miscalculated and insensitive enough to hint at what is causing her distress. The balance of sympathies seems to me meticulously judged.

In their book, *The Cinema as Art*, Ralph Stephenson and J. R. Debrix offer an admirable description of the film's opening and lead-in to the first flashback:

> The film opens to show Jo (Anne Bancroft) looking haggard and careworn, wandering like a ghost in her fine drawing room. Thus when she is on the extreme left of the screen, everything gradually fades to dead white except her figure. She turns her head to the blank part of the screen and, as it were, looks back at her past which then gradually materializes on the screen – we see a younger Jo, laughing and attentive, romping with the children.[18]

The phrase 'wandering like a ghost' is very suggestive: Clayton always disliked conventional flashbacks, and the one here is similar to the first flashback in *The Bespoke Overcoat* – a memory, or even a fantasy, of the past, being watched by a person in the present as if he or she were almost a participant. It has the effect of giving the flashback, and the past, a living immediacy; but it also suggests a subjective colouring of the person's present predicament as well as (indeed, more than) a narrative step backwards. The contrast between Jo's haggard face in the present and her happy face in the past – similar to the opening of *The Innocents* – is a shrewd strategy of narrative suspense: what, in the interim, can have changed her expression so dramatically? It is in this scene at the barn that she has first met Jake and fallen in love; the two have married with the somewhat reluctant blessings of their respective fathers. Jake's father (Alan Webb) is ironic and disparaging: Jo's father (Sir Cedric Hardwicke) fearsome and intimidating; both are rather sceptical about how their respective children will cope. The decision of Jo's father to pay for two of her boys to go to boarding school will be one of the first sources of marital tension. Father figures are never very positive in Clayton, as we have noted, but the deaths of these two characters in the film – and Clayton does love his funeral scenes – will both occur at crucial stages in the Jo–Jake relationship.

Clayton varies his flashbacks well and the second comes by way of a soundtrack introduction to the character of Philpot ('Why does Philpot have to stay with us?' 'She's been turned out of her flat') who then visually materialises. Philpot was one of the best of Maggie Smith's early screen characterisations, richly comic but with a disturbing edge. 'Wives don't usually like me,' she says. 'They get so ratty, people's wives ... I mean ... I've been told that I'm frigid, but I don't see how you can tell ...?' The scene is brilliantly choreographed. Whilst Philpot is talking, Jo is trying to clean round her. After wondering whether she is frigid, Philpot proceeds to sit on the fridge. The dramatic edge of the scene comes from her being in the way – as she will be in the relationship; and its life comes from a feeling delicately and comically conveyed of people competing for space. 'I think you're marvellous,'

Philpot goes on, and then, on the line 'Of course, Jake's the most fabulous husband and father. He's *the* most fabulous ...', her leg drapes over Jo as the latter is trying to get into the old-fashioned icebox. Philpot has to move, leaving the line, like her leg, moment-arily dangling in the air. It is the first illustration of what Michael Billington called Pinter's heightening of 'the story's central irony: that Jo is surrounded by women who gush about her husband's creative sensitivity while she has to live with the reality of his moral indifference'.[19]

This is spelt out more explicitly in Philpot's next scene. Having breakfast in bed, she gushes over Jake's brilliance as a writer ('his understanding is so extraordinary, his innate ... the way he draws his characters ... swift strokes ... so swift'), but Jo's mind is on something else entirely: the story the children told her of Jake's catching Philpot when she fainted. Her first suspicion of his infi-delity leads to their first row, over the washing-up in the kitchen. 'Does Philpot faint much?' asks Jo (more bluntly than the novel's 'Is Philpot given to fainting much?'); the argument that follows is a finely nuanced piece of writing, acting and direction as Jake's anger rather than confusion suggests his guilt and amplifies Jo's anxiety. Again, the scene is carefully choreographed: Jake is at first slightly concealed by a curtain as they wash the dishes, which makes his response seem evasive; Jo is later slightly concealed by this curtain, as if she is retreating from full confrontation out of fear of what she might find. Later, when they return from the cinema, the argument is renewed. 'What did you think of the film?' Jo asks Jake. When he only gestures a response she snaps 'What did you think of the bloody film?', her annoyance about one subject a displacement of her anxiety about another. (Her anger at her psychiatrist's holidaying in Tenerife is another example of this.) Jake admits he kissed Philpot but denies sleeping with her (a lie), but the suspicion has been planted, and the ironic contrast between sensitive writer and insensitive husband is further emphasised.

The contrast will be reinforced by Jake's affair with the actress, Beth Conway (Janine Gray). Our suspicions are once again alerted when during the aftermath of the party Beth starts talking of

Jake's writing and describes it in terms almost identical to those used by Philpot: 'He's got such extraordinary understanding, such swift, you know, kind of illumination of people'. The extraordinary understanding both of them highlight suggests a connection between them, but this does not extend to his own wife, whose state of mind will baffle him. This will be in the future. At this early stage in the narrative it is not certain that Jake has slept with Philpot, but enough doubt has been planted, as well as implications about areas of guilt elsewhere in her life, to suggest Jo's troubled state of mind as she leaves the house at last to go shopping at Harrods.

The breakdown in Harrods is perhaps the film's most famous sequence. People float noiselessly past Jo's field of vision; mannequins evoke her own sense of hollowness; peering at caged animals she sees herself behind bars, a prisoner of her own body and character; a piano tuner's exercises mimic her own internal discord; Delerue's music cocoons her until it stops on an indeterminate chord and leaves her stranded. At this point the camera cranes behind her, a movement that conveys a sense of the soul leaving the body and emphasises her total isolation: and then, just as Hitchcock in *Psycho* cut from a high shot to a big close-up of the murdered detective – the impact coming from the contrast between the sizes of the image – Clayton cuts to a big close-up of Jo as she begins to cry and then cannot stop. It is reminiscent of the earlier large close-up, with her on left side of frame, that has led into the flashback, but now she fills the frame – it imprisons her, cutting off, as it were, her route back to the past, and she is trapped, isolated in an imperative present tense. At first people drift away, embarrassed; in a moment other women will come to help her. Michael Billington was one critic who found the scene overdone: 'Even Anne Bancroft's famed breakdown in Harrods' Food Hall carries overtones of privileged despair, as if it were inherently more tragic than a nervous collapse in the Birkenhead Safeway's.'[20] This echoes Jake's own comment to the doctor (which, in viewings at which I have been present, have drawn gasps of exasperation from women in the audience): 'I mean, breaking down in Harrods like that. Harrods of all places!' (It is a line from the novel: Penelope Mortimer deserves credit for that.) Rather than carrying overtones of privileged despair the breakdown expresses maximised humiliation and embarrassment, emotions which recur painfully in Clayton and which he always records with unusual intensity. One thinks of the reaction to Lampton's mispronunciation of 'brazier' in *Room at the Top* (the hysterical laughter, Joe's class humiliation), or the distorted laughter when the governess in *The Innocents* is told that the man she says she has seen at the window is actually dead. Such moments always happen to Clayton's leading characters when they feel most exposed, vulnerable and alone.

Antonioniesque angst and alienation? 'Clayton inaugurated the whole British back to the provinces movement with *Room at the Top*', said Penelope Houston, 'and in *The Pumpkin Eater* I suspect that he is showing the same freakish instinct for the mood of the times'.[21] But the relative lack of success of the film suggested, if anything, that it was ahead of its time; and in any case, Clayton, the least fashion-conscious of directors, would certainly not be interested in following the Antonioni mode. One could see it more as a continuation of the exploration of the emotional life of women begun in *Room at the Top*, but now in a different milieu; or a continuation of the tradition started by *Brief Encounter*, about the emotional malaise of a middle-class housewife for whom the problem is not the temptation of adultery but the tensions of affluence. I agree with Robert Murphy's sensitive brief commentary in his book *Sixties British Cinema*, when he contrasts the richness of the film's characterisation to the one-dimensional portraiture of the novel, and talks of the way Pinter's script gives a 'spiky and disturbing edge' to incidents which are 'little more than whimsical details' in the novel.[22]

One example of this is a remarkable scene at the hairdresser's, sandwiched between Jo's two meetings with her psychiatrist. The scene is suggested by a moment in the novel when Jo receives a letter from a Mrs Meg Evans who has seen her picture in a magazine at the hairdressers, and, assuming she is happy and fulfilled, pours out her troubles to her: her loneliness, her struggle with money, her neglect by her father and now by her husband, her love for yet resentment of her young children. Jo is left at a loss as to how to respond but comments in the novel that the letter 'contained the only evidence I had in the world that I was not alone'.[23] Pinter dramatises an equivalent scene for the film where Jo is spoken to by a woman under the hairdryer who has seen her picture in a magazine. However, the film's scene will develop in a very different direction.

Unnervingly acted by Yootha Joyce in a powerful single-scene cameo, the character is now quite disturbed, becomes gradually angry at what she interprets as Jo's condescension, and starts threatening her. 'Anyone ever clawed your skin off? You see these claws? Ever had your skin clawed off?' A moment in the novel, which has given Jo a fleeting sense of company and comfort, has been transformed in the film into a nightmare encounter where even a hairdressing salon can become a potential torture chamber. On first viewing I wondered why a scene of female solidarity in the novel had been transformed into its opposite for the film. But it seems to me now that the film wants a scene that sharpens and intensifies the heroine's dilemma rather than one that simply provides a temporary sentimental drop. It is a scene that, to quote Robert Murphy again, is 'used by Pinter to capture that opening out into a world of pain and sorrow which occurs when one is jolted out of the rut of routine existence'.[24] The woman in the hairdresser's can be seen as an externalisation of Jo's psychological state. The threat correlates to Jo's sense of self-inflicted torment; the complaints about the husband's indifference parallel Jo's; the hostility to Jo's 'patronising' attitude reflects Jo's guilt about her social status; the woman's anger expresses what Jo feels inside, which indeed is to erupt in her next scene with the psychiatrist and in her battle with Jake when she finds he has made Beth pregnant. The gaunt, strained, tormented woman at the hairdresser is a nightmare projection of Jo herself, a nightmare all the more horrifying because, like the ghosts in *The Innocents*, it stalks by daylight. The connection between the two women is concisely suggested when the psychiatrist's instruction to Jo to 'cut down on liquids as much as you can' brings a fleeting remembrance of the woman's 'I'm off liquids' in the previous scene. The connection is clinched in a key scene later in the film between Jo and her second husband Giles when she is talking about her marriage. 'My life is an empty place,' she says, echoing precisely a phrase that the woman at the hairdressers has used and suggesting that she has reached the same level of desperation. Anne Bancroft's bitterly ironic delivery of that line, followed by a brief private chuckle, indicates Jo's full awareness of where she has heard this phrase before and what it implies about her emotional state and is one of the acting highlights of the film, even though delivered off-screen.

There is another future connection between the two. The woman in the hairdresser's mentions that she has had a hysterectomy and Jo is later to have an operation to prevent her from having any more children for fear that pregnancy might damage her health and risk a further onset of acute depression. Jo's hysterical relief after the operation is at first uncomfortably close to her break-down at Harrods, but afterwards a happy mood is (temporarily) sustained. 'I want to have a great feeling of exuberance and love in it,' noted Clayton about the hospital scene, 'rather like a cork coming out of a champagne bottle.'[25] A little later he wrote: 'What we really need to do with this scene is to blow it out like a flower ... we can afford to have a little Dinah scene of embarrassment here, because it gives charm. Jo no longer has to worry about making love at this moment and this could be perhaps one of her first conversations with Dinah about this particular subject.'[26] The scene, sensitively acted by Bancroft with Frances White as her daughter, is moving because it shows Jo resuming her former intimacy with the children and becoming again the happy Jo of former years. The mood is continued as Jake enters the room – the women happily conspiratorial, the man ironic and affectionate – so that we might not notice the seemingly casual way (neatly directed and acted) in which Jake enquires whether Jo has acknowledged her gift of flowers from the Conways. The enquiry becomes significant when Jo is later to discover from Bob Conway (James Mason) that Jake has been having an affair with his wife, and that Jake's pressure on Jo to have an abortion had been due partly to his desire for the affair to continue.

The Conways are introduced in a party scene earlier in the film.

Prior to this, Jake returns home from being on location in Morocco but is prevented from telling Jo much about it by the cacophony of noise from the children. A humorous anecdote is begun but never finished because of constant interruptions. Jake's mood moves from affection to amusement to irritation whilst Jo's moves from gladness to sorrow. It is an acutely observant cameo about the difficulty of communication between husband and wife in a house full of children. (It is also one of the few moments in the novel where the heroine attempts to go beyond her perception of things to Jake's: 'I heard him thinking, weeping wife, kids, bills, joint, Saturday, nothing changed. It did not occur to me that these were my thoughts or that his could be more complex'.)[27] Jo suggests that they throw a party for Jake's associates on the film so that she can hear all about it.

How to avoid the usual clichéd party scene in a film? Clayton's solution derives from his perception of what makes this scene special: it is the first time that we see Jo in Jake's world. This in turn dictates the shooting style, which starts on Conway's speech ('Professional people are all a lot of bloody parasites, the lot of them ...') as Jo is trapped by him in a corner, and then as Clayton wrote, 'would concentrate completely on Jo and her reactions to the various people ... The room would be entirely filled with guests, and we would just follow Jo's face as she went in and out of different conversations'.[28] It exploits Pinter's gift for the swift vignette, so that he can suggest an entire relationship in two lines of dialogue (compare the restaurant scene in *The Servant*); also his gift for elaborate set pieces, like one guest's loud and extrovert tale of flagellation, another marvellous cameo in the film, this time by the infallible Gerald Sim (ranking alongside his performance as the shell-shocked soldier in *Ryan's Daughter*). It is only in the latter stages of the party when all the guests have left, apart from the Conways, that the tone, though still lightly amusing through Jake's sending up of an uncomprehending Conway, begins to shade over menacingly. Beth is speaking – a little too much like Philpot – about Jake's 'extraordinary understanding'. 'Some of the scenes', she goes on, '... actually made me really cry'. 'You must have had sand in your eyes', says Jake, at which, and with an expertly judged switch of camera angle to signal a shift of tension and emphasis, Conway says, 'Lots of sand in Morocco, was there?' It is amazing how much malevolence James Mason injects into that line. 'Every single scene must have a purpose', Clayton has written to himself, *'a purpose of progression.'*[29] The great thing about Pinter's script and Clayton's direction is that every scene fans out into different areas of the film, for purposes of narrative preparation, thematic relevance, dramatic value. The 'purpose of progression' in the party scene is served particularly by that line of Conway's, with its poisonous stab, behind the ostensible meaning, of jealousy and suspicion. (Mason accentuates this by an eloquent rhythmic jerk in his delivery of the line, followed by a nervous tug at his nostril.) It will move the plot forward through a cluster of ironies, one of which is that it is in the love scene between Jo and Jake that follows this party that Jo becomes pregnant again, the event which will, stage by stage, bring Jake's affair with Beth out into the open.

The scene between Jo and Conway, when he tells her of Jake's infidelity with Beth, makes an interesting contrast to the corresponding scene in the novel. In the book, the meeting takes place in a tea shop and has been initiated by Jo, who has found an incriminating letter to Jake from Beth. In the film the meeting is initiated by Conway, which is dramatically more suspenseful (what does he want?) and seems more plausible (as a symptom both of his jealousy and of his obvious attraction to Jo), and the setting is not a tea shop but a zoo, which is altogether more expressive. For one thing, it recalls a comment made by Jo's father to Jake when he is counselling him about his proposed marriage: 'Do you realise what you're saddling yourself with? A zoo. A children's zoo. And their keeper. Are you reconciled to having the zoo and its keeper?' Further, the zoo is an imaginative expression of mood, both a setting of ostensible pleasure that counterpoints the raw adult emotions that are being played out against a background of animal cries and childish laughter and also an evocative correlative to the predatory emotions of Conway and to Jo's caged state of entrapment. Like the party scene, this scene begins on a note of comedy with an expert cameo by Leslie

Nunnerley as a surly waitress, singularly unimpressed by Conway's excitement at discovering lemon tea on the menu. The tone changes when Conway insinuates that this might be the start of a regular assignation between him and Jo and he puts his hand over Jo's. She pointedly pulls hers away, and the rejection prompts him to produce Beth's incriminating letter to Jake. His former suave control then frighteningly erupts into ferocious rage.

'No viewer will ever forget the intercut close-ups of James Mason's mouth,' wrote Tony Sloman in his tribute to Clayton for the National Film Theatre.[30] Too true: watching the ever-closer cuts is like being sucked into the jaws of an angry animal. (The moment recalls the similar close-up of the ghost Quint as he taunts the terrified governess in *The Innocents*, or the famous extreme close-up of Celia Johnson's talkative friend in *Brief Encounter* whose ceaseless chattering frays the suicidal heroine's nerves so much that she momentarily wishes her dead.) This scene will lead to another ferocious argument between Jo and Jake, which will build to a moment when Jake will shout: 'I wish you'd shut up! I wish you'd die!'

Jo's action of quickly withdrawing her hand from under Conway's is part of a leitmotif of hands in the film. Hands as claws (the woman at the hairdresser) have already been mentioned. Early in the film there is a freeze frame of Jo and Jake clasping hands which neatly prepares for a movement from past to present and gives the impression of the depressed Jo trying to freeze the memory of a moment of happiness. The death of Jo's father is signalled in a small, moving ballet of hands as the dying man reaches for his daughter's hand to close his eyes for the last time, which takes its cue from a sensitive description in the novel. ('My father groped for my hands. I gave them to him and he lifted them, pressing them against his eyes. After a while his own hands dropped, but I didn't move'.)[31] In the novel too there is a description of Jo's feeling of alienation from her two older sons at boarding school that could fit straight into a Clayton film: 'Slowly, little by little, almost imperceptibly, I let them drift, until only fingertips were touching, then reaching, then finding nothing.'[32] Like the novel, the film is about the pain and precariousness of human contact, in which touching hands will play a significant symbolic role. When Jo, arriving late for the funeral of Jake's father, tries to take Jake's hand in sympathy, he pulls it angrily away. Earlier, as a culmination of their marital conflict and after Conway's bombshell that Beth is pregnant and that the baby is not his, hands have turned into fists and the marriage has become a boxing match.

What follows this crisis point is a bedroom scene between Jo and her second husband, Giles (Richard Johnson), which is faithful to the events of the novel but seems to have given Clayton and Pinter a great deal of trouble.[33] It includes the now famous shot of smoke going back into Jo's cigarette which Clayton, ever honest in interviews, said had been interpreted by some critics as clever use of sexual symbolism but had happened because he felt the original continuous shot – from photo to bed – did not work and would play better if reversed.[34] The intention of the scene was to give more insight into Jo's state of mind. 'She is sort of trying to reach back to the past, trying to feel a security which she doesn't have anymore, which presumably she did have with Giles', wrote Clayton in a note on the scene.[35] 'Probably too much of it, which is why she left him'. Prior to a script meeting with Pinter on 9 July 1963, Clayton wrote: 'the scene is already very good and supplies us with what we both feel necessary here: a different kind of emotional outburst from Jo. But there can be more of it, and I now think that Jo could reveal more of her true feelings about Jake and about their whole situation.' At Clayton's BAFTA memorial service, Harold Pinter recalled that even at a very late stage Clayton was still not quite satisfied and, on a terrible winter's morning of February 1964, summoned Pinter to the studio to complete the rewriting of the scene. Pinter was not best pleased but was mollified when Clayton declared the rewritten scene 'beautiful'. It is certainly finely played: Anne Bancroft's use of vocal nuance is supremely subtle and skilful. The writing too is eloquent in its sense of desolation and its almost musical use of phrases from earlier parts of the film ('I didn't want anything else') to bind the drama together. It is Jo's most reflective scene as she tries to analyse her love for Jake and what has gone wrong with the marriage. Nevertheless, I still wonder whether the scene has quite the emotional force it should have and tend to agree with Douglas McVay's criticism: 'As the camera tracks round the bedroom during Jo's "I cared" speech, one feels for the sole time in the film, a trace of stylistic excess. Wouldn't close-up have been more potent? But this is the merest quibble.'[36]

Jo's scene with Giles is intercut with one between Peter Finch and James Mason in the bar of a London club, a wonderfully droll Pinter dialogue of confrontation – two men facing up to each other in a saloon but, in true English fashion, trading not blows or shots but bluff and innuendo. It is a scene invented for the film and the only one in which Jo does not appear. It might be taken as the male equivalent of Jo's scene with the disturbed woman at the hairdresser's, with the male confrontation being as civil and decorous as the female one is heated. McVay calls it 'mutual hatred expressed via British courtesy'.[37] (In its emotional temperature, it reminds me of the scene in the flat between Alec and Stephen in *Brief Encounter* after the latter has interrupted Alec's assignation with Laura, and where Stephen's disgust, disappointment and anger are expressed through an icy man-of-the-world irony and sarcasm.) The positioning of the Jake/Conway confrontation within Jo's bedroom scene with her ex-husband is rather strange. Might it be her fantasy of a confrontation between the two men, in which Jake has no difficulty in putting his rival down and making him look foolish? It anticipates another tense and immaculately played scene – the one between Tom Buchanan (Bruce Dern) and Gatsby (Robert Redford) that will so terrify and disorientate Daisy (Mia Farrow) as she senses her romantic dream about to burst.

After the rift with Jake at his father's funeral, Jo retreats to the new house they have been talking of, the tower, which as Clayton wrote in his notes for the end scenes, 'always was, in her mind, a kind of dream of the future – in which, of course, Jake shared'.[38] Now, however, she is alone. As she roams the empty premises at night and in the early morning, Delerue over the soundtrack now gives his fullest, tenderest statement of the 'Jo theme', a plangent expression of a heart in pain. As at the opening of the film, Jo stares listlessly out of a window: it is as if we have despairingly come full circle. And then, in what Haya Clayton has described to me as one of her favourite uses of sound in all film (the sound editor is one of Clayton's regular associates, Peter Handford), we hear, above the cawing of the birds, the noise of children in the distance and drawing nearer: Jo's children, and Jake is with them. Penelope Mortimer's description of this moment in the novel was: 'I waited for him, as you wait on a hill, in a tower, in the mist, for an enemy.'[39] The film frames the moment as if the children are advancing over the hill like an invading army – which in one sense they are – but the beautiful swelling from silence to sound is also redolent of life starting up all over again. The dialogue for this end scene, Clayton suggested, 'should be constructed, at least partly, from lines heard in various scenes throughout the film. For example, the delightful line from the child, "Where's the big red ball? ... I just want to put it on the grass, I don't want to play with it".'[40] As in an earlier scene, Jake's beer can spurts as it opens and he offers it to Jo. The repetition is a way of drawing together not only the structure but the film's whole theme: the shared moments and habits and memories that bind a married couple together even in their times of tension, betrayal and breakdown. They both have a drink; Jake smiles hesitantly; Jo looks down, and the film ends.

Penelope Mortimer thought the film ending sentimentalised her novel,[41] but I agree with Robert Murphy that it is moving precisely because it is not happy or idealised but reveals matter-of-fact understanding and acceptance of compromise and loss.[42] This is what makes the film, for me, the most perceptive study of marriage in the British cinema. 'You don't know Jake. You only know me', says the heroine in the novel. 'Therefore, it probably seems absurd to you that I ever expected so much of a man who must seem to you very normal, limited, understandable, a man who, as far as you can see, did his best after all.'[43] It is one of the few moments when the heroine attempts to see the situation from a viewpoint other than her own. Although the novel is clearly intended, and partly succeeds, as a moving and courageous self-examination, the first-person narration offers a degree of partiality that Pinter's screenplay undercuts. In the film, we are less certain than in the novel that Jake is guilty of adultery, less confident that he has been given a fair hearing. Has Pinter gone too far in shifting sympathy away from the heroine? For me, the effect is a more balanced characterisation, giving both protagonists the virtues and flaws of complex, believable human beings and offering acute insights into the different needs, characteristics, and worlds of men and women.

'Have we got enough variety in it?', wrote Clayton in some notes on the first draft of the script. 'Variety of mood, tempo changes? This is a story that must never be allowed to settle down too long, like a broody hen on a clutch of eggs or Philpot sitting on the fridge. Do we have enough magic?' Nervous breakdown, marital arguments, party patter, children's bathtime, a madwoman under the hairdryer, a Jamaican King of Jerusalem at your front door: there are enough moments of rawness and radiance, sorrow and surprise, humour and horror to encompass life in all its variety. But to conclude by returning to the epigraph from the novel that introduces this chapter and closes the heroine's own story: it draws attention to what Penelope Mortimer called a key theme in the tale – the clash between fantasy and reality. 'You live in a dream world, you know that?' Jake says to Jo in the film, and I think a major conflict in her character is the tension between her idealism and the reality she has to face up to. This is the tension that Chekhov thought lay at the heart of all great art: the tension between life as it is and life as it ought to be. Penelope Mortimer could not quite define what her novel was about, but if I were to identify the theme of the film in one sentence, that would be it.

Notes

1 All subsequent quotations from the novel are from this Penguin edition but *The Pumpkin Eater* was first published, by Hutchinson, in 1962.

2 Otto Plaschkes, *Direct*, Summer 1995, p. 15.

3 This might be contrasted with Penelope Mortimer's assertion in the second volume of her autobiography, *About Time Too* (London, Weidenfeld & Nicholson, 1963, p. 102), where she claimed that 'apart from one ghoulish scene in a hairdresser's which was vintage Pinter, he stayed meticulously faithful to the dialogue'. A careful comparison between film

and novel reveals that this is not really the case. Some of the dialogue is taken from the novel but much of it is sharpened or invented by Pinter. Other details in Mortimer's autobiography concerning the film of *The Pumpkin Eater* are untrustworthy too. She refers, for example, to her 'fantasy hoards of children' being reduced in the film to 'three plain, correctly dressed, well mannered poppets and a mute toddler'; I doubt whether anyone would recognise the actual children in Clayton's film from that description, even numerically. On the central relationship, she says: 'Since she was the beautiful Anne Bancroft married to the thoroughly decent, pipe smoking Peter Finch, I, for one, couldn't see what she had to complain about.' Whether the Peter Finch character is really 'thoroughly decent' is perhaps up to the individual spectator, but 'pipe smoking'? He never smokes a pipe in the entire film. Was she thinking of a different movie?

4 *Sunday Telegraph*, 10 May 1964.

5 *Middlesex County Times*, 8 January 1965.

6 Douglas McVay, 'The House that Jack Built', *Films and Filming*, October 1967, p. 5.

7 'Jack Clayton is after all a very capable and intelligent director; if only he could forget about Art for a while and just make pictures we might really see something', *The Times*, 12 May 1964.

8 Penelope Houston, 'Keeping Up with the Antonionis', *Sight and Sound*, Autumn 1964, pp. 163–8.

9 *International Film Guide* (London, Tantivy Press, 1964), p. 86.

10 Andrew Sarris, *Confessions of a Cultist* (New York, Simon & Schuster, 1971), p. 369.

11 Jonathan Romney, 'British Film is Sick', *Guardian*, 13 November 1998.

12 *Films Illustrated*, July 1980, p. 393.

13 I elaborate the relevance of this quotation from *The Pumpkin Eater* to the theme of Nicolas Roeg's *Castaway* in *The Films of Nicolas Roeg* (London, Charles Letts & Co., 1991), p. 108.

14 Michael Billington, *The Life and Work of Harold Pinter* (London, Faber, 1996), p. 157.

15 Jack Clayton, personal note, 21 March 1963.

16 Pauline Kael, *Kiss Kiss Bang Bang* (New York, Bantam Books, 1969), p. 175.

17 'James Mason Interview with Riu Nogueira', *Focus on Film*, March–April 1970, p. 36.

18 *The Cinema as Art* (London, Penguin, 1964), pp. 101–2.

19 Billington, *Life and Work of Pinter*, p. 157.

20 *Ibid.* p. 158.

21 Houston, 'Keeping Up with the Antonionis', p. 167.

22 Robert Murphy, *Sixties British Cinema* (London, BFI Publishing, 1992), pp. 80–1.

23 Mortimer, *The Pumpkin Eater*, p. 108.

24 Murphy, *Sixties British Cinema*, p. 81.

25 Jack Clayton, personal note, 22 April 1963.

26 Jack Clayton, personal note, 9 May 1963.

27 Mortimer, *The Pumpkin Eater*, p. 83.

28 Jack Clayton, personal note, 9 May 1963.

29 *Ibid.*

30 Tony Sloman, 'Jack Clayton: the Bespoke Cineaste', *National Film Theatre booklet*, March 1996, p. 16.

31 Mortimer, *The Pumpkin Eater*, p. 91.

32 *Ibid.*, p. 20.

33 Among Clayton's papers are several drafts of this scene by Pinter. Coincidentally, there is a similar scene in Pinter's screenplay for Joseph Losey's *Accident* (1967), where, at a crisis point in his marriage, the hero sleeps with a former partner, and that scene does not quite work either. It might be worth mentioning here, incidentally, that Pinter's published screenplay, included in *Five Screenplays* (London, Methuen & Co., 1971), differs in several respects from the finished film and is clearly taken from an earlier draft. In the final film (which was cut by nine minutes after its showing at Cannes) some scenes are in a different order. For example, the scene at the hairdresser's now comes *between* the two scenes with the psychiatrist rather than after. This seems to work much better, in terms both of dramatic variety and of character continuity. It seems more logical that Jo's anger with the psychiatrist should come after an encounter at the hairdresser's which leaves her shaken. The bedroom scene with Giles in the final film is longer and better than the one in the published screenplay (Pinter, *Five Screenplays*, p. 132).

34 See Ivan Butler, *The Making of Feature Films – A Guide* (London, Penguin, 1971), p. 62.

35 Jack Clayton, personal note, 9 May 1963.

36 McVay, 'The House that Jack Built', p. 11.

37 *Ibid.*, p. 10.

38 Jack Clayton, personal note, 10 May 1963.

39 Mortimer, *The Pumpkin Eater*, p. 155.

40 Jack Clayton, personal note, 9 May 1963.

41 See *About Time Too*, pp. 102–3. Mortimer wrote that: 'In the novel the woman does a bolt to her "high hill" (a tower, for some Freudian reason), and is tracked down and captured by her innumerable children. Her husband, Jake, knowing that this is the only strategy that will succeed, delays his appearance until the capture is over. In the movie courageous Finch strides over the horizon with the mingy family tagging along behind. At first sight of him, Bancroft capitulates and accepts a loving cup or can of Worthington.' As I have indicated, I think this is a misreading of the tone and complexity of the film's ending. I also think this is a misrepresentation of the role of Jake in this last section of the film. It has always seemed clear to me that Jake is using the children in this scene as a shield, clearly recognising that this 'capture' would not succeed without them.

42 Murphy, *Sixties British Cinema*, p. 81.

43 Mortimer, *The Pumpkin Eater*, p. 155.

44 Jack Clayton, personal note, 27 May 1963.

Forbidden games: **6**
Our Mother's House (1967)

I found him whom my soul loveth. I held him, and would not let him go, until I had brought him into my mother's house, and into the chamber of her that conceived me. (Song of Solomon, 3: 4)

On my first morning in the gloomy house in Croydon I was in a bit of a funk. Eight pairs of eyes, ranging from five to fourteen, gazed at me solemnly. Not a smile, no welcoming grin even. In the little caravan in the scrubby front garden which I had been given to change in there was a jam jar stuffed with privet and some wilting Michaelmas daisies. Under it was a note. 'Let's hope you're as good as you're cracked up to be. You'd better be. Sincerely, The Children'.

I loved every second of the film which was one of the happiest I have ever made. (Dirk Bogarde, *Snakes and Ladders*, London, Chatto & Windus, 1975, pp. 247–8)

Most films about children make the adults serious and the children frivolous. Quite the other way round. (Francois Truffaut, *New Yorker*, 20 February 1960)

Jack Clayton described *Our Mother's House* in the following way. 'It's a story about children with no father, and so religious that when their mother dies they decide to bury her in the garden. They succeed in existing for six months until the father, who was no good anyway, appears and one of the girls kills him with a poker. It sounds macabre, but it's a lovely story.' This description is quoted in Lawrence Grobel's biography, *The Hustons*, where it is also noted that, 'lovely story' or not, a young Anjelica Huston cried throughout the screening and was, in Clayton's words, 'seriously disturbed' by it. (Grobel thought it reminded her of her frequently absent father, John Huston, and the domestic tension his absences caused.)[1] It is a description that immediately raises a question about the film's target audience: who precisely is the film for? Children would undoubtedly relate strongly to some parts of it, but might find other parts distressing. Amazingly, it was given an 'X' certificate on its release in Britain, which may be one of the reasons why it failed commercially: the certificate effectively excluded the constituency that the film was about and who might have had the most empathy with it. Three years later, Nicolas Roeg was to experience similar difficulties with *Walkabout* (1970).

Our Mother's House could be seen as a continuation of *The Innocents* and *The Pumpkin Eater*. It has something of the Gothicism of the former, and the same restricted setting and disturbed children; also a strong religious subtext (like Joe Lampton's aunt in *Room at the Top*, the mother has framed religious texts on the walls) and a sense of the way in which adult experience can pervert the maturation of children. Like *The Pumpkin Eater*, it has a superfluity of children and a strong sense of place. It also picks up a theme that is introduced at the end of Penelope Mortimer's novel of *The Pumpkin Eater* when the children come to visit Jo in the tower and she asks who has been looking after them in her absence. 'Dinah didn't go to school,' she is told, and then another child chimes in: 'We managed all right.'.[2] *Our Mother's House* is about how children 'manage'.

When the film was reviewed, it was often discussed as a sort of cross between *Lord of the Flies* and *The Servant*. Like William Golding's *Lord of the Flies* (which was filmed by Peter Brook in 1963), *Our Mother's House* deals with the situation of children cast on their own resources after a disaster. In *Lord of the Flies* the setting is an island and the children are all boys; in *Our Mother's House* the setting is an old Victorian house and there is a mixture of boys and girls. In both cases, though, discipline begins to break down; there are outbursts of cruelty and tyranny as one faction tries to impose its will on another; the children begin to mimic the social fissures created by their elders. In *The Servant* (1963), meanwhile, the house is invaded by a lower-class character (played by Dirk Bogarde) who begins to take over and invite in his disreputable friends: things degenerate as the invasion becomes a sort of peasants' revolt in which power relationships are turned upside down. Similar adult destruction occurs in *Our Mother's House*, but the children strike back. It might have been thought that, with all these parallels feeding into it without undermining its own originality, *Our Mother's House* had a fair chance of finding an audience. But in the 'Summer of Love' of 1967 a quirky little film about seven orphans concealing their mother's death from the world seemed in Robert Murphy's phrase 'almost perversely unfashionable and uncompromisingly uncommercial'.[3]

In this brief account, Murphy makes a rare factual error when he describes the film as a story involving 'five' children rather than 'seven'. I mention this only because, in theme and atmosphere, the film reminds me so strongly of one of Wordsworth's lyrical ballads, 'We Are Seven', in which an adult questions a young girl at a graveyard about the members of her family and the girl insists that there are seven of them, even though two lie buried beneath the earth. The poem concludes:

> 'How many are you, then' said I,
> 'If they two are in Heaven?'
> The little Maiden did reply,
> 'O Master! We are seven'.

> 'But they are dead; those two are dead!
> Their spirits are in heaven!'
> 'Twas throwing words away; for still
> The little Maid would have her will,
> And said, 'Nay, we are seven!'

Max Beerbohm once composed a cartoon about this poem, in which an old man is leaning over a young girl and saying to her fiercely: 'Look! Seven minus two equals five!' What we have in *Our Mother's House* is something very Wordsworthian: children who choose to assimilate the idea of death in their own way and into their own world of logic and imagination, confronted by an adult world that appears actively to seek to destroy the child's intuitions and illusions. In the poem, why is the old man so insistent on destroying the girl's confidence in her own intuitions? Is it exasperation at childish obstinacy, or envy of an innocence he has lost? The 'father' Charlie Hook will have a similar outburst at the end of *Our Mother's House*, the adult actively attempting to destroy childhood innocence and illusion – but it will be he who is destroyed. The danger to adults of childhood innocence has been explored in other films, notably in those of Alexander Mackendrick, but *Our Mother's House* has an atmosphere all of its own. The nearest to it, I think, for its combination of the grotesque and the poignant in its depiction of childhood, is René Clément's great film, *Jeux Interdits – Forbidden Games* (1952) which is also about how children come into contact with, and adapt to their own purposes, the rituals surrounding death.

'The time must shortly come', said Clayton in a note to his screenwriter Jeremy Brooks (6 July 1966), 'when we must decide what *Our Mother's House* is trying to say'. The novel had been brought to his attention by his close friend the Canadian novelist Mordecai Richler, and he had found it instantly fascinating: the fatherless house with children thrown on their own resources for survival would obviously have an immediate personal appeal. A letter from the novel's author Julian Gloag to Clayton (26 September 1966) seems to suggest that Fox was initially interested in the property and that Eleanor Perry, at that time best known for her screenplay for an extremely successful American independent film about disturbed adolescents, *David and Lisa* (1963), had completed a script. However, MGM and Martin Ransohoff acquired it for Clayton, who commissioned Jeremy Brooks, the literary manager of the Royal Shakespeare Company, to write the screenplay. When Brooks's screenplay turned out to be too long and rather too close to its source, the adaptation was completed by Haya Harareet, who tightened the structure and particularly changed the ending to make it more thematically consistent and psychologically plausible than in the novel.

At an early stage Richard Burton had been considered for the role of Charlie Hook, though it was felt that he might cost more than the film could afford. In the event Dirk Bogarde was cast, to the great satisfaction of all. 'I can't imagine anyone more likely to bring the necessary subtlety to a part which it would be all too easy to play in a stereotyped manner,' wrote Julian Gloag to Clayton (26 September 1966). The only other casting problem came with the role of Diana. The part had originally been assigned to Jenny Agutter, but she was withdrawn to take up a better-paid role in Andrzej Wajda's *Gates of Paradise* (1967), much to the chagrin of Clayton, who felt her mother and her agent had reneged on a verbal agreement. The part was reassigned to Pamela Franklin, who makes up for being slightly too old for the role by giving a performance of great emotional power that adds particular force to the latter part of the film.

Franklin had made her screen début for Clayton in *The Innocents*. Of the other seven children only two had ever appeared on screen before: Sarah Nicholls, who plays Gerty, and who had been one of the family in *The Pumpkin Eater* (her father, Anthony Nicholls, plays Mr Halbert in *Our Mother's House* and had a small role as a consultant surgeon in *The Pumpkin Eater*), and Mark Lester, who on the basis of his performance here was to be recommended by Clayton to John Woolf for the title role of *Oliver!* (1968). (It might be remembered that Woolf wanted Clayton to direct *Oliver!* but he refused, because he felt strongly that Fagin was an anti-Semitic characterisation. The direction was undertaken by Carol Reed, who was to win an Oscar for it.) Margaret Brooks, who gives a remarkable performance as the oldest child Elsa, was the daughter of Jeremy Brooks. The others were all amateurs, but acquit themselves well. When asked once what made him think he could direct a cast of children whose work would require ensemble acting in long takes and could not be assembled by montage, Clayton replied, drily: 'Utter conceit'. In fact, because he never shouted and seemed to have infinite patience and respect for young performers, they rapidly gave him their trust. In his notes to Jeremy Brooks about the first draft screenplay (18 August 1966), Clayton was very alert to what children should and should not be required to do, in terms of dialogue, for the sake of a convincing performance. 'Children can rarely maintain the tempo of an adult actor,' he wrote, 'and I also think that children embarking on over-long sentences tend to get boring. In order to try and get the flow very fast, we should attempt to reduce the children's dialogue to single line exchanges.'

The film was shot entirely on location in Croydon at a very modest budget of just over £200,000. Dirk Bogarde took a reduced salary, a generous gesture which had its own payback for it was this performance, more than any other, that attracted the attention of Luchino Visconti and was to result in his being cast in *The Damned* (1969) and, most famously, in *Death in Venice* (1971).[4] Also offering his services at reduced rate out of belief in the project and loyalty to the director was composer Georges Delerue, whose score is as evocative of the innocence and terror of childhood as Elmer Bernstein's great score for *To Kill a Mockingbird* (1962). There was to be some payback for Delerue too. If one notices a distinct similarity between Delerue's main theme and that composed by Quincy Jones for Steven Spielberg's *The Color Purple* (1985), the reason is that Spielberg had loved both Clayton's film and Delerue's score, and had used Delerue's music as a guide to indicate to Jones the style he wanted. Delerue was rightly to be paid for the influence his score exerted on Jones.

In an interview with Gordon Gow, Clayton described the style of the film as 'slightly feet-off-the-ground, and not a truly realistic subject, although it does exist within a realist area'.[5] The mood comes from both the strangeness of the situation and the fact that things are seen from the children's perspective and therefore seem larger than life. It was Clayton's first film in colour – a rather odd choice, given the claustrophobic interior nature of the subject. However, the colour is used very expressively. It is for the most part low-key and shadowy, which, as Raymond Durgnat noted, 'accords well with mother's invisible presence'.[6] However, this texture is punctuated by sharp infusions of brighter shades to intensify dramatic moments, like Hubert's (Louis Sheldon) switching on the light to convince the children that mother is truly dead, or Diana's (Pamela Franklin) discovery of the transparent scarlet negligée prior to her encounter with Charlie.

The early scenes crisply establish atmosphere and character. Autumn leaves set the season: a huge Bible dominating the frame evokes the oppressive religious atmosphere in mother's room; the abrasive manner and even the red hair of the housekeeper, Mrs Quayle (Yootha Joyce), instantly set her at odds with the tone of the house and the mood of its inhabitants. The mother's death is signalled by her hand stretching for her bell and then falling limply, knocking onto the floor a gold watch which stops, as if marking not only the time of death but a different dimension of 'normal' time. 'We have no *time* to show time or to properly develop the relationship between people in time', wrote Clayton in his personal notes (20–21 August 1966). Although one is dimly aware of time's passing, the stronger impression is of the action taking place in a kind of suspended time until the fantasy is played out to the finish and the children can rejoin the real world. When they step out of the house at the end of the film ('Come on, we haven't got all night,' one of them says), it is as if a spell has been broken. Previously, one feels, they have been existing in a dream-like condition of shock. It is only at the end that Gerty can say to Elsa, in my favourite line of the film: 'You mean it's not a secret anymore? I can tell Miss Bailey'? – exactly what a child in those circumstances would say, but also a hopeful sign that the secret can be brought into the real world and exorcised by sympathetic adulthood. (The line was Haya Harareet's: it does not appear in the novel, nor in Jeremy Brooks's second draft screenplay.) The last shot of the avenue is a reprise of the first, this time at night, as one ponders what the future will now hold as they move into the world of experience. Like a lot of Clayton's endings, it has the feeling of a threshold being crossed.

Out of fear of being sent to an orphanage and separated, the children have decided to bury the mother in the garden and conceal her death from the adult world. Clayton creates both tension and comedy from the conflict between these diminutive children and the magnitude of what they are doing. The barely comprehended reading of their mother's will is introduced by a below-table shot of little legs that can hardly touch the floor. A bank clerk (Gerald Sim) looms awesomely over his counter as they attempt to cash their mother's welfare cheque, her signature dutifully forged by the skilful Jiminee (Mark Lester). In the opening scene of the mother's death, the range of moods has been particularly well characterised: Diana hysterical; the puritanical Dunstan (John Gugolka) expressing his fear and distress by bullying a younger child; the youngest, Willy (Gustav Henry), becoming more subdued and miserable not because he fully understands what has happened but simply because he senses something is wrong. As the situation develops, the children have to deal not only with the prying, inquisitive outside world – schoolteachers, neighbours – but with tensions that develop among themselves.

'In the book, I don't think really enough is made of totally enclosing them with their guilty secret from the world', wrote Clayton in his draft notes (20–21 August 1966). 'In other words, I think that Mother's House becomes a tomb ... they are enclosed by what they have themselves created.' One has a sense of this early in the film, when they leave the house for the first time since their mother's death to go to school, and a subjective shot from Elsa's point of view makes the front gate seem a huge distance away. In other words the real world out there looks threatening; safer by far to return to the tomb – or womb – of their mother's house. But there are dangers here too. The fierce puritanism of the household has gripped some of the children. When Gerty hitches a ride with a motorcyclist and is thought to have endangered their secret, she is tried in the 'tabernacle' they have created in the garden shed, with Diana convinced she can hear her mother's voice and asking what punishment should be meted out. Dunstan shines a torch in Gerty's eyes – a gesture at torture, but also (with the light hitting the face) a reference to exposure to harsh reality. Diana rocks menacingly back and forth in the rocking chair as she summons up the spirit of 'Mother', the slight blurring and crumbling of the colour here suggesting the 'dissolution and substitution of personality', as Durgnat puts it.[7] We are suddenly in the territory of *Les Enfants terribles* or even *Psycho* (the fetishisation of mother's wig), and the enactment of the punishment – taking away the comb and cutting Gerty's hair – is powerful and distressing, the horror intensified by amplification of Gerty's screams. Incidentally, in the novel, Gerty will fall ill after this incident and die, which seems not only gratuitously morbid but a further strain on credibility: the children might get away with hiding one body, but two? Also, such an event would turn them into monsters. The film compassionately and wisely allows Gerty to survive her illness,[8] and by the time of her recovery there is another member of the household – Jiminee's young friend Louis (Parnum Wallace), who has been invited by Jiminee to leave home and join them. Mother's house is being transformed into an orphanage run by the inmates.

It is at this point that the adult world invades, or is ineluctably sucked into, their fantasy. The screenwriters cleverly telescope two scenes from the novel into one: the appearance of the teacher, Miss Bailey (Claire Davidson), who is looking for the missing Louis and who has become increasingly suspicious about the situation in the family, and the appearance of their 'father', Charlie Hook (Dirk Bogarde), who has been secretly summoned in a letter by Hubert when he felt discipline and authority amongst the children was beginning to break down. Clayton worried that there might be too much exposition, repetition and psychological complexity to get over convincingly in this scene, but in fact it is extremely well written and acted and seems to move things forward without repetitive explanation. Immediately prior to Charlie Hook's entrance, the situation with Miss Bailey has been growing tense and unpleasant: the children's obduracy, their ganging up on the young teacher, have begun to seem menacing. Charlie's entrance is a surprise (a neatly timed close-up of Dirk Bogarde registers the slight shock of this delayed entrance, the star not appearing until the film is half over – *Psycho* in reverse); but, crucially, it also defuses the tension. Moreover, in shrewdly assessing the situation and manoeuvring Miss Bailey out of the house, Charlie gets most of the children quickly on his side: after all, he has got them out of a tight spot.

Bogarde's performance is a consummate one. As films as varied as *Hunted* (1952), *The Spanish Gardener* (1957) and *Accident* (1967) have shown, he has always been a fine actor with children. Crucially here, and with the undoubted collaboration of Clayton, he picks up the tempo of the film just at the moment when it is beginning to flag. Some critics unfairly thought Bogarde was simply reprising his performance in *The Servant*,[9] but there is a world of difference between the reptilian Barrett in Losey's film and the Charlie Hook of *Our Mother's House*, who is on one level an unscrupulous opportunist but who is also alternately bewildered, bemused, charmed and likeable. 'It would be nice', wrote Clayton in a note to Jeremy Brooks (18 August 1966), 'if we could see that Charlie really enjoyed the children – indeed their adulation fulfilled in him some definite need. Who, for instance, could listen to his boasting stories with much greater credulity than they?' The scenes of games and stories are delightfully done, and if Dunstan seems a little too easily won over (a reservation Haya Harareet felt about the script), the conflict between Diana, who approves of Charlie, and Elsa, who does not, adds another layer of tension to the final part of the film. The irony is that, as Clayton noted, Charlie opens up the world for them, which previously has been a fearful place beyond their front gate: he takes them on a drive, he takes them canoeing on a lake. 'In fact,' noted Clayton (in his draft notes of 20 August), 'Charlie, poor Charlie, really makes the present ending possible. He actually makes it possible for them to go out and be healthy.'

It is Charlie who will bring things to a crisis. With the aid of Jiminee's forgery skills, he has been cashing in mother's money and inviting women round for parties, including Mrs Quayle, who has insinuated her way back into the household by convincing Charlie that she knows about his financial frauds. One morning Diana comes into the bedroom with Charlie's morning tea only to find Charlie and another woman in mother's bed. It is one of the most powerful scenes of emotional disillusionment in Clayton's work. A hostile review in the *Monthly Film Bulletin*[10] felt this scene misfired because it was shot through red gauze, giving it an inappropriate adult romanticism, whereas it should have been shot with absolute clarity. But the red haziness of the scene does not feel like romanticism to me. The suffusion of red into what has been a predominantly sombre film has a shock effect of its own, the colour having clear overtones of loss of innocence and the veil being suggestive of Diana's confusion; it also anticipates the blood-letting to come. Although he reassures Diana later, in a beguilingly acted scene between Bogarde and Franklin, stage by stage Charlie is dismantling their fantasy. The furniture has been removed from the tabernacle; an estate agent has been in to assess the value of the house; a confrontation is inevitable.

It is at this confrontation that Charlie shatters their final illusion about their beloved mother. She was a whore, he says, and none of the children is his. He smashes her picture, stamps on it, and throws it on the fire. 'What a life,' he says to Diana, who lifts the poker and in telling, agonising slow motion smashes it across his skull. In the novel it was Hubert who did the killing, but in the film it seems more logical that it should be Diana, his tirade against the mother being the culmination of her disillusionment and the crushing of the last of her illusions. 'He's dead', they say starkly, with none of the hesitant euphemisms they used about their mother's death. The house is now dark, suddenly terrifying. A loud knock at the door announces the presence of a fresh danger waiting outside. The voice of Mrs Quayle is heard, shouting for Charlie. She tries to get in and suddenly fear becomes a black gloved hand reaching for the door chain – the 'evil grasp pursuing them', to borrow a phrase that David Thomson uses to describe the chilling moment of the hand reaching for the children in Charles Laughton's *The Night of the Hunter* (1955).[11] No longer their refuge, the house becomes something from which they must escape. A key detail is changed here from the novel: Charlie is not buried in the garden because, as Elsa tells Gerty: 'He doesn't belong in the garden. He didn't love us.' The children leave the house and move uncertainly into the real world they have kept at arm's length for as long as their childhood has allowed.

Clayton made haunting films – appropriately enough for someone who believed in ghosts. They stay with you and invade your dreams, even when they walk a knife edge between the plausible and the implausible. This is particularly true of *Our Mother's House*. 'It is after all a bit naughty of Clayton', said Raymond Durgnat, 'to offer us an almost *impossible* plot'[12] (though one of the most haunting of all films – Hitchcock's *Vertigo* – also does that). Is it credible that the school would not be more suspicious of the children's behaviour, would not check up a bit more about the ailing mother? The novel accentuates this implausibility through its emphasis on the passage of time (of around a year). The film elides it by making time seem nebulous and dream-like – as if time stops in that house, like mother's watch, until a second, very different death reactivates it. Is the children's innocence plausible? The younger ones might still idealise the mother, but, given their ages, would not the older ones be likely to be aware of the true state of affairs? (The 'shock' revelation appears not to have been shocking enough to have the impact required for an audience of 1967.) There is also something curiously old-fashioned about the household. Why no television? no radio even? (Given the mother's religious puritanism, one could imagine the reasons, but it is strange that no explanation is offered.) Small wonder that some critics described the situation and setting as 'sub-Dickensian', an impression which is intensified by the characters' curious names. The film, thank goodness, renames the housekeeper 'Mrs Quayle' rather than 'Mrs Stork' and the teacher 'Miss Bailey' rather than 'Miss Deko'. Pleasingly though, it keeps the father's name of 'Hook', a relevant allusion to *Peter Pan*, for *Our Mother's House* is also a story about children who do not wish to grow up. And, given Spielberg's enormous admiration for *Our Mother's House*, is it fanciful to think that it might have been in some part of his mind when he came to make his long-awaited film of *Peter Pan* but called it instead *Hook* (1991)?

Yet if *Our Mother's House* strains credulity on a realist level, its operation on an imaginative plane is very compelling. For Dirk Bogarde the film was a frightening allegory about people who try to exist by themselves but when democracy starts hardening into authoritarianism, appeal to an external authority for help, which brings the whole thing crashing down. This version of the story involves children, but there are numerous political parallels. Clayton could never make a film that did not have some personal meaning for him and it would not be hard to think of reasons why this material would particularly appeal: the fatherless family; the tension between innocence and experience, romanticism and reality.

There is a curious moment in the film when Hubert is inspecting a toy soldier and he looks through the window curtain and sees a veiled image of cavalrymen riding their horses past the house. In the context of the film, it is impossible to know whether the image is real or imagined; whether the toy activates the image in Hubert's mind or whether it represents some sort of yearning of his to be outside the house and this situation. In a note on the first draft of the script (18 August 1966), Clayton wrote: 'For reasons I cannot explain, I am anxious to have Hubert at dawn looking through a window and seeing a troop of cavalry exercising their horses past the house.' It is intriguing that Clayton could not explain the reason for wanting the shot but went ahead with it anyway, allowing the instinctive to prevail over the rational. I suspect that one of the things that particularly appealed to him about *Our Mother's House* was precisely its anti-rationality: the determination of a group of people (children, in this case) to keep the rational world at bay for as long as possible. Nearly all Clayton's major characters have a spell in which they create an intensively subjective world that becomes an idealised space in which they can momentarily live out their romantic dreams. One thinks of the weekend idyll of Joe and Alice in *Room at the Top*; the enchanting children who, for a while, bring a fullness to the life of the governess in *The Innocents*; Jo's 'dream world' in *The Pumpkin Eater*; Gatsby's dream; the whole 'dream come true' theme of *Something Wicked This Way Comes*. It is an ideal but it is also a fantasy that must be brought down to earth. As Hubert says, in a telling sentence in the novel: 'He was frightened. The dream wasn't ending at all.'[13] The dream inevitably ends. The world allows no hermits, as D. H. Lawrence observed in *Lady Chatterley's Lover* (Chapter 10). Yet the dream *must* end, for to be enclosed for ever in that kind of 'self-created supernatural' (Tony Sloman's phrase)[14] risks alienation and madness. Still, the intensity with which Clayton creates this feeling probably explains why so many of his endings take the form of an exorcism: an expiation, or casting out, of demons, be they psychological, creative or cinematic. *Our Mother's House* feels like a personal, private battle with inner demons: flawed, obscure, old-fashioned in places it may be, but there are many more passages in it that seem touching, tender and true.

Notes

1 Lawrence Grobel, *The Hustons* (London, Bloomsbury, 1990), p. 601.

2 Penelope Mortimer, *The Pumpkin Eater* (London, Penguin, 1964), p. 158.

3 Robert Murphy, *Sixties British Cinema* (London, British Film Institute Publishing, 1992), p. 81.

4 Dirk Bogarde, *Snakes and Ladders* (London, Chatto & Windus, 1978), p. 248. Here Dirk Bogarde writes of the film's failure at the 1967 Venice Film Festival. 'Our hopes, reasonably high, were very soon damned by faint praise and light applause ... I hoped never to see Venice again.' An ironic wish if ever there was one, for, as he goes on: 'I immersed myself in a deep and useless conversation with Clayton trying to work out, far too late, just where we had gone wrong; so immersed was I that I quite failed to notice my future standing at the bar watching me. Luchino Visconti.'

5 *Films and Filming*, April 1974, p. 12.

6 Raymond Durgnat, *Films and Filming*, November 1967, p. 20.

7 *Ibid.*

8 Haya Clayton told me of a scene she had written and wished to include at this point in the film. During Gerty's illness, Dunstan and Diana go to a pharmacy to try to get some medicine for her: from outside the window, Diana can see Dunstan arguing with the chemist. When Dunstan comes out, he starts running and Diana struggles to keep pace with him. 'Did you get some medicine?' she asks. 'No', replies Dunstan, 'he said I needed a prescription'. 'Then why are you running?' Dunstan stops and opens his hand – to reveal a packet of polo mints he has stolen from the chemist's. Clayton never explained why he cut the scene; perhaps he felt it might dilute the tomb-like atmosphere and claustrophobic intensity of the scenes in the house. Haya felt the scene would have served a purpose in showing that, although Diana and Dunstan seemed to be the most righteous and cruel of the children – Diana pronouncing the punishment on Gerty, Dunstan carrying it out – underneath they cared and were worried enough to try and get some medicine for her. It also usefully showed that beneath his religious piety, Dunstan is not as rigid or unfeeling as he might seem. (That will be important later to explain why he is charmed and won over by Charlie, a conversion which might otherwise seem rather abrupt.) This further relates to a moment in the film that I always find moving. When Gerty recovers, her first response is typically: 'I want a biscuit'. It is Dunstan who immediately says, 'I'll get it' and runs off to find one for her, his sense of relief conveyed by the speed and spontaneity of that gesture.

9 See, for example, David Shipman, *The Story of Cinema: Volume Two* (London, Hodder & Stoughton, 1984), p. 120.

10 *Monthly Film Bulletin*, October 1967, p. 153.

11 *Sight and Sound*, April 1999, p. 21.

12 Durgnat, *Films and Filming*, p. 20.

13 Julian Gloag, *Our Mother's House* (London, Secker & Warburg, 1963; quotation from Pan edition, 1966, p. 103).

14 Tony Sloman, *National Film Theatre booklet*, March 1996, p. 17.

7

Clayton in America: *The Great Gatsby* (1974); *Something Wicked This Way Comes* (1983)

It seems to me that quite a few of my stories, as well as my one acts would provide interesting and profitable material for the contemporary cinema, if committed to such lovely hands as Miss [Faye] Dunaway's or Jon Voight's. And to such cinematic masters of direction as Jack Clayton, who made of *The Great Gatsby* a film that even surpassed, I think, the novel by Scott Fitzgerald. (Tennessee Williams, *Memoirs*, New York, Doubleday & Co., 1975, p. 178)

Fantasy is the difference between what we have and what we want. We all dream constantly and we try only a little less constantly to make our dreams a part of what we call reality. We usually succeed; reality is merely the sum of dreams that have been made to come true. (That many of the dreams were bad ones means that the world needs not fewer dreamers but better ones!) Few of us settle for less than we want, although sometimes we confuse what we want with what others have. Why does anyone want less than a world of love? (John Brook)[1]

The Great Gatsby

Jack Clayton was always a controversial director for so American a subject as *The Great Gatsby*. He was the preferred choice of Ali McGraw, who at that time was married to the head of Paramount, Robert Evans, and had suggested the idea of a film of *Gatsby* to him with her in the role of Daisy. By the time the project was confirmed, Clayton was attached to it but McGraw had begun an affair with Steve McQueen and left her husband. Clayton was unfazed by questions about his fitness to direct an American classic. '*Gatsby* is about a class and a society both of which I know very well', he told Penelope Houston. 'Apart from the romantic side of the film, and Gatsby's obsession (and I think I understand obsession very well), it is a story about class, which is something I love.'² The theme of class would connect *Gatsby* directly in Clayton's work with *Room at the Top*. It is powerfully conveyed in *Gatsby* through the contrasting photographic texture – light and dark – for the Gatsby/Daisy romance and the Myrtle/Wilson marriage, the latter being the grim flipside of the romantic main theme of why 'rich girls should not marry poor boys'.

There is also the familiar Clayton theme of lost innocence, where characters either sacrifice their dreams or romantic vision for ambition or greed (like Lampton in *Room at the Top*), or collide head-on with corruption and experience (like the children in *Our Mother's House*). *The Great Gatsby* is about the death of a particularly single-minded innocence and romanticism, the high price to be paid for, as Fitzgerald put it, 'living too long with a single dream'. So Clayton was an imaginative choice of director, one who could bring an outsider's objectivity to the material but also a real emotional empathy.

Clayton certainly knew his Fitzgerald. He had first read the novel as a teenager and it had remained one of his favourites. He had once been announced as director of a projected film version from Laurence Harvey's production company of Budd Schulberg's *The Disenchanted*, a novel inspired by Schulberg's encounter with Fitzgerald, but nothing came of the venture.³ Even ten years after *Gatsby*, and notwithstanding the critical mauling he had received in some quarters, Clayton did extensive preparatory work on a screenplay, *One Last Glimpse*, that was based on the friendship between Scott Fitzgerald and Ernest Hemingway. (See Chapter 10.) Moreover, prior to filming *Gatsby*, Clayton did his customary thorough preparation (he knew that two previous versions – one in 1926 with Warner Baxter as Gatsby and one in 1949 with Alan Ladd – had both failed). He consulted literary experts, including the doyen of Fitzgerald scholars, Matthew J. Bruccoli; he read up on the most recent Fitzgerald scholarship (his papers contain a large section specially typed out of Milton R. Stern's analysis of *Gatsby* in his 1970 book on Fitzgerald, *The Golden Moment*). Most particularly he discussed the script in detail with Fitzgerald's daughter, Scottie Smith. She gave much useful advice and, contrary to what the critic David Shipman (among many others) asserted,[4] always insisted that her father would have loved the film.

Truman Capote submitted a first draft screenplay which Clayton felt to be flawed. 'There is far too much dialogue and exposition', he wrote in a letter to Capote (18 January 1972). 'There is also a feeling that many of the scenes are about the same thing: same people, same setting and most important of all, the same even, emotional level within each scene.' The question of variety preoccupied Clayton. The way to solve the problem, he thought, was not by a series of short, sharp scenes but a contrast between scenes or within them. When he saw the last section of Capote's script, he had to say (in a letter of 28 January 1972) that, having found the first part too long, he now found this too short: up to and including the Plaza sequence, the script was 112 pages, from there until the end, it was barely 12. 'It's like a great fish that is all head and no tail', he wrote to Capote. 'What we have to do is to make it seem to go fast, and yet develop from it every dramatic possibility.' Clayton was articulating a problem that he felt the novel posed for adaptation anyway: that it is somewhat un-balanced. The first two-thirds is perhaps too leisurely – it takes Fitzgerald half the novel to bring Gatsby and Daisy together – whereas the last third is the most exciting and interesting part of the tale in cinematic terms. In his 'notes on structure' to himself, Clayton wrote that, although it was always his intention to render the novel faithfully, the first half of the book should be com-pressed to ensure that they got to the Gatsby/Daisy romance somewhere between a third and a half of the way through the script.

For students of the novel genre and of adaptation generally, the thoughts of a first-class film-maker like Clayton about the narra-tive problems of a text are invariably valuable. They give great insight into narrative structure, interpretative lines and those differences between film and literary narrative which mean that what may work in one form may not work in another. No one who has read, for example, David Lean's letter to Santha Rama Rau that sets out the narrative problems of E. M. Forster's *A Passage to India* could fail to learn something both about the novel and about film.[5] Clayton's notes are similarly judicious and illuminating. As well as problems with the structural balance of the novel he put his finger on two other elements which he felt would cause problems. The first had to do with the series of coincidences that lead up to Myrtle's death. There is the whole business of who is driving which car: why do they keep changing cars? Why does Gatsby's car have to stop at Wilson's garage for gas: as Clayton noted, we know it was a chauffeur-maintained car, so would it not be full anyway? In plot terms, we know why they have to stop, because we need to see what is developing between Wilson and Myrtle, but can the detail be made to seem more plausible in the film? Also, how does Myrtle manage to escape from the locked room at Wilson's garage, and just in time to be run over by Gatsby's car? These narrative details are deftly rendered in the film, so one is never tempted to query their plausibility, but they work because of Clayton's alertness to the difficulties in the first place.

The second problem is perhaps more acute and the handling more controversial. The present-day romance between Gatsby and Daisy is suggested in the novel in just one line of Gatsby's dialogue: 'Daisy comes over quite often – in the afternoon.'[6] 'I think you have to see it,' Clayton said to Penelope Houston. 'The sequence is also the method of finding out about the past between them, without using flashback.'[7] The inclusion of the modern-day romance – and the way it was done – was to be the subject of much criticism, but it is worth pointing out that Clayton's sense of a structural deficiency in the novel at this stage had been acknowledged by Fitzgerald himself in a letter to Edmund Wilson:

> The worst fault in it, I think, is a BIG FAULT: I gave no account (and had no feeling about or knowledge of) the emotional relations between Gatsby and Daisy from the time of their reunion to the catastrophe. However, the lack is so astutely concealed by the retrospect of Gatsby's past and by blankets of excellent prose that

no one has noticed it – though everyone has felt the lack and called it by another name.[8]

When Capote failed to deliver a screenplay that was acceptable to Paramount or Clayton,[9] the director considered a number of alternatives, including Robert Towne, Gore Vidal, Christopher Hampton, Stewart Stern and Carol Eastman. Previous valued collaborators, such as Mordecai Richler, John Mortimer and Harold Pinter were also considered but proved to be unavailable. (Coincidentally, Pinter was soon to script the film adaptation of another Fitzgerald novel, *The Last Tycoon*, for Elia Kazan, with the main female role going to the young actress Ingrid Boulting, who can be briefly glimpsed as an extra during one of the party scenes in *Gatsby*.)[10] Eventually the job fell to Francis Ford Coppola, who had recently won a screenwriting Oscar for *Patton* (1970) and was Paramount's golden boy on account of *The Godfather*, which was shortly due for release. 'The whole feeling we have to achieve between Gatsby and Daisy', wrote Clayton in a note to Coppola (24 February 1972), 'is that this is not just a sexual love affair but the absolute essence of the word "romance". It is for Gatsby the whole meaning of his life. And this is what we must try and get onto the screen: *the magic of romance.*' Because of this, Clayton felt, he would need a European cameraman. 'On the basis of the best that I have seen here in America', Clayton wrote, 'none of them have a romantic quality that I feel Gatsby needs'. His selection for cinematographer was the brilliant English cameraman Douglas Slocombe. Clayton went on: 'Also on the colour, I am going to play to the full, as in the book, the effect of the sun – and, of course, the sun indoors, so that there will constantly be a glare from the windows – a great feeling of whiteness.'

Coppola wrote a screenplay in six weeks that did not entirely meet with Clayton's approval. There are copies of the script that have posted on them on adjoining pages xeroxed extracts from the novel, as if at times they were filming direct from the book (as Visconti is said to have done with *Death in Venice*, one of Clayton's favourite films, and whose influence on *Gatsby* is noticeable). An early Coppola draft had ended the film with the shot of the framed photo of Daisy and Gatsby's father asking, 'Who is this girl?' That was changed later, probably because it was felt that such an ending might give the impression that the film was really about Daisy. A line that was to cause some controversy in Coppola's second draft of April 1972 was 'Poor boys don't marry rich girls', which Clayton changed round to 'Rich girls don't marry poor boys', probably because, as the line is said by Daisy, it makes more sense for her to speak from her own point of view. Scottie Smith thought the line was out of character as Daisy had waited for Gatsby a while after he had gone to the war; but, as his personal notes about Daisy reveal, Clayton clearly felt that it was absolutely in character and did express something crucial about Daisy and her class. As he put it in a note to himself after his meeting with Coppola (6 March 1972): 'She truly belongs to Tom, or she belongs to Tom's background and class.' In the same note he makes a very interesting and astute comment on Daisy: 'She is as obsessed with herself as Gatsby is with her – and that is, in fact, strangely enough, their common link.' Much of the narcissistic imagery associated with Daisy in the film, and Mia Farrow's performance in the role, is traceable to that intuition of Clayton's about her character.

The casting attracted great publicity. Haya Clayton told me that at one time her husband considered Jack Nicholson for the role of Gatsby, as he had greatly admired his performance in *Five Easy Pieces* (1971), particularly in his scene with his father: there was a quality of vulnerability behind the toughness that he thought Gatsby required. However, after a ninety-minute meeting at a London airport with Robert Redford he was persuaded that he had his ideal Gatsby, Redford having, as he put it, 'the possibility of danger' behind the romantic Wasp image. Finding the ideal Daisy was more difficult. He tested Katharine Ross, Candice Bergen, Lois Chiles and Faye Dunaway; he also considered Tuesday Weld, Natalie Wood, Julie Christie and Cybill Shepherd, who were either unavailable or who ruled themselves out by refusing to be tested. Despite having a temperature of 103 because of 'flu, Mia Farrow was persuaded by Clayton to do a test and was by his account sensational. She landed the part – and then caused consternation by announcing she was pregnant, which complicated but in the event did not seriously hamper Clayton's shooting schedule. A candidate for Daisy, Lois Chiles, was eventually cast in the smaller but important role of Jordan Baker.

Other complications included the engagement of Shirley Russell as costume designer, who then backed out because of personal problems, which led to a delay of four weeks as they looked for a replacement. (The costumes were eventually designed by Theoni Aldredge, who at that time was mainly a stage designer for Joseph Papp's public theatre in New York, but who was to win an Oscar for her work on *Gatsby*.) As a cost-cutting exercise, reducing the budget by $4 million, it was decided to shoot some of the film at Pinewood studios in London. The exteriors for Fitzgerald's wealthy East Egg community had been mainly shot at Newport, Rhode Island. Fitzgerald's valley of ashes – the symbolic dividing line between the rich of Long Island and the urban masses and containing both Wilson's garage and the all-seeing sign of occulist Dr T. J. Eckleburg – was recreated at Pinewood.

Some post-production decisions were also a little delicate. There was the casting credit of Tom Ewell as Fitzgerald's Owl-Eyed Man whose role, apart from a fleeting appearance at the funeral, had been edited out of the final film, entirely for reasons of length and nothing whatever to do with the quality of the performance. (In the publicity, he receives a credit as 'Special appearance by ...'.) There was also the question of how to credit the contribution of Nelson Riddle, who had been recommended to Clayton for the music by André Previn but whose role was somewhat difficult to define (musical arranger? musical director? composer?). In the event, he was credited as musical 'supervisor' over the main titles with an additional caption at the end that reads: 'Arrangements and additional music composed and conducted by ...'. Riddle's contribution is important not only for the dramatic cues – the plaintive love theme for Gatsby and Daisy, the evocative musical motif for Daisy's green light, the tense music for Wilson's murderous mission – but also for his selection of source music that evokes the period but also enlarges the theme. For example, there are two songs that are given particular prominence: 'What'll I Do?' and 'Ain't We Got Fun?' Gordon Gow has shrewdly noted that 'perhaps it was significant that these popular songs came with question marks. Prosperity wasn't for everyone nor was it a guarantee of security'.[11] The first song, 'What'll I Do?', not only evokes Gatsby's romantic longing tinged with self-pity but is also a comment on the rich society people, whose lives have all the material comforts but seem empty of purpose. 'Ain't We Got Fun?' is a song that builds a satirical self-doubt into its ostensible celebration of pleasure and the Roaring Twenties – it seems not entirely convinced that this hedonistic pursuit is all that satisfying – and its acid lines about the division between rich and poor ('There's nothing surer/The rich get rich/And the poor get poorer') are at the core of the film's thematic substance. Riddle deservedly was to win an Oscar for the music and he paid special tribute in his acceptance speech to Clayton's support.

In his rough notes about the script, set design and colour, Clayton made a number of observations that usefully illuminate his approach to the subject and how the style would reflect his intention. 'I think the film should have a golden look', he wrote. 'By this I mean, not necessarily that the colour gold is constantly there but that a feeling and a glow of a kind of gold warmth is in it.' This obviously relates to the film's romanticism and its obsession with money; but it also reflects the story's physical and emotional temperature. 'I intend in fact to keep throughout the film a constant feeling of extreme heat', he went on. 'I want people to perspire all the time and I want to see even stains on people's dresses. It is part of the story, the heat.' As for the overall intention about the basic style of the film, he wrote:

> *Gatsby* is an enormously romantic story which at the same time is a tragedy. Not just for Gatsby but for all the characters that take part. So first of all it has obviously and is going to be treated by me very romantically. As it is a story basically about obsession, it is absolutely necessary that the film has constantly a kind of mystery to it. Mystery, mystique and absolute touching sadness.

The film opens with a shot of Gatsby's house and then shots of objects or settings – the yellow car, the pool – that are to play an important part in the narrative. As the credits unroll we hear an echo of one of Gatsby's parties across the shots of deserted rooms, as if the house is haunted. The camera roams across the golden items on Gatsby's dressing table and is drawn hypnotically to the photos of Daisy Buchanan which begin to dominate the credit sequence. Only one slightly incongruous image disturbs the mood: a fly on an unfinished sandwich, suggestive of time's passing perhaps but also of incipient decay under the luxurious surface. (It is only at the end of the film that we realise that we are seeing the house shortly after Nick and Gatsby's father have left it to attend Gatsby's funeral.) The house is Gatsby's Xanadu, a hollow monument that is not, however, for himself but for the unattainable defining love of his life. Daisy is, as it were, Gatsby's Rosebud: like Kane, he dies with her name on his lips. Fitzgerald's novel was published in 1926 and the character of Gatsby can be seen, in some ways, as a forerunner of Charles Foster Kane. Critics have even, in Robert Redford's tone as he introduces himself to the film's Nick Carroway (an immaculate performance by Sam Waterston), detected a vocal echo of Orson Welles. Like Kane, Gatsby is wealthy, frustrated, of limitless potential and limited perception. He might even be an anticipation of Rick in *Casablanca*, with his mysterious, possibly murderous past ('They say you killed a man') and that inextinguishable romanticism; they even share a similarly soggy letter that betokens the dissolution of their love affairs. What Gatsby particularly stands for is an aspect of the American Dream – its promise and betrayal. He has the idealism and the flair to achieve anything he wishes in material terms; but his dream is a chimera; the society which he wants to enter and conquer is shallow and alien to him; and he will draw unto himself finally only rejection and violence.

Into this world will stumble the film's narrator and observer, Nick Carroway, who will be the go-between in the reunion of Gatsby and Daisy. His potential clumsiness in this role is indicated in his first scene: he cannot navigate a rowing boat from one end of the bay to the other without getting soaked. He is visiting his wealthy cousin Daisy (Mia Farrow) and her husband, an old college chum Tom Buchanan (Bruce Dern), at their luxurious home. The couple seem to have everything and the setting is a study in whiteness (Tom is a fervent believer in white supremacy). Unobtrusively but adroitly, however, Clayton locates spots of tension and even horror in this set-up. Despite Daisy's claim that 'It's romantic, isn't it?' she seems on edge, clearly discomfited by a phone call for her husband that another guest, Jordan Baker (Lois Chiles), tells Nick is from Tom's mistress. Tom is also testy when Daisy describes him as 'hulking' – an image of his gracelessness about which he is obviously sensitive. When his mistress, Myrtle Wilson (Karen Black), later similarly calls him 'clumsy', it sets in train a rising anger and brutality in Tom that culminates in a sickening moment when he breaks Myrtle's nose with one slap across the face for repeatedly mentioning Daisy's name. That sudden violence in the film precisely captures the shock of the novel's single sentence 'Making a short deft movement, Tom Buchanan broke her nose with his open hand'.¹² It shows Tom's capacity for offhand, almost careless destructiveness, which will be Nick's final judgement of both him and Daisy. ('Oh Daisy ...' Nick will say, in a tone of mixed exasperation, reproach yet affection in their final scene together after the tragedy, when she breezes into the hotel and talks to Nick precisely in the manner of their first scene together, as if nothing has happened in between.) It also tellingly links the name 'Daisy' – which Myrtle keeps whispering as blood streams from her nose – with destruction. It will not be the only occasion in the film when the single word 'Daisy' will be followed by the spilling of someone's blood.

The Buchanans' home is being watched by a mysterious figure, Jay Gatsby, staring at the green light that glows at the end of their dock. We hear a lot of Gatsby before we see him and, as his neighbour, Nick is well aware of the Gatsby parties that attract people from miles around. After the first party, Clayton dissolves to the glasses on the advertisement of Dr T. J. Eckleburg – another God-like watcher over the action – which signals a movement into a different social sphere, Fitzgerald's famous valley of ashes (both an inspiration from Eliot's *The Waste Land* and a prophecy of the Depression). Here we are introduced to the Wilsons, as Tom stops at their garage to fill up with petrol and to introduce Carroway to his girl. The photographic texture of the film is notably gloomier here – a contrast in social scale but also in psychological tone to the earlier scenes – and it is here that Tom has arranged his tryst in town with Myrtle Wilson that has culminated in her broken nose. At that party, in a moment before Tom's violent outburst, Nick has been privy to Myrtle's description of how she and Tom first met. As she whispers the tale, the sound subjectively dips to convey Nick's concentration on her words; and it becomes a privileged moment for Myrtle as she describes how the affair is a desperate relief from her marriage to George Wilson (Scott Wilson), who is poor and spiritually broken. 'All I kept thinking', she whispers to her companion, is 'You can't live forever.' This is a telling contrast to Gatsby, who is committed to the idea of one love for eternity. Karen Black plays Myrtle as a character on heat (strikingly in contrast to the cool fronts of Gatsby and Jordan) and sensuality oozes out of her, as does a hunger to escape from her present surroundings. When Wilson locks her up in a room in the garage, she smashes the window with her bare hands and then starts licking her own blood – a compelling reiteration of her frustration and desperation.

It is at the second of Gatsby's big parties that Nick meets his neighbour for the first time. Clayton has been criticised for the length and ornateness of these party scenes, as if he were compensating for the dance marathon movie he did not direct (*They Shoot Horses Don't They?*). David Shipman talked of the film as a 'funereal spectacular'.[13] Yet there is a sense in which these scenes are appropriately enervating rather than exhilarating: empty people, first seen by Nick as shadows silhouetted against a tent, insubstantial, slightly grotesque, participating in pleasures that seem more strenuous than spontaneous. The film has a graceful Viscontian languor that becomes at times less like an evocation of Fitzgerald than a deconstruction of it: every detail of an ostentatious, narcissistic society scrutinised as if to reveal (to paraphrase Dorothy Parker on Ernest Hemingway) that way down deep it is very superficial. In a perceptive review in the *New Yorker* (11 April 1974) Penelope Gilliat saw behind the film's seeming slowness and languid atmosphere. 'This sometimes drowsy film', she noted, 'pierces, with Fitzgerald's moral breeding, to the weakness in the society's fabric: lack of intelligence and resolve going unperceived, like lack of heart.' She also talks of the notes of 'sharp humour' in the film, which at this stage are particularly registered in the contrast between Carroway's modest style of living and his neighbour's ostentation. Gatsby has a 'lawn' whereas Nick just has 'grass'; the lavish banqueting arrangements for Gatsby's first party in the film are cross-cut with Nick's personally prepared steak in a small frying pan.

Clayton was also criticised for changing – melodramatising – the first meeting between Nick and Gatsby. Clearly, however, it could not be handled as in the novel: Nick getting into a conversation with someone whom he assumes to be a party guest but who gradually introduces himself as Gatsby. (Nick might not know him but an audience would instantly recognise Robert Redford.) Having Nick escorted from the party into the house by an usher who is shown to be carrying a gun might seem to be taking the film into *Godfather* territory, but it usefully lends visual and rhythmic variety to the scene and is not an inappropriate disclosure, given Gatsby's hinted connections with bootlegging. The first scene between them – all pauses, gestures and hesitations – is well played, particularly by Redford, who seems instantly to inhabit Gatsby's mystery, reserve and romanticism. It remains his finest character performance on film.

Nick will act as facilitator for the reunion between Gatsby and Daisy, the love of his life. 'I took the liberty of silverware,' says Gatsby, preparatory to the meeting between him and Daisy in Nick's house, the glittering tea service seeming quite incongruous in the setting but being one of the film's frequent and successful attempts to inject into the oppressive romanticism a delicate deflating comedy. Sam Waterston as Nick is important here, always alert and expressive in reaction shot. The comedy is a way of enlarging the film's mood and avoiding Fitzgerald's tendency, in his other work, to sentimentality and self-pity (as James Thurber said of him, 'A sense of humour might have saved him'). And it is connected to a reminder that Clayton had given himself in his notes: 'Don't forget that Gatsby has to be at times an almost comically pathetic figure.'

Unlike in the novel, Daisy's first sight of Gatsby is in a mirror reflection as he appears behind her. Mirrors are omnipresent in the film, appropriate for a society that is vain and narcissistic but also appropriate for a film about the fragility of romantic illusions. (In the later hotel scene when Gatsby tells Tom Buchanan of his love for Daisy, her instinctive movement will be towards the hotel mirror – as if by looking at herself she can somehow avoid facing things head-on and hang onto a romantic illusion that is in imminent danger of disintegration). When Nick begins to introduce them, Gatsby says, 'We've met before'. Redford imbues this line with much sensitivity: the falling cadence in 'before' has great weight, since this one word carries all of Gatsby's hope and ambition and his conviction that you *can* repeat the past. The romantic atmosphere is sustained as Gatsby conducts Daisy round his house – dissolves, champagne, pink light – gathering to the famous moment when he shows Daisy his collection of silk shirts. Tossing them around the bedroom ('everything about them in moving, floating colours', wrote Clayton in his notes for the scene), Gatsby turns to see that Daisy is moved to tears by their beauty. At this point we get three of the most pointed shots in the film: Gatsby and Daisy reflected in a multitude of mirrors as she weeps at the gorgeous profusion of shirts; the pianist Klipspringer (Edward Herrmann) concluding his singing of 'Ain't We Got Fun?' in one of Gatsby's cavernous rooms; then the huge billboard spectacles of Dr Eckleburg – yellow spectacles that watch broodingly over a golden summer that will be shattered by a fatal road accident involving a yellow car. These three shots represent roughly a move from hollow romanticism to off-key humour (but brought to an abrupt end, as if the fun is over) to sinister foreboding. For the sensitive observer, Clayton's film encompasses a wide variety of moods. This is continued in the next sequence, involving Nick and Jordan: a casual romantic couple in counterpoint to the more intense Gatsby/Daisy, Tom/Myrtle complications around them. (Perhaps slightly too casual: I have always found Lois Chiles's performance vocally dull and strangely inexpressive and lethargic – a weakness in an otherwise terrific cast.) Jordan's driving has nearly caused a crash – prefiguring the tragic crash of the second half of the narrative. Jordan, however, says it takes two to make an accident. This, in turn, will resonate in the film as an omen of the future tragedy and is a reminder that, like Joseph Losey's film *Accident* (1967), *The Great Gatsby* is about tragic human collisions.

The most controversial aspect of the adaptation are the love scenes between Gatsby and Daisy. The critic Janet Maslin was typical of many in berating the film for including these: 'the novel very deliberately avoids invading the couple's privacy once they have been reunited'.[14] But as we have seen, Fitzgerald himself did not argue that this omission was part of his narrative deliberation: on the contrary, he conceded it was the novel's greatest flaw. Weren't Clayton and Coppola, then, quite entitled, indeed, obliged, to try and rectify it? Clayton was striving through his imagery for this 'very essence of romance'. The touching of Gatsby's gold ornament; the candlelight; dancing in the dark; 'Do you remember ...?' whispered over the soundtrack; the ring with the green emerald that becomes a material(ist) correlative to the green light at the end of the dock that stokes Gatsby's obsession – all these are blended into a romantic concoction so highblown that it seems bound to burst. What Clayton is striving for looks similar to what David Lean tried to do in *Ryan's Daughter* (1970) and for which he was similarly derided: to contrive a romantic sequence that could be recognised simultaneously as an *impossible* romantic dream. In his superb review of *Gatsby*, Gordon Gow was one of the few critics to pick up the fact that the 'images of beauty' in the film are also 'often ironic'.[15] Gow sees the irony primarily signalled by the juxtaposition of these romantic images with something harsher that undercuts them; but it is also signalled through dramatic irony and is indeed implicit in the image itself. Maslin reports how her preview audience sniggered through much of the film, the biggest snigger reserved for 'the last part of the picture, most notably for the scene in which Farrow and Redford kiss and their images are studiously reflected in a pool stocked with expensive Japanese goldfish'.[16] An alert audience might have been picking up on those details that could be said to be modifying, even ironising, the romanticism at this point – the hollowness of the house, the echoey music, the shimmeringly transparent surfaces.

If Clayton is drawn to the pool, it is because it is there that Gatsby will meet his death. Indeed the impression is that he might even be thinking of this very moment at the point of his death for, as then, the curtains of the cabana move in the breeze. 'Daisy?' Gatsby will say, his last word, and one that will usher in his killer. The last we see of the pool, there is a gun, not goldfish, lying at the bottom.

At another stage in her analysis, Maslin talks of *The Great Gatsby*'s 'maverick stupidity: the film is neither faithful enough to qualify as even a run-of-the-mill screen adaptation nor is it guided by even the faintest glimmer of adaptive imagination'.[17] No remark more perfectly encapsulates the film-makers' dilemma when adapting a classic: they are invariably accused either of timidity or of betrayal, either of being overly reverential to the original or of being unfaithful to the source. I recall with what dignity, in a tele-vised interview, Clayton responded to criticism such as this, only observing that he had had no idea that there were so many experts on Scott Fitzgerald in the world. In contrast to Maslin's accusation of 'maverick stupidity', I would offer Penelope Gilliat's perception of Clayton as a very serious film-maker with 'a shapely compre-hension of an author's intelligence',[18] which certainly corresponds closely to my opinion. Whether or not one is persuaded by Clayton's method, this is incontrovertibly an adaptation that has been carefully thought through and in which every detail has its justification.

As an example of fruitful fidelity, I would cite the argument scene in the Plaza Hotel. It is faithful to the text of the novel and is finely acted and filmed, catching all of the scene's sweaty em-barrassment, its inadvertent comedy (the agitated movement of all of them when Gatsby discloses his love for Daisy), its tension and anger, conveyed particularly in the four quick cuts as Tom and Gatsby square up to each other and where, just in the slight smile across Gatsby's face, one has the sense that he might once have killed a man. For a cinematically skilled moment impossible to match in a novel, I would recall the visually precise dissolve from Eckleburg's yellow spectacles to the broken bloodstained head-lamps of Gatsby's yellow car – a dissolve that sucks us inexorably towards the tragic conclusion of the drama. As an example of a sensitive Clayton addition to Fitzgerald, there is that moment near the end of the film where Gatsby's father and Nick are driving past the Valley of Ashes. The old man is reading from his son's book where he has written down his childhood resolutions, but Nick is distracted by the sight of Myrtle's sister emerging sadly from the garage in the act of disposing of some of the Wilsons' rubbish. According to James Monaco in *American Film Now*,[19] Francis Ford Coppola was critical of Clayton's handling of this scene because it took away the audience's attention from the details of Gatsby's little book which, Coppola said, crucially revealed not only Gatsby's common roots but his driving ambition. But it is typical of Clayton that, unlike Fitzgerald, he did not want us to forget the Wilsons at this juncture nor to lose sight of the fact that the story is of other people's tragedies as well as Gatsby's.

Was Clayton miscast? Coppola undoubtedly saw *Gatsby* as a very American tale, one indeed with which he himself could identify, Gatsby possibly being a symbol of his own dreams of money and success. Coppola's public gripes about Clayton's direction – which were to lead to a heated argument on an aeroplane in which Clayton told Coppola in no uncertain terms what he thought about his unprofessionalism – seem essentially to amount to this: *Gatsby* is a quintessentially American story, so what is an Englishman muscling in for? But *Gatsby* has a lot of European overtones as well – only finally is it 'a story of the West after all'. It has something of the high style and intricate romance of Ford Madox Ford's *The Good Soldier*. Some of its imagery (Wilson's garage that is surrounded by a wasteland of ashes) and its themes (the romantic idealism that will be crushed by the brutality of the modern century, symbolised here, as in *The Magnificent Ambersons*, by the automobile) were similar to those in *The Waste Land*, whose author, T. S. Eliot, admired the novel greatly. There was no American filmmaker who could have come close to Fitzgerald's romanticism or to suggesting a similar vision to that of Fitzgerald, with the arguable exception of George Stevens. Stevens's dreamy and erotic view of materialism in *A Place in the Sun* (1951) has a very Fitzgerald-like feel, but is actually an adaptation of Dreiser's *An American Tragedy*. The film-maker at that time who was most often compared with Fitzgerald was, strangely, Michelangelo Antonioni. Both were acute analysts of the spiritual malaise of the rich; both were creators of emotionally alienated worlds of brittle surfaces that echo with the sound of loveless money; both arguably shared the same artistic flaw of self-pity and narcissism. Antonioni, ironically, has often been used as a stick with which to beat Clayton, particularly over *The Pumpkin Eater*. But Clayton would have argued that *Gatsby* belongs not just to America but to everywhere; that its observations on class, society and obsession are not confined to a specific time and place but are timeless and universal; and that his particular concerns, characteristics and strengths as a director matched Fitzgerald's very well. If the critics did not unanimously agree, he had the endorsement of Fitzgerald's daughter for the validity of his vision, and the support of Tennessee Williams for the quality of his artistry. These are considerable testimonials.

Something Wicked This Way Comes

'Dad, don't talk death – someone'll hear you.' (Will Halloway)

'I believe you.'
'You do? But we're not grown ups.'
'That's why I believe you.' (Charles Halloway to Jim Nightshade)

The nine years between *The Great Gatsby* and *Something Wicked This Way Comes* were the most difficult of Clayton's career. They saw the collapse of a number of cherished projects which, in some cases, he had brought very close to fruition (see Chapter 10). In 1978 he suffered a serious stroke which deprived him of speech. He kept this a secret known only to a few close friends while his partner Haya and a speech therapist nursed him patiently back to sufficiently good health to work again. A project that surfaced and resurfaced over this period was *Something Wicked This Way Comes*, which was to become arguably Clayton's most flawed and traumatic film. Even in its altered form, it remains the work of a great cineaste.

The full tale of bringing this project to the screen has often been told.[20] Briefly, the author Ray Bradbury wrote a short story entitled 'Black Ferris' which had been published in the magazine *Weird Tales* in 1948. After seeing and loving Gene Kelly's *Invitation to a Dance* in 1956, Bradbury had turned the story into a screen treatment in the hope that Kelly would direct it, but although Kelly was very enthusiastic about the material he could never raise the finance. Bradbury decided to write up the material as a novel and *Something Wicked This Way Comes* was published in 1962.

In the early 1970s the production team of Robert Chartoff and Irwin Winkler had optioned the property, and it was at this stage that Bradbury had suggested Sam Peckinpah as a possible director, with Jason Robards (who was later to play the father, Charles Halloway, in Clayton's version) as Mr Dark. When this lapsed, the director Mark Rydell was brought into the discussion but the project still did not progress. The rights were then acquired by Kirk Douglas, who wanted his son Peter to produce the film and Clayton to direct it. This idea received the enthusiastic support of Bradbury, who was a vocal admirer of Clayton and had indeed sent him an encouraging letter after seeing and admiring *Gatsby*. 'People are going to like it', he wrote. 'It's going to make money. Don't kill yourself yet.' In fact, the two had met twenty years earlier when Bradbury had been writing the screenplay for John Huston's film *Moby Dick* (1956), which Huston had wanted Clayton to produce. It had not been the friendliest of collaborations, to say the least, and Bradbury remembered that, on one occasion, when he and Huston almost came to blows in a restaurant, it was Clayton who intervened and hustled Bradbury into a cab.[21]

Clayton worked for months on the screenplay with Bradbury, but the production stalled when it appeared that a condition of its being made was that Kirk Douglas should play the role of the father. This was unacceptable to Clayton – not because of any animosity towards Douglas, whom he liked and admired enormously, but because he thought Douglas's screen persona was just too dynamic and extrovert for the role. 'I always saw Halloway as a mild, reflective man who understood that in terms of

"success", his life had been a failure', wrote Clayton in a letter to
Peter Douglas (11 April 1977).

> If Halloway does not fully reflect this on the screen, we lose so
> much of the point of the story. For the beauty of Halloway is that
> this mild, gentle character develops under the strain of terror and
> through his love for his son, into a man of bravery and action. This
> is mainly why the ending of the film is so uplifting, because it's a
> big triumph for a small man.

Kirk Douglas would not bring that kind of resonance to the role.
As Clayton drily remarked: 'In the Library scene where Mr Dark
crushes Halloway's hand, if I were in the audience I would know
that it was Mr Dark's hand that was in danger and not Kirk's.'

In the event, Kirk Douglas would not have been available to
play the role, so the project was temporarily on again, to be produced by Paramount. But it then became caught up in a power
struggle between the studio president, David Picker, who had
backed the project, and the new chairman of the board, Barry
Diller, who – as chairmen often do in this sort of situation –
exerted his authority by cancelling a project that had been
supported by the former regime. Enraged at having the project
rejected before Diller had even had time to read the screenplay,
Clayton stormed into Diller's office and, in one of his legendary
tempers, threw several chairs through Diller's plate glass windows
– which were not open at the time.

Between then and 1981 there was talk of Steven Spielberg
directing it as his follow-up film to *Close Encounters of the Third
Kind*, but this also never materialised. It was at the beginning of
the 1980s, with a change of management personnel at the Disney
organisation, that interest in the subject was revived. When Kirk
Douglas approached Clayton again as a possible director, he was
involved in pre-production preparation for a film, *Revelations*, but
when that stalled, he became available and started work again on
the screenplay, from scratch, with Bradbury. The major change
they decided on at that stage was to set the story in an earlier
period, the 1930s. Clayton felt it would be more credible in that
period for two young boys to be so excited at the prospect of a

carnival that they would get up in the middle of the night to watch it arrive: setting it in the era of television would make that crucial excitement less plausible.

Although the project might have seemed a rather grim one for Disney – the novel is about the effect on a small town in Illinois of the visit of a sinister carnival – the tale has many characteristics of the dark fairy tales at which the Disney organisation had excelled in its heyday. There is a wicked witch, as well as magic mirrors, that recall *Snow White*, and a cruel carnival as in *Dumbo*. The movie's theme of an innocent boy with an ineffectual father thrown into a world of malevolence and monsters has similarities to the story of *Pinocchio*. The new regime at Disney probably thought it worth reviving that Disney tradition of the frisson of fright that accompanies the flight of fantasy. Moreover, Ray Bradbury was a huge Disney fan who had been a member of the Mickey Mouse Club when he was 12; the novel had always seemed closer in style to Disney than to, say, Henry James.

How Clayton would fit into this regime was another matter. His appointment as director raised a few eyebrows. In his none-too-flattering book on Disney, *The Disney Version*, Richard Schickel described Clayton as the 'kind of reliable second-rater that was comforting to a cautious studio management'.[22] This is insulting both to the management and to the director: it would be truer to say that the choice was both imaginative and risky. It was imaginative in that Clayton had made one of the eeriest and most elegant of all horror films, *The Innocents*, based on a story by another American master; he was a superb director of children and therefore ideal for a story seen mostly through the eyes of two boys; and his work revealed a recurrent fascination with the tension between innocence and experience, reality and dream that is at the heart of *Something Wicked*. It was a risky choice in that, contrary to Schickel's description, Clayton was an idiosyncratic maverick rather than a 'reliable second-rater'; his films often eluded the attention of mass audiences and their high quality often only became apparent to critics over the fullness of time.

Clayton was later to describe his experience of working with the Disney Corporation (*The Times*, 22 September 1983) as 'torture, absolute torture. I said to them when I started, I've never done a special effects film before so please give me the very best people you've got. That turned out to be three old men and some very antique machinery. I think it turned out well enough in the end, but it took a long time getting there'. Clayton had got some of his own way in terms of creative personnel, including the controversial casting of the then relatively unknown Jonathan Pryce as Mr Dark (Clayton had seen him on stage in *Hamlet* and in Trevor Griffiths's *Comedians* and thought he would bring a seductive as well as sinister quality to the role) and the brilliant English production designer, Richard MacDonald, who in particular did a wonderfully stylised American small town of the late 1920s, straight out of Disneyland's Main Street and the folksy imagination of Thornton Wilder. He had two excellent child actors for the boys, Vidal Peterson as an appropriately sensitive Will and Shawn Carson (the nephew of Karen Black) as the more adventurous darker-hearted Jim Nightshade. He also at that stage had Georges Delerue, as always his first choice as composer.

Principal photography was completed by the end of 1981, though there continued to be some disquiet over the special effects. The turning point came with an unsuccessful preview of the film in Los Angeles in July 1982, where, to quote Disney's head of production, Tom Wilhite, 'the preview cards were just average, or below. There was no magic to the picture. Things that worked fine on paper just didn't work on film'.[23] It was generally felt to be too claustrophobic and downbeat. In the process of studio revision, Clayton felt it 'lost a lot of its subtlety. It was much on the lines of *The Innocents* originally, playing on the audience's imagination, whereas this version relies on special effects. I don't mind it as it is now, but obviously I'd much rather have it as it was'.[24] Basically Clayton felt that he had been fobbed off with Disney's second-division special-effects team during principal photography while the major talent was engaged on *Tron* (1982). It was only at a later stage that Disney's chief special-effects man, Lee Dyer, could get fully involved on *Something Wicked* and give it more 'spectacle' and 'magic'. 'If I'd had Lee from the very beginning', Clayton was to say later, 'a lot more of the subtleties would be there now – things that we couldn't put in afterwards. At least it's got characters in it and a lot of love – unlike a lot of special effects films I could mention, where the people making them didn't seem to think it was necessary to have a story'.[25]

One casualty was Georges Delerue's score, which Disney executives thought was too sombre and not strong enough for the picture. Clayton took that hard, for he was an unreserved champion of Delerue's music and thought the score exquisite.[26] When Jerry Goldsmith turned out to be unavailable because he was working on the score for *The Twilight Zone* (1983), the relatively inexperienced James Horner was assigned to write the music and produced a score which Clayton felt was loud and over-dramatic in comparison with Delerue, but which, in fairness, did succeed in creating atmosphere and driving the narrative forward in the new film and which was often singled out for critical praise. One could summarise the difference by saying that, whereas Delerue had written a score in keeping with the film Clayton originally wanted to make, Horner wrote a score that fitted the film in its final form.

Yet there are still some tremendous moments in the film, and some unforgettable images. A fabulous opening shot of a train steaming forward like a breathing monster out of a black sky announces the approach of the carnival. It is one of several details in the film that strongly reminds one of Hitchcock's *Shadow of a Doubt* (1943), where another idealised American small town will be infiltrated by a demon arriving by train and the truth about whose terror will be discovered in the library. As in the Hitchcock film, it will be a craving among the townspeople for excitement, a dissatisfaction with their lot (the barber lusts after beautiful women, the schoolteacher longs to bring back her youth, the tobacconist is obsessed with money), that bring these demons into their midst. Also as in the Hitchcock film, a crucial object in the narrative is a ring, which here entices susceptible townspeople to enter Dark's world, momentarily fulfil their deepest wishes and then confront their worst nightmares. Disappointment is part and parcel of life's merry-go-round but here the merry-go-round goes wrong, either reversing time or accelerating it dangerously into the future.

The two young boys, Will Halloway and Jim Nightshade, who

have seen the carnival arrive, are like two halves of the same personality: Jim is the darker, more adventurous, more devilish side of Will's cautious, quieter, blander character. Together they have glimpsed more of the sinister side of this carnival than they should. As punishment, they are pursued by a green dust,[27] an emanation of the Dust Witch (Pam Grier), and together they are compelled to dream the same dream: an invasion of their bedroom by tarantulas. This was one of the special-effects sequences added later, following the sight of a tarantula that had scared the boys earlier in the carnival tent, and perhaps also suggested by the description in the novel of Mr Dark's right hand as a 'princely tarantula'.[28] 'We've not left anything to the imagination,' commented Lee Dyer on this sequence, and Clayton was to feel it went over the top: he had in mind one tarantula, not scores of them. Nevertheless it is still the creepiest scene in a Disney movie for forty years.

The finest scene in the film, though, which could alone justify the whole enterprise, is the scene in the library in which old Mr Halloway and Mr Dark confront each other. Quizzing Halloway earlier on the whereabouts of the two boys, Mr Dark has clenched his hand in tension: the blood that leaks forth has dripped on the face of Will who, with Jim, is hiding in terror under a grating below. We are under no illusion, then, about the powers of darkness that Halloway will be required to overcome and defeat. In the novel at this juncture the narrative comes to a halt for three long chapters whilst Halloway instructs the two boys on the forces of evil – the philosophising all but takes the urgency out of the situation. The film has prepared this confrontation differently. The relationship between Will and his father is less sentimental, more troubled, in the film than in the novel. Halloway is haunted by an incident in the past when Will fell into a lake and he was unable to come to his son's rescue because he could not swim. Will was actually rescued by Jim Nightshade's father, in some ways the shadow side of Halloway's personality: irresponsible, adventurous but active and alive in a way old Halloway is not. Halloway's guilt and melancholy cast shadows over his relationship with his son: he has a stench of advancing death about him, feeling unable even to climb the wall ladder to the boy's bedroom, and having a heart, as the screenplay says, 'too old, too tired, too full of yearning and regrets'. As a librarian 'dreaming other men's dreams', as Dark has put it, Halloway has never been put to the test. It is only in the meeting with Dark by the cigar store that he realises the danger the boys are in and that this time he cannot stand aside. But is he strong and brave enough? There is a palpable adult, as well as childish, fear in that library as they hear the front doors close and realise Mr Dark has entered their domain.

In an open letter in support of the film – not a gesture every novelist makes – Ray Bradbury described the library scene between Jason Robards and Jonathan Pryce as 'pure tour de force, Academy Award material'.[29] The two actors are at their finest here, Robards showing a stiffening of obstinacy and irony in his character that nevertheless does not mask the fear and vulnerability, whilst Pryce has a truly demonic slyness and cruelty. As with his other victims, Dark homes in on Halloway's weak point – his age – and tempts him with the prospect of a return to youth. Each page of a book represents a year and as Halloway spurns each offer as it passes, Dark tears out a page, the rip being accompanied by a bright orange flash. This is one of the more subdued of the added special effects, and it works very well – as a brief light quickly extinguished, like youth itself, or as a flame that burns, like regret, leaving only the taste of ashes. An earlier special effect that showed Dark's crushing of Halloway's hand and bone coming through the skin had the preview audience gasping and was toned down: it was felt (probably wisely) to be too gruesome for its context, and the crushing is now only glimpsed – is heard more than seen. With Halloway now immobilised with pain, Mr Dark goes searching for the boys hiding amongst the library shelves. A shot of his face flecked by shadow, with his footsteps echoing on the wrought-iron staircase, seems the very personification of fearful evil. His quiet appeal is particularly directed at Jim Nightshade, as if knowing of Jim's anguish at his father's desertion ('I'm the father you've been waiting for ... my son') and having already sensed Jim's precocious hunger for experience. He promises Jim sexual knowledge, 'to know what grown ups do behind locked doors when children are asleep' – a line that sounds more like John Mortimer than Ray Bradbury, recalling Mortimer's line in *The Innocents* about 'rooms used as if they were dark woods'. (Although uncredited, Mortimer, Clayton claimed, made a considerable contribution to the tone of *Something Wicked*, subduing the sentiment and whimsy and giving it a harsher edge.) There is a heart-stopping moment when the boys are discovered. Peering out anxiously from between the shelves they are unaware – unlike us – that behind them two disembodied, black-gloved hands are rising like the tentacles of an octopus to seize them from their hiding place. 'Lose their tongues,' he instructs the Dust Witch so that the boys are unable to shout for help (an uncomfortable moment, one might think, for a director who until recently had himself lost the power of speech) and the boys are hurried to the carnival.

The final scene gave the makers of the film enormous trouble. At this stage Clayton had more or less to step aside and let the special-effects team take over, and it shows. I agree with David Castell, who remarked when reviewing the film for the *Sunday Telegraph* (2 October 1983) that 'it is only in this final assault of special effects that a film of intelligence and subtlety becomes over-literal'. Yet it is in no way inferior to the novel and there is a coherent concept behind the imagery used. Will's father has followed the boys to the Mirror Maze, and Mr Dark again confronts Halloway with a magnified image of his failure as a father and as a man: the mirror is 'your glass of darkness – its name, regret ... its sum, despair'. The Mirror Maze expands on an image that has occurred in the early part of the novel when Wills suddenly thinks that his dad 'looks ... like me in a smashed mirror!'[30] The idea is taken further by Lee Dyer, who links it to the earlier drowning incident between father and son. 'The whole point of it', said Dyer, 'is that Will almost drowned years ago and was saved by Mr. Nightshade because Halloway can't swim. That's never resolved. It's resolved in a talk between father and son, but it's never really resolved in Halloway's mind. We wanted him to relive this in the mirror maze and *resolve* it, once and for all'.[31] Separated by this glass from his son, Halloway is roused when he hears Will assert his love for his father over Dark's claim that he hates him and summons up the strength to break through the mirror and pull his son to safety. The boy's sobbing cry – 'Oh Dad, I love you!' – that breaks Dark's spell seems a very Disneyesque moment, but it is worth recollecting that it is handled in exactly the same way in the novel.

In the meantime, Mr Dark is preparing to put Jim on his fiendish carousel and launch him into the future. Halloway rescues the boy, at which point the storm which has threatened and which Dark fears now breaks and Dark finds himself trapped on his own carousel. In the visual design of the film, whereas green lighting has been associated with evil spirits (as in the greenish ectoplasm of the Dust Witch that has followed the boys to their homes and unleashed the tarantula nightmare), the bluish white of the lightning has been associated with good. This is why Dark has been torturing the lightning-rod salesman (Royal Dano) in an attempt to force him to reveal the time of the storm: he knows that lightning can harm him and the Dust Witch. Eventually it is indeed a bolt of lightning that transfixes Dark on his carousel and leads to his death. At this point the whole evil construct of the carnival is sucked up into the air and swallowed by the storm clouds. Evil has been vanquished by love.

'I think the message of the film is pretty much the same as in every Disney film,' said Jason Robards during the shooting of the movie. 'We're not making *La Dolce Vita* here'. True, up to a point. Certainly evil is defeated; the father redeems himself by coming to his son's rescue; the ending is triumphant in content, even if it might seem a little hollow in tone and execution. Why, then, did the film fail so badly at the box office?

'Probably the major problem concerning the disappointing box office reception for *Something Wicked*', wrote Clayton in a letter to Walt Disney Pictures Corporation (18 July 1983), 'was due to the advertising describing it as a horror film ... I think *Something Wicked* should be advertised as a very classy fantasy picture.' How and where to target the film seems to have been a major problem, and it might simply be that Clayton and Disney were not a compatible combination. For all the stress on the children's point of view, it is not really an escapist children's film: it is an adult fantasy that is both Grimm-like and grim. Despite the happy ending (though what happens to those townspeople who have succumbed to Dark's temptation?), the overall atmosphere remains oppressive. The film deals obsessively with both outer and inner demons, and with fears of ageing and death. It keeps returning to the theme of fatherhood – the weak father (Halloway), the absent father (Nightshade), the surrogate father (Dark) who offers corruption under the guise of compassion – and how fathers fail their sons. In this respect, it reminds me very much of Steven Spielberg's *Hook* (1991), another film with a Disneyesque premise and sentimental happy ending but which is so full of paternal anxiety – where Peter Pan has to fight for the soul of his son against the seductive temptations of Hook – that it is less feelgood than feelglum. The similarity is so great that I would be surprised if *Something Wicked* had not exercised a considerable influence on Spielberg. In any case, both films failed to find an audience because in both cases a childlike fantasy became, in execution, more like an adult panic attack. *Something Wicked* uncovers behind the American Dream and the American love affair with youth a whole host of nightmarish ogres of the imagination. If the film's Main Street reminded some critics of Disneyland, then the carnival itself is more subversive than ever, turning Disneyland dark side out.

Given the film's mature and disillusioned exploration of what Ray Bradbury's screenplay eloquently calls 'the fearful needs of the human heart', it is perhaps not surprising that *Something Wicked* intimidated audiences more than entranced them. For all the uplifting ending and the comforting narration of Arthur Hill that frames the story, adults might still find Jonathan Pryce's Mr Dark and Pam Grier's Dust Witch a little too disturbingly seductive to be easily dismissed, and they might find Jason Robards's anguished portrayal of a lifetime of regret striking too painful a chord. On the other hand, children might be scared out of their wits by the tarantula scene and the hunt in the library. It is an uneasy combination for a mass-audience film.

Nevertheless, if it is doubtful whether the millions who saw

Disney's *The Love Bug*, say, can remember much about it, the comparative few who saw *Something Wicked* will not have forgotten the experience. Like another film set in the Depression that is a chilling evocation of childhood terror and brings an odd English perspective to an American subject – Charles Laughton's *The Night of the Hunter* (1955) – it changes the quality of your nightmares. And in their unpublished account of the making of *Something Wicked*, the authors Randy and Jean Marc Lofficier drew an interesting comparison with the contemporaneous Ridley Scott film, *Blade Runner* (1982). Both films were supported by the authors of the original novels (Ray Bradbury, Philip K. Dick); both had voice-over added and different endings provided; both were controversial, having good reviews but indifferent commercial returns; and both were taken out of the hands of their directors. *Blade Runner* has since achieved cult status and has been reissued in a director's cut version. A director's cut of *Something Wicked* would be very welcome – and preferably with Georges Delerue's original score.

Notes

1 I discovered this quotation amongst a collection of Jack Clayton's papers. It had been typed up separately, as if it had some particular significance for him. Certainly the tension between dream and reality occurs a lot in his films, with characters who are dreamers pursuing their dream with great intensity or being brusquely awakened into reality.

2 Penelope Houston, *Sight and Sound*, Spring 1974, p. 78.

3 See *Films and Filming*, April 1960, p. 27.

4 David Shipman, *The Story of Cinema, Volume Two* (London, Hodder & Stoughton, 1984), p. 121.

5 See Kevin Brownlow, *David Lean* (London, Faber & Faber, 1997), pp. 646–51.

6 *The Great Gatsby* (London, Penguin, 1964), p. 120. All subsequent quotations are from this edition, but the novel was first published in 1926.

7 Houston, *Sight and Sound*, p. 79.

8 Letter to Edmund Wilson, Spring 1925. Quoted in *The Letters of F. Scott Fitzgerald*, ed. Andrew Turnbull (London, Penguin, 1968), p. 361.

9 A partial account of the reasons for the rejection of Capote's screenplay is given in George Plimpton's *Truman Capote* (London, Picador, 1998), pp. 365–6. It does seem generally agreed, however, that Capote was too ill to deliver an acceptable screenplay in the time allowed by Paramount. His

first draft (submitted November 1971) had some flashes of Capote wit and bitchiness, particularly in the one-liners for the party scenes. 'See that skinny looking monkey woman?', says Tom. 'If Darwin had got a look at her, he wouldn't have had to invent his theory.' (Bruce Dern, who is wonderful in the film at conveying Tom's unconscious humour, might have relished that line – but is it in character?) Another party guest remarks of an acquaintance that 'she's had her face lifted so many times she has to sleep with her eyes open'. Overall, though, the script seems verbose, ungainly in structure, with too much voice-over and exposition. There are some choice phrases (Wilson has 'the voice of a born loser'; Tom is described, before striking Myrtle, as 'not really drunk yet, but he's not too far from the curve of the road'), but overall there is a lack of momentum, and the characters do not leap from the page: indeed, Daisy barely comes through at all. One interesting detail is that, in Capote's screenplay, Myrtle's death was going to be shown. This occasioned the following response from Clayton, who favoured not showing the accident (letter to Capote, 18 January 1972): 'I know it would be a great pity to lose our almost only action sequence but there are advantages too. We would not know about the accident until Tom arrives on the scene (consequently might think Daisy and Gatsby are dead). It also takes away the coincidence – of our not seeing it – of Myrtle being killed by the yellow car. If we don't see it, the fact that Daisy was driving might come as more of a surprise.' Coincidentally, there had been a great debate about whether to show Alice's car crash in *Room at the Top*: as with *Gatsby*, Clayton felt the drama better served if they did not.

10 That fine actress Brooke Adams can also be spotted making her screen début in a party scene in the film.

11 Gordon Gow, *Films and Filming*, June 1974, pp. 45–7.

12 *The Great Gatsby*, p. 43.

13 Shipman, *Story of Cinema*, p. 121.

14 Janet Maslin, 'Ballantine's Scotch, Glemby Haircuts, White Suits and White Teflon: Gatsby 1974' in *The Classic American Novel and the Movies*, ed. Gerald Peary and Roger Shatzkin (New York, Frederick Ungar, 1977), pp. 261–7.

15 Gow, *Films and Filming*, p. 46.

16 Maslin, 'Gatsby 1974', p. 262.

17 *Ibid.*

18 Penelope Gilliat, *New Yorker*, 11 April 1974.

19 James Monaco, *American Film Now* (New York, Plume, 1979), p. 339.

20 The most detailed account is a fine article by Stephen Rebello in *Cinéfantastique*, Vol. 13, No. 5, June–July 1983, pp. 28–49.

21 See the interview with Ray Bradbury by Mitch Tuchman in *OMNI*, May 1983, p. 30.

22 Richard Schickel, *The Disney Version* (London, Pavilion, 1986), p. 402.

23 Rebello, *Cinéfantastique*, p. 43.

24 *Screen International*, 24 September 1983, p. 14.

25 '*Something Wicked This Way Comes*: Adding the Magic', *Cinefex*, No. 12, April 1983, pp. 6–27.

26 This article by Brad Munson is another interesting account of the making of the film. It is perhaps worth mentioning that Delerue recorded a suite from his rejected score in one of the survey recordings of his film music (London sessions: Volume 3, Varese Sarabande VSD 5256). The main theme is a particular favourite of Haya Clayton and, at her request, was played at the BAFTA memorial service for Clayton in 1996. Now that many great film scores of the past are being recorded or re-recorded, I regard a recording of Delerue's music for the films of Jack Clayton as one of the major omissions of the current film discography and surely a leading candidate for future issue.

27 Originally the boys were to be pursued by a giant mechanical claw that was to scratch at their bedroom window and leave a trail of snail slime. However, this proved to be technically unworkable. Similarly, the special-effects department was planning to show the construction of the carnival by elaborate computer graphics but it did not work (it might also have been too much of a reminder of the night-time erecting of the circus tent in *Dumbo*). In the finished film the arrival of the carnival is much closer to Clayton's first conception: that the boys would see the train arrive and then virtually in the next instant the carnival would magically, supernaturally be *there*.

28 Ray Bradbury, *Something Wicked This Way Comes* (London, Grafton Books, 1983), p. 167. All subsequent quotations are taken from this edition. The novel was first published, by Hart Davis MacGibbon, in 1963.

29 3 August 1983. In later interviews (notably in *Outré* magazine, 1995), Bradbury has been less supportive of the film and has indicated that relations between him and Clayton were much more fraught and tense when they were collaborating for Disney than they had been when working together earlier for Paramount. I am grateful to John C. Tibbetts for drawing my attention to this article. For an interesting account of Bradbury's screenwriting career, including *Something Wicked This Way Comes*, see John C. Tibbetts, 'The Illustrating Man: The Screenplays of Ray Bradbury', *Creative Screenwriting*, Vol. 6, No. 1, Jan.–Feb. 1999, pp. 45–54.

30 *Something Wicked*, p. 20.

31 *Cinefex*, p. 21.

8

God's lonely woman: *The Lonely Passion of Judith Hearne* (1987)

The performances that have made the most impression on me, that have the deepest effect – when I narrowed it down to three out of the many – I realised are all those of character actresses. Judy Holliday in *Born Yesterday*, Giulietta Masina in *La Strada* and Maggie Smith in *The Lonely Passion of Judith Hearne*. In each what inspires me is their skill coupled with a presence, and by that I don't mean beauty, though there is something beautiful about them. In particular I thought about Smith playing an alcoholic in *The Lonely Passion*. It's her face: she manages to convey so much in her fragile face, she physicalises it so that it is so graceful. It is the same watching Masina. They are very economical and specific about the choice of movement that they make. I think of the scene in *The Lonely Passion* where Smith has just moved into a boarding house, she goes into her room, it's a horrible room and she turns around. It's very Maggie Smith, but so right for the character, as she just puts her hand on the mantelpiece and it's almost like she is looking around saying: 'Oh my god. But I'm going to be fine, it's a new start'. But we don't see her face, it's all in her body, the way her arm is holding her up and keeping her there as she surveys this nasty boarding-house room. Moments like that followed by the camera are beautiful – it's like an arc. When you are cutting a film you need to have that whole sweep, you have to see her coming into the room and that gesture has to come at the right moment or too much film is used and you can't cut it in afterwards because you need the whole movement of her entering the room. Then it's the way that she holds her mouth sometimes, or the expression in her eyes. She is a lonely, lonely woman with a drinking problem and Smith manages to say all these things about this woman and it keeps twisting and twisting me in the gut because it is so exquisitely placed. It's like her fingers – she has very graceful bones in her hands and you know that this woman doesn't eat that much. The whole character of Judith Hearne is articulated in that physicality ... Though Smith and Holliday's characters are victims, they don't play them as victims – they have a pride. Maybe it comes from within the actress, I don't know. But there is never a sense of underdog. You care about them, but without them ever asking you to do so. (Saskia Reeves, *Sight and Sound*, September 1995, p. 119)

I'm fascinated by loneliness and what really attracted me about *Judith Hearne* is that loneliness and loss of faith, which are both very important things in life. It doesn't really have anything to do with religion *per se* – you can lose faith in anything in your life, in your circumstances. ('Clayton's Passion: An Interview with Philip Bergson', *What's On*, 4 January 1989, p. 63)

'Things are going to be better here than the other places ... a new start,' says Judith Hearne in her new boarding house. It could almost be Clayton himself returning to the British cinema after a generation's absence.

Brian Moore's début novel, *The Lonely Passion of Judith Hearne*, was published in 1955 to immediate acclaim. As a study by a comparatively young author of middle-aged frustration, it is comparable in perception and depth to James Joyce's story 'The Dead' in *Dubliners*. Almost from its publication, it had been talked of as a possible film property. John Huston had wanted to film it in 1962 with Katharine Hepburn but Allied Artists, who were putting up the money, wanted Rosalind Russell instead and the project lapsed. Over the years it was mentioned as a possible vehicle for Rachel Roberts with director Daniel Petrie, and for Deborah Kerr with Irvin Kershner as director. José Quintero wanted to do it on stage with Geraldine Page. When screenwriter Peter Nelson acquired the rights of *Judith Hearne* in 1982, he had talked to Shirley MacLaine about doing it, with Mike Nichols directing. But Nichols wanted to update it to the 1980s and change the locale to Boston.

Clayton tried to option the screen rights for the book in 1961, 1964, 1970 and 1973. At an early stage he had talked to Spencer Tracy about the possibility of playing the role of James Madden – Clayton said he did not really expect him to agree but it was a great excuse to talk to one of his screen idols over the phone – and there is a personal note in his files for 8 July 1966 which suggests that he raised it as a possible screen project with producer Ray Stark, vaguely discussing Vanessa Redgrave for the main role 'providing one could make her look a little older and plainer'. But it was twenty years before the opportunity to make the film finally came, when United British Artists brought it to Clayton's attention via his agent, who was also on the board of HandMade Films. By that time Maggie Smith – who had made such an impression on Clayton in her small but crucial role in *The Pumpkin Eater* – seemed the ideal choice, as was to prove true. Bob Hoskins, who had scored a great personal success with his role in Neil Jordan's *Mona Lisa* (1986), was an equally felicitous, bankable choice as co-star. In interviews Clayton was at pains to point out that both were accepting a third of their normal salary in order for the film to be made.

As was his normal practice, Clayton sent a copy of Peter Nelson's screenplay to Brian Moore for comments. 'It is always much better to get the author on the side of the film before it starts rather than hear his complaints after it has been finished', Clayton told Nelson in a letter (19 March 1987). In fact, Moore thought the script a 'very good rendition' of his book, making some suggestions to increase the authenticity of the dialogue and some for dramatic changes which were accepted only in part. Interestingly, he made no objection to the film's change of setting from Belfast to Dublin.[1] One effect of the change is to make the parallels between the material here and Joyce's *Dubliners* very apparent, particularly the criticism by both authors of the stranglehold religion has on the country. (Coincidentally, John Huston's last film, his 1987 adaptation of *The Dead*, the longest story in *Dubliners*, had opened shortly before *Judith Hearne*.)[2] Clayton said he did not remember why the setting had been changed, but it might just have been that Dublin, more than Belfast, provided the 1950s ambience that the film needed. In fact, only ten days of the seven-week filming schedule were actually shot in Dublin, with Blessington Street providing the exterior of Mrs Henry Rice's appalling boarding house. The remainder of the film was shot at Shepperton studios; and, as Clayton explained in an interview with Roderick Mann for the *Los Angeles Times* (27 December 1987), 'we had to shoot the church desecration scene in London because the Irish wouldn't permit us to do it in Dublin. Frankly I was surprised we were able to find a priest in London who'd let us use his church'.

As usual, Clayton left the writer alone to come up with a first-draft screenplay, but then conferred closely about changes. Clayton's main suggestions after the first draft centred on four aspects of the film. Rather than having one long flashback dealing with Judith's relationship with her aunt, Clayton felt the pace would be better if the flashbacks were split up and slipped into key points of the narrative, giving necessary background information whilst moving the narrative forwards. He felt more humour could be drawn out of the material (the film is certainly funnier than the novel), and that some suggested fantasy scenes (Judith in a coffin, Madden in a doorman's uniform whirling around in a revolving door, Madden as Samson shackled to the bedposts) should be cut because they might produce the wrong kind of laugh. Clayton made a distinction between 'fantasy' and 'the fantastic' – 'the first is rooted in reality and the second is quite unbelievable'. The scenes being proposed tended to fall into the second category and had 'no place in the reality of a story of this kind'.[3] It should be stressed here that a first-draft screenplay is always an exploratory rather than a definitive document, and that comments made by a director should not be construed as criticism but as part of a developing dialogue between writer and director as they exchange ideas, clarify their thoughts and move towards a common goal.

A major part of their discussion concerned the ending, which is substantially different from the novel's and which, in the event, was to provoke the most criticism. This will be discussed in more detail in due course, but, although there was some disagreement over detail, Clayton and Nelson agreed fundamentally in wanting a more explicitly upbeat ending than the one in the novel. 'It's not because I'm against sad endings', Clayton told the *New York Times* (26 December, 1987). 'But in film I love *developing* characters' (the word 'developing' there being used as an adjective). 'In the book she starts and finishes at the same point. In the film she winds up a much freer woman than when she started.' One might compare this with the ending of *The Pumpkin Eater*, where it seems momentarily the heroine is back where she started but then, in the final two minutes, resurgent new life and hope course through the film.

Judith Hearne is arguably Clayton's finest and most completely realised film since *The Pumpkin Eater*. One reason is that the material brings out so many of his strengths: his capacity to elicit brilliant performances; his talent as a 'four wall, interrelationship director', as Bruce Dern called him,[4] who could locate, dramatize and animate the suspense lurking in seemingly ordinary, confined spaces; and the sensitivity to feminine feeling which Pauline Kael defined as his ability to 'show women's temperatures and their mind–body interaction'[5] and which makes him, to my mind, a 'woman's director' quite unparalleled in British film. Anne Bancroft's astute observation on Clayton's indifference to conventional screen heroes but his fascination with the heroic in unconventional people (see page 109) is particularly relevant to *Judith Hearne*, which shows deep compassion for the courageous way Judith grapples with her isolation and despair.

Of Clayton's previous films, the one that has most in common with *Judith Hearne* is probably *The Pumpkin Eater*. Like the earlier film, *Judith Hearne* deals sympathetically with the situation of a middle-aged woman under stress – in Judith's case, intensified by loneliness and the loss of her closest relative, her aunt. When her hopes of the possibility of a romantic relationship with James Madden turn out to have been built on sand, she gives in to her one great weakness, alcohol, which in turn leads to a terrible crisis of religious faith. As in *The Pumpkin Eater*, there is a moment of planned incongruity to counterpoint yet intensify the heroine's anguish: in the earlier film, a religious fanatic appears at Jo's door and requests money just as she is about to receive the devastating phone call from Conway about his wife's pregnancy ('You will be blessed for this', says the religious man); in *Judith Hearne*, when Judith realises she has disastrously misinterpreted Madden's interest in her and runs away in despair shouting 'O my God', she rushes past a solitary woman chanting 'Mother of God, pray for us ...'. Also like the heroine in *The Pumpkin Eater*, Judith's fluctuating fortunes and happiness are very much reflected in the places she inhabits – from the comfort of the recital rooms of her youth to the chill of Mrs Rice's lodging house; from the temporary refuge at the home of her friend Moira and her family (however they might mock her) to the Shelbourne hotel where she will spend the remains of her savings and which represents the luxury she craves. Her final destination is the bleak nursing home where she will be forced to convalesce after her breakdown. All these are punctuated by visits to the church – at the opening of the film when, as a child, she has a fit of the giggles and has to be restrained by her aunt (the clasped hands are a typical Clayton image and also indicate how the aunt will maintain a grip on her throughout her life); at the Mass she attends with Madden, where we hear her thoughts and hopes as the testy priest remonstrates with his congregation; at the confession where, humiliatingly, she finds herself in a session given over to children and fails to persuade the priest of the seriousness of her plight; and finally and most terrifyingly, when she vandalizes the altar and pulls desperately at the tabernacle door for some sign of God. 'Red light filled her eyes', says the novel at this point;[6] Clayton has her collapse backwards onto the red carpet. As she enters the church the novel has said: 'She passed the Holy Water font. What use? Only water, dirty water in a cold marble bowl.'[7] Clayton and Smith convey this mood in a gesture: her hand slapped violently into the font and creating an angry splash as she enters. I have suggested before how Clayton's work is remarkable for the palpable absence or failure of father figures. Here the 'absence' of the (heavenly) Father is felt with terrifying force and precipitates an acute psychological crisis.

Alexander Walker once observed of Clayton that 'an attachment to places – a very English characteristic – is a strong element in his temperament'.[8] Clayton invests places with great emotional weight and value. One thinks of the grandeur yet ghostliness of

Bly House in *The Innocents*; the different environments of *The Pumpkin Eater* that culminate in the heroine's retreat to the old tower at the end of the film; the Victorian house of *Our Mother's House* which sets the moral atmosphere against which the action is to be judged; or Gatsby's house in *The Great Gatsby*, which seems more hotel than home and is a private monument to a romantic dream. If Joe Lampton is less defined by setting in *Room at the Top*, it is precisely because he is in flux and on the move and trying to escape from his roots. For Judith Hearne, the definition of who and where she is is provided by two pictures: one of her aunt and another of The Sacred Heart. 'When they're with me', she says to herself at the end of the novel, 'watching over me, a new place becomes home.'[9] These two pictures will have a similar importance in the film – Judith will place them either face down or to the wall when she is unhappy or is doing something of which she is ashamed – but the ending will not share the melancholy fatalism of the novel, which has something of the sad finality of the phrase 'for life, as it were' that closes Henry James's *Washington Square*.

It would be hard to over-praise Maggie Smith's performance, which Pauline Kael in *Hooked* properly called 'staggering' and compared with Katharine Hepburn's great performance in George Stevens's *Alice Adams* for its acute observation of social embarrassment.[10] It is meticulously detailed: one remembers Judith's slight stiffening and hesitation before entering the breakfast room for the first time, as if entering a lion's den (truer than she knows); or the way, when Madden is telling her of his idea to open a hamburger joint in Dublin, her eyes keep wandering to the drink in his hand (it is a detail one might miss on a first viewing but is crucial not only because it is a clue to her alcoholism but also because it explains why she does not quite pick up his drift, which is to have unfortunate consequences later). When Judith tells Moira and the family about her relationship with Madden and embroiders the romantic possibilities, Maggie Smith delicately conveys a sense that she is drinking the sherry to excess because she is rising to, and resisting, the sarcasm and disrespect she can feel in the air. She clutches the sherry glass with both hands, which becomes a telling gesture – not only cherishing it but steadying it. Judith's Sunday visits to the family have been indulged and she has been subtly patronised and pitied. Her habitual greeting, 'It's only me', might provoke giggles from the children but is, in fact, a revealing statement of self-denigration. (Since seeing this film, I have never used the phrase again.) There is a surprising and powerful moment near the end of the film when Judith is convalescent in the nursing home and being visited by Moira. 'You know, Moira', Judith says, 'I never liked you, that's the honest truth.' The original indication of dialogue delivery in the first draft of the script said 'suddenly'; it was changed to 'with rueful honesty'. It is actually not a sudden comment but a considered one, suggesting that Judith is almost past caring what impression she gives but also offering the promise of a new relationship that is based on truth rather than pity on one side and need on the other. Moira's reaction is very moving. 'Well, I hope we can change all that,' she says, quietly. Prunella Scales (who, of course, played one of the office girls in *Room at the Top*) acts this moment brilliantly, rising to the challenge of Smith's perform-ance, saying the words as if hardly anything has happened but conveying on her face the shock felt by someone who has been suddenly struck.

As Saskia Reeves suggested, the great thing about Smith's performance is that there is no self-pity: she does not play the role as a victim. She can be very funny, particularly in the hospital scene with her friend Edie (Aine Ni Mhuiri) when they get the giggles and Judith seems unable to keep control of her hat: momentarily, the character is endearingly close to Stan Laurel. She can also be very forceful, proudly standing up to Mrs Rice's insinuations and expressing her religious doubts with such fervour, rather than apology, to the priest (Alan Devlin) that he is roused to anger: she strikes the nerve of his own possible unbelief. Maggie Smith is particularly magnificent when the loathsome Bernard suggests to Judith that her drinking might land her in the madhouse. Judith's reaction is not simply hurt and fear but an explosive *rage*. This may touch on her own guilty feelings about once thinking of confining her bedridden aunt to an asylum (and

how deftly the film has implied that Judith's drinking problem
may have started here, taking a little nip of her aunt's sherry –
egged on by her friend Edie – as she carries the drink to the invalid
upstairs). It certainly anticipates the repressed anger within her at
her life's missed opportunities, anger that will surface violently in
her act of desecration of the church.

Perhaps Bob Hoskins's performance as Madden, the landlady's
brother who has recently returned to Ireland after thirty years in
America, is not quite on the same level of imagination. It does not
have the emotional authenticity or nuancing of the other performances: it seems, by comparison, a bit bluntly conceived. Technically,
however, it is very skilful. Like Dirk Bogarde in *Our Mother's House*,
Hoskins seems to know instinctively when to pick up the pace
(cleverly done, because the quickening of pulse corresponds to
Judith's own feeling when she is around Madden), yet in the
midst of his brashness there is also sensitivity and vulnerability.
In one of Clayton's most elaborate feats of cross-cutting, both
Judith and Madden reach a crisis of frustration at the same time,
she relieving hers in her room by taking to the bottle, he relieving
his by a brutal and clumsy rape of the maid Mary (Rudi Davies)
who, to his fury and jealousy, has been carrying on with Bernard.
The crisis has come about on their learning from Madden's sister,
Mrs Rice, the truth about each other – that Judith is not a wealthy
spinster but an impoverished occasional teacher of the piano, and
Madden is not an enterprising hotelier but has been a humble
hotel doorman. Such mutual misunderstanding has earlier created
a comedy of sorts, particularly in the fine scene at Mass, where
their internal thoughts voiced over the soundtrack comically
counterpoint the external proprieties of the service (the priest, as
so often in the film, is in a testy mood and denounces the congregation's lack of time for God: a deeper irony is that he will not have
time for Judith). Their thoughts also expose their complete delu-
sions about each other. Madden notices the rings on Judith's
fingers, assessing their value and musing wanly, 'It's a pity she
looks like that.' 'Devout and respectable', thinks Judith about him,
adding 'that limp – you'd hardly notice it'. She has picked up the
impression of Madden's devoutness from seeing his crossing

himself, not realising the gesture is an instinctive, defensive reaction to the lascivious thoughts he is harbouring about Mary.

The relationship between Judith and Madden, then, becomes a comedy/catastrophe of failed communication and misunderstanding. Ironically, Madden's kindest, most selfless gesture to Judith in the entire film is one she does not see: covering her with a coat after she has been knocked unconscious during her argument with Bernard and lies prostrate on the bed. Even in their final scene, Madden, now a cab driver, is misreading the signs: if Judith was staying at the Shelbourne before she got ill, surely this means she has money? Their final embrace at the hospital will be so moving because what draws them together at that point is not love but an overwhelming sense of their mutual loneliness; moreover, the embrace is a signal not of commitment but of goodbye. The panic in Hoskins's eyes, as Madden seems to stare into the abyss that is his future, is his finest moment in the film.

Still, I agree with Pauline Kael when she says that Hoskins's performance does not have the surprise of Ian McNeice's as Madden's nephew, 'the landlady's son ... a Dickensian horror with lewd pink flesh and yellowish hair'.[11] This is Brian Moore's description of Judith's first sight of Bernard as he swivels round in his wing chair to face her: 'He was a horrid looking fellow. Fat as a pig he was, and his face was the colour of cottage cheese ... His stomach stuck out like a sagging pillow ... He was all bristly blond jowls, tiny puffy hands and long blond curly hair, like some monstrous baby swelled to man size.'[12] McNeice brings a real bravura to the role, the mother's boy taken to the point of grotesquerie, and creepily fascinating because of his wit and wicked sense of mischief. As Kael noted, McNeice catches not only the 'sybaritic slime' that is Bernie but also the playfulness that could attract an inexperienced convent-girl like Mary, who gets precious little pleasure and laughter elsewhere in that monstrous boarding house.

McNeice's marvellous performance is matched by Marie Kean's as Mrs Rice who, if anything, is even better here than she was as Mrs Malins in Huston's *The Dead*. At one stage in the novel, Moore talks of Mrs Rice's 'bland eyes showing nothing of what went on behind them'.[13] There is the same quality in Kean's performance, where the surface gentility and charm mask her venom. Her timing of the lines is almost supernal, like her sudden comment on Judith's flowers – 'I know they're gardenias. What do you take me for, a dimwit?' – which cracks like a whip-lash across the surface decorousness to disclose the disquiet and malice beneath. By contrast, there is her serene 'Toast, Bernie ...' – absolute calm under fire – after another dreadful breakfast row has led to the precipitate departure of Madden and Judith and has left a little extra untouched food for the son on whom she dotes. The three breakfast scenes in the film, each more tense and tetchy than the last, are impressively staged, gruesomely funny but staying the right side of caricature to catch the range of emotions around the table: Judith's nervousness, Madden's blustering defensiveness on the subject of America, the flinty disapproval of the schoolteacher Miss Friel (Sheila Reid), all orchestrated into discord by an impassive Mrs Rice and a deliberately provocative Bernie. Also, seldom have the behavioural excesses of a stroke victim been rendered more truthfully, less sentimentally, than in Wendy Hiller's portrayal of the aunt, nor well-meaning kindness motivated by habit and duty more than genuine affection handled so affectingly as by Prunella Scales in her role as Moira.

Praising McNeice's performance as Bernard, Pauline Kael remarked that the picture 'needs the baroque touch that McNeice provides to help offset the shallow, virtuous ending'. In the novel, Judith is left at the nursing home facing an uncertain future. In the film, Madden reappears and visits her, proposing marriage. But it is another grotesque misunderstanding: hearing from Bernie that she was staying at the Shelbourne hotel, he has assumed Judith must still have money and she has to shatter his illusions. In this respect the film's ending is rather like the ending of Wyler's *The Heiress* (1949), in which the heroine finds the strength to reject a suitor to whom she was once devoted because she sees through his motives. Wyler's ending is as different from that of the Henry James novel on which the film is based (*Washington Square*) as Clayton's is different from Brian Moore's, but each has its own validity. 'In the end she is going off in that car to her own life', Clayton said (*New York Post*, 31 December 1987).

'She has progressed. With even the most terrible incidents of your life, you either emerge from them a more whole person or you'll be destroyed.' It is an important statement because it contains the essence of why Clayton was so insistent on a more upbeat ending, on some development in Judith, why this meant so much to him. When asked about this in relation to his own life, he replied: 'Five years of total terror as an air gunner on a Lancaster in World War II. I had to receive pills not to fall asleep flying to Berlin and back. My fear of flying lasted for ten years after the war.' He could also have cited – but at this stage was not yet ready to discuss it – his remarkable and courageous recovery from a stroke that could have destroyed his career.

At the close of Peter Nelson's first-draft screenplay, Judith and Madden bump into each other at a cinema after she has seen *Singin' in the Rain*. They chat briefly before parting and then Madden comes running after her to arrange a meeting for the following week, before going off to see the film himself. Walking away, Judith, as the screenplay said, 'suddenly skips up and down the curb imitating the light-hearted steps she saw Gene Kelly do in the movie'. It is a charming conception but perhaps not quite in character – a little too flamboyant for someone so inhibited – and too extrovertly optimistic for a film that makes its points more quietly. In his biography of Maggie Smith, Michael Coveney describes the actual ending as follows:

> When Judith later leaves the home, she hands a crumpled piece of paper to the taxi driver on which is written Madden's address. The camera once again lingers, searching for clues, anxious to know if, at last, this is to be the really brand new start she deserves. But Maggie's taut mask, frankly lined with a history of disappointment, is giving nothing away.[14]

This is not quite what happens. In a final revised version of the screenplay (dated 2 March 1987) there is a note in Clayton's handwriting that describes the ending as follows:

> JUDITH gazes at the slip of paper for a long moment. Then JUDITH lowers the window and tosses the paper out. A faint smile appears on her lips as she sits with her head high.

EXIT ROADWAY OUTSIDE EARNCLIFFE – DAY.

As the taxi passes through the gates and rolls away through the green landscape.

FADE OUT.

THE END.

Clayton clearly felt that one aspect of Judith's new start was an explicit rejection of Madden. Anything else might have signalled that she was still clinging to her illusions.

The release of *The Lonely Passion of Judith Hearne* turned out to be something of a disaster. It was premièred in Los Angeles in the Christmas week of 1987 in order to qualify for Oscar consideration. Unfortunately it opened in the same week as Hector Babenco's *Ironweed* (1987), starring Jack Nicholson and Meryl Streep, another film about life's failures and even gloomier and longer than Clayton's: *Judith Hearne* was, I suspect, rather undervalued as a result. Certainly, the LA reviews tended to be negative. 'Angst isn't quite art,' said the *Los Angeles Star* (23 December 1987) in a review that was representative of a critical feeling that here was an honourable film that was, in the last resort, depressing. To borrow the phrase of the *Star*, it had 'not transcended its harrowing material into genuine tragedy', perhaps because Clayton was not actually aiming for tragedy but building towards something hopeful rather than harrowing. Nevertheless, there was widespread expectation that Maggie Smith would garner an Oscar nomination, if not the statuette itself: it was a major surprise when she was overlooked by the Academy.[15] (But they loved the film in Norway, the country of Ibsen.)

The British release was even more catastrophic. A row between Cannon distributors and HandMade Films over alleged non-payment by Cannon in connection with four UK video releases of HandMade films led to HandMade's threat of a lawsuit ten days before *Judith Hearne* was to have its first screening. Cannon retaliated by pulling the film from its UK première date and refusing to show it in its cinemas until the issue had been resolved. The result was that a national release was delayed for a year: the film was not premièred in London until January 1989. Although Clayton thought that HandMade's handling of the affair was naïve – he said *he* would not have started threatening lawsuits until *after* the film had been released – he also considered Cannon's attitude 'awful' (*Edinburgh Evening News*, 30 January 1989). Nevertheless the film went on to win awards for Maggie Smith and Bob Hoskins (voted best actress and actor in the *London Evening Standard* British Film Awards of 1989) and Maggie Smith was to win a British Academy Award.

'It's absolute luck, timing', Clayton was to say in an interview for the *Los Angeles Times* (27 December 1987). '*Room at the Top* isn't one of my favourite films, but it came out at exactly the right time. Whereas *The Pumpkin Eater*, which I consider a much better film, came out at the wrong time and did not do well ... Personally I'm a great admirer of Steven Spielberg, who knows the market better than anybody. He has a great sense of timing.' But if the film was a marketing disaster, it had more than enough for the discerning cineaste. The reunion with composer Georges Delerue was particularly felicitous, Delerue contributing one of his inimitably delicate scores that cut to the heart of the drama: the skeletal strings that underscore Judith's depressed binge in her room are particularly eloquent of a mind stretched to its nerve ends; the exquisite harmonies that close the score leave a gentle trail of hope and humanity.

Judith Hearne shows unmistakable traces of Clayton's stylistic signatures: the circling camera shot at those moments where the leading characters lose control; the amplification of sound at extreme moments of psychological disturbance, in this case when Judith shouts defiance at God in the church; the slow dissolves that melt past and present into a continuum of felt time.[16] The geography of Mrs Rice's boarding house is exploited with particular dramatic effect, as characters jostle for positions of power and advantage on the stairs, behind doors, in rooms. A lot of spying goes on as mean-spirited adults behave like malicious children and inform on their fellows out of spite and vengefulness. It is a film of sometimes unsparing cruelty, not only in incidents like the squalid, clumsy rape of Mary by Madden, but more subtly in those smirks at Judith's defensive airs that become cumulatively terrifying slices off her self-esteem. Yet it is redeemed by an

occasionally comic, always compassionate spirit that finds something noble in the way life's 'failures' refuse to give up. In this
regard, it reminds me very much of John Huston's splendid
movie, *Fat City* (1972), where the intensity with which his characters dream their dreams is contrasted with the harsh environment
in which they must live their lives, and where he finds dignity in
the way people who have been battered almost to the floor by life's
vicissitudes nevertheless refuse to admit defeat. Small wonder
that Clayton, in a private screening of that film in producer Ray
Stark's house, almost came to blows with Peter Bogdanovich and
Ryan O'Neal when they made disparaging remarks about
Huston's direction.[17] Like Huston, Clayton is a tender chronicler
of the courageous spiritual processes of lowly people whose hopes
are defeated by destiny but who nevertheless endure.

Notes

1 This occasioned some adverse critical comment, though Alexander Walker
was one who thought the change of setting an improvement. 'Clayton and
his screenwriter Peter Nelson have re-located Brian Moore's novel south of
the Irish border – and gained in pain by it', he wrote. 'Dublin is a malicious
capital. There's nothing like Irish smiles for rubbing salts in the wounds
their owners' tongues have already opened' (*London Evening Standard*, 5
January 1989).

2 Because he was heavily involved in the preparation of his own film, Clayton
had to turn down a request from Huston to be ready to take over direction
of *The Dead* in case Huston died before completion. (Huston had prepared
a similar request three years before while working on *Under the Volcano* but
had survived the production. Indeed, Michael Caine would often recall the
occasion when a sickly Huston bade him a final farewell from his supposed
death bed after *The Man Who Would Be King*: 'the next time I saw him', said
Caine, 'he'd done four more films'.) Clayton arranged for Karel Reisz to
stand by but Huston lived long enough to see his film through.

3 Jack Clayton, personal note, 6 January 1987.

4 Bruce Dern, *Films Illustrated*, October 1975, p. 52.

5 Pauline Kael, *Hooked* (London and New York, Marion Boyars, 1990), p. 411.

6 Brian Moore, *The Lonely Passion of Judith Hearne* (London, Flamingo, 1994),
p. 241. All subsequent quotations from the novel are from this edition. The
novel was first published by André Deutsch in 1955.

7 *The Lonely Passion of Judith Hearne*, p. 238.

8 Alexander Walker, *Hollywood England: The British Film Industry in the*

Sixties (London, Michael Joseph, 1974), p. 163.

9 The Lonely Passion of Judith Hearne, p. 255.

10 Kael, Hooked, p. 409.

11 Ibid., p. 412.

12 The Lonely Passion of Judith Hearne, pp. 9–10.

13 Ibid., p. 136.

14 Michael Coveney, Maggie Smith: A Bright Particular Star (London, Victor Gollancz, 1992), p. 257.

15 For the record, the nominees for Best Actress that year were Cher (Moonstruck), Glenn Close (Fatal Attraction), Holly Hunter (Broadcast News), Sally Kirkland (Anna) and Meryl Streep (Ironweed). Another controversial omission was Lillian Gish for her performance in The Whales of August, though, so the story goes, the feisty Miss Gish professed herself content that she was spared the humiliation of losing to Cher. An impassioned letter by Terrence Bradley to the Los Angeles Times (20 February 1988), offered the following opinion on the nominations. 'This year the unforgiveable has been committed. Maggie Smith gave by far her finest performance on film in The Lonely Passion of Judith Hearne. It will be truly remembered as one of the great performances of all time. I realise that it's too late to right the wrong that has been committed but, for me, the Academy Awards will never be as meaningful.'

16 In the novel there is a moment where Judith thinks that 'it was so much easier to go back now: going forward was so frightening' (p. 85). This is an interesting comment in relation to Clayton's films and his use of flashback. It recalls Gatsby's 'Can't repeat the past? Of course you can', or Jo's flashbacks at the start of The Pumpkin Eater which partly reflect her terror of moving forward and leaving the house.

17 The story is told in Lawrence Grobel's The Hustons (London, Bloomsbury, 1990), pp. 648–9. O'Neal and Bogdanovich sat and joked through the screening of Fat City and at the end one of them said: 'I wish that old fart would give up directing.' At this Clayton rounded on them both for what he called their childishness and declared that Huston had more talent in one fingernail than they had in their entire bodies. 'I'm disgusted with you both,' he concluded. He and O'Neal almost came to blows.

9

Death makes a call:
Memento Mori (1992)

Being over seventy is like being engaged in a war. All our friends
are going and gone and we survive amongst the dead and the dying
as on a battlefield. (Muriel Spark, *Memento Mori*, London, Penguin,
1961, p. 37)[1]

I'm sure you're all dying ... I mean, I'm sure you'd all like a nice
cup of tea'. (Mrs Mortimer, greeting her elderly luncheon guests in
Memento Mori)

There was one film genre Jack Clayton seemed determined to
avoid: comedy. 'I don't think I could do a comedy', he told Judith
Crist of the *New York Herald Tribune* (26 April 1959) when being
interviewed at the time of the American opening of *Room at the
Top*. 'That's the greatest and hardest thing in the world and very
special.' (The sentiment might have been reinforced by the fact
that his film had opened in New York in the same week as Billy
Wilder's *Some Like It Hot*, a very special film comedy that would
intimidate anyone.) The question cropped up again at the Oxford
Union when he was asked if he was thinking of following *The
Innocents* with a comedy. 'That's a very specific talent which I don't
think I have', he replied (*Oxford Mail*, 24 February 1962). Certainly the three film comedies on which he had served as producer –
Sailor Beware, Dry Rot and *Three Men in a Boat* (all 1956) – are not
really of a vintage to have done much for his enthusiasm for the
form (although in *Sailor Beware*, Alfie Bass does a nice turn as a
church organist who plays the instrument in his stockinged feet
and, as the bridgegroom still fails to appear, finds 'Art Thou

Weary' staring at him on his music stand). As associate producer on Henry Cornelius's *I Am A Camera* (1955), Clayton said he 'took bets about which line would get a laugh. I must have made a hundred bets throughout the film and lost all of them' (*Los Angeles Times*, 27 December 1987). It is indeed a desperately unfunny film and at one stage provides an object lesson in how not to direct a party scene (which Clayton may have recalled when he came to direct the party scene in *The Pumpkin Eater*, which *is* very funny). Even the humour of John Huston's spoof thriller, *Beat the Devil*, on which Clayton was associate producer and which has at least an underground reputation as a cult classic, was lost on him. Although great fun to make, with Truman Capote pounding out some terrific one-liners even when troubled with raging toothache and not having a clue about what was supposed to happen next, Clayton thought it an awful film.

All the more remarkable, then, that Clayton's last film, made for BBC Television, should be a black comedy and one handled with such finesse and style as to garner the most unanimously favourable set of reviews he had achieved on any of his films since *Room at the Top*. Muriel Spark's novel *Memento Mori* had been published in 1959 and had immediately attracted Clayton's attention as a possible film project, partly because he admired its style and dialogue but particularly because he related to the theme. 'I really believe what the book says,' he told Jane Garner (*The Stage and Television Today*, 2 April 1992), 'that people should be told to remember they must die – from an early, early age. Children should be told that after their birth the most natural thing is death.' The feeling, no doubt, derived in part from the experience of five years of flying missions for the RAF during World War II. As we have already noted, death and/or funeral scenes occur frequently in his work, involving the key characters and always carrying great weight. *The Bespoke Overcoat* is, in a sense, one long death scene, and one might also remember the deaths of Alice in *Room at the Top*; Miles in *The Innocents*; the two fathers in *The Pumpkin Eater*; the mother in *Our Mother's House* and then the 'father' at the end of that film; and Gatsby, Myrtle and Wilson in *The Great Gatsby*. So it is not surprising that the theme – and indeed the main character – of what was sadly to prove Clayton's last film should be Death itself. What is more surprising is the tone: a touch macabre, but mellow not morbid. It combines the gravity of Ingmar Bergman's *The Seventh Seal* (1956) with the mordant wit and truculent tenderness of the BBC's classic sitcom *One Foot in the Grave*.

A project dealing with the themes of old age and death might not have seemed a particularly commercial proposition in the youth-oriented cinema of the 1980s and 1990s, but the subject had been given a fillip by the unexpected critical and commercial success of *Driving Miss Daisy* (1989). Nevertheless, in the past Clayton had declined American offers of finance, feeling that, because of America's different attitude to death, any attempt to adapt the material to an American setting would be doomed to fail. It would lose the character of what he called 'Muriel's beautiful dialogue': moreover, it would cause the dilution and disappearance of one of the novel's major characteristics, which is precisely its Englishness. Part of the strength of the material, which the film preserves, is its dark observation of some aspects of Englishness: eccentricity of manners, sexual furtiveness, snobbery and class cruelty. If one is initially reminded of the gentility of Ealing comedy it is not the cosiness of a *Titfield Thunderbolt* (1952) that comes to mind but the cutting edge of a *Kind Hearts and Coronets* (1949) and *The Ladykillers* (1955) – darkly funny films that play dangerous games with death.

Given the Englishness of the theme and the nature of the subject, a natural home for the project seemed the BBC, which is where it ended up, somewhat against Clayton's inclinations in that he had previously resisted the temptation to work for television. It meant a much tighter schedule than he was used to – a twenty-eight-day shooting schedule made even more difficult by the fact that he was suffering from 'flu. But for producer Louis Marks, Clayton's prestigious name had the effect of attracting an extraordinary rollcall of acting talent. As he was to observe, there was around a thousand years of acting experience present on screen in the final film, with a cast list that reads like a Who's Who of British film since 1940: Michael Hordern, Cyril Cusack, Renée

Asherson, Maurice Denham, Robert Flemyng, Preston Lockwood, Barbara Hicks, Thora Hird, Muriel Pavlow, not to mention comparative youngsters such as Maggie Smith, John Wood and Zoë Wanamaker. 'I think the truth of the matter', said Marks, 'is that all these artists came into the film because they wanted to work with Clayton because his reputation is so very high in the film world'.² Clayton was disappointed that, despite this being a strong period for BBC Film Drama – contemporary films such as Mike Newell's *Enchanted April* (1991) and Anthony Minghella's *Truly Madly Deeply* (1990) were significant international successes – *Memento Mori* was never given a proper theatrical distribution. It was to be shown in two parts, to great acclaim, in the 'Masterpiece Theatre' series on American television (25 October and 1 November 1992) and was also to be successfully screened at the Film Festivals of Telluride, Montreal and Berlin. As Marks observed, the film industry's loss was television's gain and some compensation was provided by the plethora of awards received – for John Wood as best actor (Evening Standard Award); for Clayton, Jeanie Sims and Alan Kelley for best television drama (Writers' Guild of Great Britain Award); for Oliver Bayldon as best production designer (British Academy Award), as well as BAFTA nominations for best single drama, best actress (Maggie Smith), best photography, best sound and best editing.

An early draft screenplay was completed by Peter Prince in March 1990. It was worked over by Clayton, Jeanie Sims and Alan Kelley and submitted to Muriel Spark, whose initial response was decidedly unenthusiastic. In a letter to Louis Marks (12 August 1990), she expressed the view that the script had little or no commercial exploitability; that it was aggressive and even sadistic towards old people; and that its final scene between Taylor and Charmian was awful in its 'syruppy sentimentality'. In a detailed response to Clayton (14 September 1990), Jeanie Sims put up a spirited and eloquent defence of the script. In fact, apart from minor modifications suggested by Spark on matters of expression, the script was left essentially unchanged, and can perhaps stand as a salutary example of the adage 'If it were all in the script, why make the picture?' In other words, what might seem dubious when read coldly on the page is quite transformed when brought to dramatic life by expert acting and direction.

For example, a scene that Spark thought unnecessarily sadistic and clichéd when she read it in the screenplay – the altercation between the critic Guy Leet (Maurice Denham) and the poet Percy Mannering (Cyril Cusack) – is one of the comic highlights of the film. The comedy derives partly from the incongruity between the intense emotion displayed and its cause (Percy is in high dudgeon because Leet, in his volume of memoirs, has referred to him as a 'quite competent versifier', which he regards as a mortal insult); and partly from the imagery, a duel being fought with the geriatric weapons of a walking stick on one side and an umbrella on the other. Also it should be said that the characters of the two – a charming rake and an irascible rascal in their declining years – have been established with such droll affection already that one can relish the humour without fearing that it will lead to serious harm.

Also, contrary to Spark's assertions about the script's aggress-iveness and sadism, as Jeanie Sims points out, it is more com-passionate towards its characters than the novel and this is nowhere more apparent than in the ending. In the novel, the narrative ends with a listing of what all the main characters died of. 'I was a little annoyed at the way she ended it', Clayton said in an interview with Michael Church (*Observer*, 19 April 1992). 'It was as though she'd run out of ideas. And I thought why leave everyone feeling despondent? The message of it is that children should be taught early on that death is simple, inevitable and not to be feared. If you accept that, you have enormous scope for enjoying life.' The film ends with Charmian (Renée Asherson) and her former maid Jean Taylor (Thora Hird) reunited at a nursing home where they are both staying and, in a reversal of rules, Charmian reading to Taylor from one of her novels. When there is a mysterious phone call for her, no doubt to remind her of her mortality, Taylor says she is far too busy to come to the phone right now. It is the happiest ending of all of Clayton's films and because the performances have such charm and quiet dignity, any suspicion of sentimentality is banished; the scene instead breathes a serene wisdom and what one might call an experienced optimism. It has its psychological plausibility too, for, as Clayton said, 'both of them were never really frightened of death anyway, and it just shows they've got wonderful days ahead'.[3] In fairness it should be said that Muriel Spark considerably modified her initial misgivings as the production progressed, probably on learning of the casting (Maggie Smith is a prime Spark interpreter). By that time she obviously realised she was in good hands for she had seen *Judith Hearne* on television and had kindly written to Clayton to tell him 'what a splendid show' she thought it was. 'To me Maggie Smith is always magical,' she wrote in her letter (2 April 1991). 'I loved the casting and indeed the whole treatment.' When *Memento Mori* began shooting on 11 October 1991, it had the blessing of a 'good luck' telegram from the author.

Dame Lettie Colston (Stephanie Cole) – penal reformer, charity worker, hospital visitor, racist and snob, in roughly reverse order of significance – has been receiving obscene telephone calls. She has discussed them with Miss Taylor, the former maid of her sister-in-law Charmian, when visiting her in hospital but keeps being distracted by the patient in the bed next to Taylor, the perennially jolly Granny Barnacle (Margery Withers) who has a way with language and asks Lettie about her 'obese' phone calls. Lettie turns for solace to her brother Godfrey (Michael Hordern), but he has trouble – and foibles – of his own. When not paying for the privilege of looking up the skirts of Olive Mannering (Zoë Wanamaker), he is struggling to look after his wife Charmian, an eminent novelist experiencing a revival but who is now very forgetful and keeps calling any new housemaid 'Taylor' after her former maid. In fact, the new mistress of the house is Mrs Pettigrew (Maggie Smith), who, while caring for Charmian in a manner close to the intimidatory tactics of Charles Boyer's Gregory Anton in George Cukor's *Gaslight* (1944), is blackmailing Godfrey with incriminating love letters she has found between him and the recently deceased Lisa Brooke. Although the affair was long ago – half a century, in fact – Godfrey feels the revelation might devastate the already frail Charmian if they ever came to light: hence he is put under pressure to include Mrs Pettigrew in his will.

There is an odd fact about the phone calls that so terrify Lettie. The speaker simply says, 'Remember you must die', and hangs up. Others among her circle have received identical calls but, in contrast to her fear, have responded differently: for example, Godfrey blusters, Percy Mannering shouts defiant obscenities down the receiver and Charmian responds with ineffable polite-ness. 'Thank you', she says to the caller. 'At my age there are many things I don't remember but that is not one of them.' Also none of the recipients seems to hear the voice in the same way, some finding it youngish and cultured, others old and crude. Who could be playing this spiteful practical joke? And for what motive? Mrs Pettigrew, out of spite at her dashed hopes of a killing from Lisa Brooks's will? Godfrey's son Eric (Peter Eyre), who dislikes his father, is jealous of his mother's literary eminence, which undercuts his own paltry literary efforts, and is always short of money and might wish to hasten the end of his relatives in order to benefit from their respective legacies? Encouraged to do so by his friend Miss Taylor, who is worried about Charmian in the clutches of Mrs Pettigrew, a retired police inspector, Henry Mortimer (John Wood), takes up the case.

The secret of success in an ensemble piece such as this is in its casting, and the cast here is flawless: there is not a weak link anywhere. At the same time there is a frisson of unpredictability about some of the leading performances. Maggie Smith might initially seem too young for the role of the 73-year-old Mabel Pettigrew (though the novel does say that 'she did not at all look her age under her make-up'),[4] but the comic precision of her performance, visually and vocally, eliminates any possible reserva-tion. Just as Saskia Reeves noticed the eloquent delicacy of her hands in *Judith Hearne*, here she has a manner of suggesting deviousness simply through the way she cocks her head: it gives her dialogue almost literally an odd slant, cloaking nearly all her words with a suspicion of irony and double dealing. It is a coura-geous performance because Mrs Pettigrew is given no redeeming features: only in her pained response on hearing that Lisa Brooke has left her just £50 in her will ('I almost spent that on her soddin' wreath!') does one get a hint of a twisted humanity – a woman whose ruthless behaviour might be motivated by her sense of having all her life been unjustly undervalued. Clayton had to fight for Michael Hordern in the role of Godfrey: the word was that Hordern could no longer remember lines but, having the actor's assurance that this was not the case, Clayton adamantly supported his casting and the performance more than rewards the director's confidence. One of the epigraphs to the novel is a quotation from W. B. Yeats's *The Tower*:

> What shall I do with this absurdity –
> O heart, O troubled heart – this caricature,
> Decrepit age that has been tied to me
> As to a dog's tail?

It is a quote with particular applicability to Hordern's Godfrey, a man whose sensual nature is ill-matched to an ageing frame and which can only express itself, when stimulated by the sight of Olive's thighs, in low rumbles and growls of unconsummated desire. It is a hilarious sound, the kind of noise which, as John Naughton described it (*Observer*, 26 April 1992), 'causes water buffaloes to riot'. Credit for casting Renée Asherson as Charmian belongs to Clayton's long-time casting director, Irene Lamb. Best remembered for her French princess who is so delightfully wooed by Laurence Olivier's Henry V in his classic 1944 film, Asherson had rarely registered on screen since, but her performance here is nothing short of exquisite, skilfully managing to suggest at once a butterfly mind unable to rest on anything long and at the same time a rock-like moral integrity behind the airy manner. When Mrs Pettigrew brusquely interrupts Charmian's first meeting with Inspector Mortimer and says coquettishly, 'I don't think I've met a policeman before', Charmian's annoyance is apparent in her crisp rejoinder: 'You do surprise me.' Asherson delivers the line superbly. (It is a nice structural point too, for Mrs Pettigrew will encounter another policeman later in the film when waiting for Godfrey outside his solicitor's office and, to her chagrin, will be moved on, the policeman clearly suspecting she is soliciting in another sense.)[5]

Elsewhere Thora Hird as Taylor gives her definitive screen

performance of kindly old age, whilst Zoë Wanamaker's Olive displays an alternative sort of kindness from a younger more broad-minded generation, whilst also suggesting, as Philip Strick has noted, something of the compliance of the departed Lisa Brooke who so entranced Godfrey and Guy Leet.[6] (We never see Lisa but her presence is strongly felt in the film: she is another of Clayton's palpable ghosts.) Maurice Denham as Leet and Cyril Cusack as Olive's grandfather, Percy, have a fine time in roles one feels a more conventional film might have reversed: the unexpected casting adds piquancy here just as the feud between these grumpy old men is, one suspects, a displaced form of affection – the antagonism adds flavour and vitality to their lives. As Inspector Mortimer, John Wood gives a performance that seems absolutely perfectly for period (the late 1950s): with his brylcreemed hair and a sharp mind hiding behind a scrupulously polite exterior, he could be a contemporary of such radio heroes as PC 49 and Paul Temple, where crime detection seemed to walk alongside old-world courtesy and consideration. One other leading performance must be singled out: Stephanie Cole's as Lettie Colston. Clayton has a habit of photographing her from a slightly low angle so that she always seems to be leading with her chin: the imperious intimidating posture is capped by the wonderful costuming touch of her hats, which in themselves look outsize and aggressive. Like Maggie Smith as Mrs Pettigrew, Stephanie Cole plays the role unsentimentally and with absolute truth to a character who is part monster; yet, like Smith, she still wrings comedy from the character's stupefying moral blindness and also great poignancy from her mortal panic.

Amongst a fine supporting cast, mention should be made of Margery Withers as Granny Barnacle, Taylor's friend in the next hospital bed, who adds delicious touches of comedy with her relentless cheeriness and mangled use of language that so exasperates Lettie but endears her to Mortimer. When Mortimer enquires during one visit why she is singing 'I do like to be beside the seaside', Granny Barnacle explains that she is being moved to one of those 'convoluted' homes. It is an upset Taylor who has to explain to him in a whisper that she is actually being moved to a convalescent home for patients for whom there is no hope. A mood of jollity is thus counterpointed by intimations of separation and death; and there is a gentle coda as Granny Barnacle brings the celebratory song to an unexpectedly contemplative close as if, contrary to what Taylor says, she does realise what is happening to her.

Performances of this quality need a context to do them justice, and it is provided here by a narrative structure that is both teasingly complex and absolutely coherent. While retaining much of Spark's original dialogue, the writers have tightened the narrative structure, adjusting the order of events to give greater logic and momentum to the plot. The Alec Warner character, who always seemed a rather awkward device in the novel, has been eliminated, his investigative role taken over exclusively by Mortimer; Mrs Pettigrew has been made a little more explicitly villainous in the film, which effectively gingers up the narrative and adds suspense; and, as mentioned earlier, the ending has been changed, so that it is less dark than the novel but structurally neater and more satisfyingly rounded. It is an ending more characteristic perhaps of someone nearer the age of the characters than Muriel Spark was at the time of writing the novel, just as the octogenarian John Huston's rendering of *The Dead* seemed to give the story written by a 30-year-old James Joyce an extra gravity and grace. By the time of making *Memento Mori* Clayton had turned 70. At that age, he had become, as one of the characters says, 'one of us'.

Given that *Memento Mori* is mainly an interior drama with quite a large cast of characters, the writers did a skilful job in giving variety to the sequence of scenes whilst also making clear the complicated cross-currents of the relationships. Although they had worked extensively on the scripts of all previous Clayton films, this is the first film on which Clayton and his script editor Jeanie Sims were actually credited and it is a script that has a lifetime of professional experience in it – clear, compact, compelling. It has a distinctive character, too. In a tribute to Clayton for the Washington retrospective of his work in 1995, John Mortimer wrote that Clayton 'taught me, more than anyone, about how to write for the screen ... he taught me how to start each scene with some ironical comment on, or with a surprising contrast to, the one that went before'.[7] The implication is that a screenwriting strategy such as that will give variety (by setting a different tone from what has gone before) but also lend cohesion (by contrasting or connecting with the previous scene). This approach is evident in *Memento Mori*, notably in a naughty transition from a scene when Godfrey is rumbling appreciatively at a glimpse of Olive's stocking-tops: a voice says, 'If you could just hold it up a bit more', which momentarily seems a declaration of Godfrey's unspoken desire but is actually introducing the following scene, when Charmian is being asked to hold up a copy of her book so that it can be photographed by the admiring press.

Similarly deft shifts of tone and tension are plotted across entire scenes. One example is the scene late in the film when Mrs Pettigrew and Godfrey's son, Eric, are awaiting Godfrey's return from visiting Charmian at the nursing home in order to intensify the blackmailing pressure. It is clear that Mrs Pettigrew resents Eric's interference in her plan and is about to start moving in on him when Godfrey enters with unexpected good humour (he has been reassured by Charmian's knowledge and forgiveness of his previous infidelity). He promptly upstages both by cheerily ordering Eric from the house ('or I'll call the police') and giving Mrs Pettigrew a day's notice to quit. Still chuckling as he hears the doorbell and moves to open the door, Godfrey is startled by the presence of the police, who seem to have anticipated with supernatural speed his desire to eject Eric (they have, we learn afterwards, come with bad news about Lettie's violent death). The changes of mood, of character dynamics, of power relationships in this scene (reflected in camerawork and composition within the frame) are plotted with a sure dexterity. In particular, Michael Hordern – in the new confidence with which he moves, in the relish with which he delivers his devastating decisions to Eric and Mrs Pettigrew between savouring mouthfuls of his favourite whisky – gives a display of consummate comic timing: every gesture, every line is made to count.

Performances of this calibre can give the mistaken impression that all a director has to do is to wheel the actors on and let them loose. Perhaps more than in any other of his films, Clayton's direction here seems like the art that conceals art. Nevertheless, a credit scene where the camera slowly tracks towards a clock, framed photographs and a stopped pendulum, followed by a dissolve to an insistently ringing telephone, encapsulates at the outset the themes of time, age and death. One remembers from *The Pumpkin Eater* and *The Lonely Passion of Judith Hearne* how well Clayton photographs homes and hospitals: in the scenes with Taylor, one can almost smell the antiseptic, and the shots of regimented rows of NHS pensioners make a cumulatively powerful contrast between their stoical suffering and the floundering fear of their upper-class visitor Lettie. In her review for the *Independent on Sunday* (26 April 1992), Allison Pearson drew attention to one particular scene in the hospital where Lettie, on her way to see Taylor, is bundled out of the way by hospital staff rushing to save a patient. Lettie still grumbles about such rude behaviour even when told of the circumstances, but the camera at this point is resting on Taylor, half attending to her visitor but really more interested in the bed opposite. 'In one scene', writes Pearson, 'Taylor looked across the ward through a screen where she saw a nurse placing a rose on the bed of a patient who had just died. The shot was not remarkable in itself but for what it told us about Taylor's compassion, her *noticing*. We see why she saw it.' It is a fine example of what Pearson rightly calls the 'infinite suggestiveness' of Clayton's direction.

Compassion, comedy and a touch of Agatha Christie: Clayton has to draw out suspense in the telling also. Every time Mrs Pettigrew enters Charmian's territory, the camera shifts subtly to reflect an alteration in the balance of power. This is particularly noticeable in the scene when she interrupts Charmian's first interview with Inspector Mortimer, and the sinuous camera movement as she enters seems to leave Charmian upstaged and somewhat stranded in the frame. A high level of comic tension is reached in a power game played between the two under Godfrey's nose, a scene which deploys a Hitchcockian counterpoint between sound and image. A small argument develops between Mrs Pettigrew and Charmian about whether the latter has remembered to take her pills that morning. Verbally the scene is about memory, but visually it is a struggle of wills, rendered in a little finger ballet as Clayton's camera closes in on hands and pills, Pettigrew pushing the pills nearer, Charmian pushing them away; each move resembles a manoeuvre in a deadly game of chess. Disdaining the wide screen, Hitchcock used to say that he could not get the detail he wanted, the close-up of a fingernail. Clayton generates suspense in this sequence precisely through the close-up of a fingernail, particularly of the intimidatingly blood-red, painted fingernails of Mrs Pettigrew who, at one stage, does a little finger dance around the pills, like a spidery predator tantalising its victim before moving in for the kill.

The revelation that the mystery telephone caller is Death itself is handled more persuasively in the film than in the novel, partly by being saved until nearer the end, which sustains the suspense. If this narrative twist is no great surprise, the concept itself is interesting. In his book on the composer Gustav Mahler published in 1937, conductor Bruno Walter would describe the different movements of Mahler's Ninth Symphony as representing the different faces of Death, from Death as fearful foe at the outset to Death, in the prayer-like final adagio, as consoling friend. Similarly, in *Memento Mori*, Death comes in a different guise according to whoever faces it; everyone hears the voice differently and responds differently. Charmian is polite, Taylor is in no hurry to come to the phone, Percy shouts imprecations, and the literary Leet quotes Robert Frost ('But I have promises to keep/And miles to go before I sleep') to suggest he is not quite ready to conclude his journey. Lettie, meanwhile, has to meet a violent end as a reflection of her fear and unpreparedness: Death has, as it were, to take her by force.

In his *Sight and Sound* review, Philip Strick referred to the established Clayton theme, from *The Innocents* to *The Lonely Passion of Judith Hearne*, as a 'baleful collusion between women on the verge of nervous breakdown and children on the verge of excessive enlightenment'. He called his films 'dark carnivals' – which, if agreed, would give particular centrality to *Something Wicked This Way Comes* – and described *Memento Mori* as 'another reflection of a bright eye overtaken by autumn, another outcry on behalf of lives that have achieved too little and must now exhaust their strength in the losing battle against decay'.[8] Although there is obviously more to Clayton than this, Strick's concise cluster of characteristic themes usefully shows that *Memento Mori* has more in common with his previous work than might first seem to be the case. There seems in particular a continuity of theme from *The Lonely Passion of Judith Hearne*: a similar tenderness towards disappointed lives; an unblinking sensitivity to the ravages of age on all aspects of human faculties; and a certain waspish observation of the way crotchety adults regress and begin to ape the behaviour of spiteful children. As in *Judith Hearne*, there is a lot of tale-telling, sneaking and eavesdropping. Eric spies on his father, and at one stage Mrs Pettigrew is leaning so hard on a door to overhear a private conversation between Charmian and Godfrey that she almost falls headfirst into the room when the door is unexpectedly opened from the other side.

Yet Strick's phrase about 'lives that have achieved too little and must now exhaust their strength in the losing battle against decay' seems closer to the tone of the novel than of the film. Clayton's *Memento Mori* has its fair share of the darker human motives – greed, murder, snobbery, psychological cruelty – but pulsing through more strongly are the positive emotions: Taylor's devotion to Charmian, Olive's protectiveness towards her grandfather and indulgence of Godfrey, Godfrey's abiding, if unenlightened, love for his wife. Even Lettie has a soft spot for her nephew, Eric; and the feud between Guy Leet and Percy Mannering spices up rather than sours their relationship. More than a 'losing battle against decay', I find in the film a moving assertion of loyalty, affection and continuity. If the fact of death is faced, then life can be savoured all the more. The final scene catches this admirably. So too does the wonderful comic set piece of Mortimer's tea party, an Agatha Christie-type round-up of all the main characters (and suspects) to review the situation, but which collapses in disarray through the sheer weight of geriatric foible – one guest cannot stay awake, another cannot hear, someone keeps upsetting the crockery, and one of them has turned up at the wrong event anyway. Surveying in somewhat shell-shocked manner his departing guests, Mortimer comments to his wife (a delightful performance by Anna Cropper) that they have 'a sort of stubborn gallantry, with echoes of a romantic and glamorous past'. One feels it is Clayton's own tribute to people of his generation and particularly to his cast, who carry so much history of British cinema on their shoulders. When you think the credits are over, Clayton caps his tale with a cheeky final shot (of the ringing of a modern telephone) to suggest the continuing relevance of his theme. By saying to his audience 'remember you must die', Clayton has made his most life-affirming film.

There is nevertheless a postscript. *Memento Mori* was to prove the final film score of Georges Delerue, who died in 1992. As always, the score seemed to catch the spirit of the film with exactness: a saucy tango to accompany Olive's displays before Godfrey; a delicate piano theme for Charmian that seems to epitomise the character's fragility and grace. A pupil and protégé of Georges Auric, Delerue had come to Clayton's attention with his score for François Truffaut's *Jules et Jim* (1961). Although neither could speak the other's language, they got on instantly. Clayton would play music in the places where he felt the film would need it and show the film to Delerue with those, as an indication of the mood he was after. (For *Judith Hearne*, for example, he put on pieces from *Our Mother's House* and *The Pumpkin Eater* as a guide to intention and style.) What developed across five films on which they collaborated (I am including the rejected score for *Something Wicked This Way Comes*) was one of the most important, underrated and creatively productive director–composer partnerships in the history of the cinema.

In May 1988 Clayton was interviewed about Delerue by the Belgian film magazine *Soundtrack*; in their edition of 21 September 1992, after Delerue's death, they reprinted Clayton's comments. His conclusion can stand as a fitting tribute to a superb composer and collaborator: 'I just hope I never have to make a film without Georges to do the music because not only is he a beautiful musician, he is also a beautiful man. He understands everything that I think and he composes music not only to my taste but to my heart.'

Notes

1   All subsequent quotations from the novel are taken from this edition. The novel was first published, by Macmillan, in 1959.

2   Louis Marks, *The Stage and Television Today*, 2 April 1992, p. 20.

3   *What's On*, 1 April 1992, p. 47.

4   *Memento Mori*, p. 55.

5   The visual pun on 'soliciting' in this scene recalls the jokey pun, also involving Maggie Smith, in *The Pumpkin Eater*, where Philpot muses about her frigidity before actually sitting on the fridge.

6   Philip Strick, *Sight and Sound*, June 1992, p. 56.

7   Quoted in the programme that accompanied the Clayton retrospective at the National Gallery of Art, Washington DC, 9–23 September 1995.

8   Strick, *Sight and Sound*, p. 55.

10

Unfinished business: the unrealised projects of Jack Clayton

> When you see the end of things coming close and staring at you, it's not what you've done that you regret but what you didn't do. (Charles Halloway, *Something Wicked This Way Comes*)

> I cannot make a film and will not make a film unless I know that I believe in it and all its ingredients. (Jack Clayton, letter to Peter Douglas, 1 April 1977)

Why did Clayton make so few films? It was a question he was often asked and which caused him some disquiet. 'I hate myself for not having produced more', he told Philip Bergson;[1] and to Michael Church he observed: 'I *do* wonder why I've made so few.'[2] The nine-year gap between *Gatsby* and *Something Wicked* was particularly remarked on, but the comment in Ephraim Katz's esteemed *Film Encyclopedia* – 'Nearly a decade had gone by before he could land another assignment'[3] – is highly misleading: it suggests a director who, for that period, was neglected and out of fashion. This was not the case. In fact, when *Something Wicked This Way Comes* opened to generally favourable reviews from the London critics, who welcomed him back to the screen after an absence of nine years, Clayton wrote courteous 'thankyou' letters (to, for example, David Castell of the *Sunday Telegraph*, Philip French of the *Observer* and Nigel Andrews of the *Financial Times*) whilst also pointing out that he had not actually been idle during this period but had worked extensively on no fewer than seven different projects which for various reasons had fallen through.

Nevertheless, the fact remains that, as the critic Jerry Roberts stated: 'Jack Clayton may have the smallest filmography in English language movie history for a director of his stature. Even artists in the director's pantheon such as Stanley Kubrick and David Lean, who famously take the similar three to six years between pictures that Clayton takes, have directed more movies.'[4]

The reasons, then, for Clayton's meagre output need some disentangling. One was his obsessional commitment to the job in hand. He was not a director who could keep several projects juggling in the air. His work on *The Great Gatsby*, from the inception of the project to his completion of the supervision of the European dubbed versions, took three years. Also he was not a director who took on films simply as an assignment: he never made a film he did not want to make. This inevitably meant turning down a lot of projects. As we have seen, he turned down *Sons and Lovers*, *Saturday Night and Sunday Morning* and *The L-Shaped Room* because they were too similar in theme and milieu to *Room at the Top*.[5] 'If your output is as small as mine', he told the critic on *The Times* (22 September 1983), 'it's always important to try and do something different.' Despite his love of Horace McCoy's novel, he turned down the opportunity to direct *They Shoot Horses, Don't They?*, because he felt he could not take over a colleague's preparation but would wish to prepare the project from scratch, which the studio, with the film already cast and ready to go, was not prepared to allow.[6] Also there were properties that he desperately wanted to do but had to wait years for the rights to fall into his hands. He had expressed an interest in filming *Judith Hearne* as far back as 1961; he finally filmed it in 1987. *Memento Mori* had appealed to him as a possible film project when it had first been published in 1959; it did not come to fruition until over three decades later.

Finally, of course, there were the cancellations. I have suggested elsewhere that the Catch-22 of working in the film industry is the danger of monotony if you become pigeonholed and the prospect of unemployment if you refuse to be. You must be individual enough to be distinctive but not so unique as to be forbidding. This applies equally to directors and stars. The history of the cinema is littered with the unusual – and unused – footages of great creative personalities (Stroheim, Flaherty, Welles, etc.) whose ability seemed too prodigious for the industry. If some cineastes might hesitate to put Clayton in such company, few would dispute one fact: he did not make as many films as his talent warranted. Some of this can be put down to fastidiousness, but much of the responsibility can be attributed to the industry itself. It is fascinating but also depressing to consider how different Clayton's career profile might have looked if even some of his projects that were in an advanced state of pre-production had made it to the screen. Some had magnificent potential and their cancellation is on a par with Orson Welles's failed projects as an example of the cinema's capacity to waste good material. I am thinking particularly of those three projects in the 1970s – *Casualties of War*, *Massacre at Fall Creek*, *Silence* – which offered the promise of great cinema and whose cancellation was a devastating blow to Clayton and, I think, undoubtedly and understandably, contributed to his serious illness at the end of the decade that could almost have ended his career. These will be discussed later (pp. 217–22).

The following account gives brief details of some of the projects on which Clayton was involved but which for various reasons either never materialised on screen or were made by someone else. It reveals a lot about Clayton and perhaps even more about the industry in which he worked throughout his adult life.

A Child is Waiting (1961)

Clayton was approached by writer Abby Mann and producer Stanley Kramer as a possible director for this subject (which dealt with the care of mentally damaged children in a special school). He interviewed Ingrid Bergman about the possibility of playing the main role, though feeling afterwards that she was not really drawn to the subject; he was also considering Kim Novak. He withdrew from the project when Kramer insisted on a January 1962 starting date for filming. Clayton believed this did not allow sufficient time to make the required improvements to the script, which he felt needed a less conventional approach, a sharper focus and to be less verbose. 'I am being this outspoken', he wrote to Mann in a letter of 13 October 1961, 'because I have lost none of the original love I had for the subject nor my enthusiasm to make the film.' Clayton admired Mann's writing – Mann had won an Oscar for his screenplay for Kramer's *Judgement at Nuremberg* (1961) – but, in addition to reservations about the script, he felt the project needed careful planning in terms of casting and atmosphere and also time for proper research of the background. Kramer's schedule did not allow for this. 'I could not embark upon a subject of this specialised kind', Clayton wrote, 'without personally spending some time absorbing the real background of it in homes and hospitals'. In a courteous cable in reply, Mann informed Clayton that the project was going ahead with Burt Lancaster, Judy Garland and Frank Sinatra (who seems to have dropped out at a later stage) and with another director, who turned out to be John Cassavetes. The film was not a success, either critically, commercially or artistically.[7] One can only speculate how a film of that subject by Clayton, who was to reveal himself as a master director of the disturbed world of childhood, might have turned out.

Among the other scripts brought to Clayton's attention at this time, which he decided not to direct, were *The Lion* (made by Jack Cardiff in 1962) and *To Sir With Love* (filmed by James Clavell in 1967).

The Looking-Glass War (1965–6)

Discussions had begun with Columbia for this as a possible project for Clayton after *The Pumpkin Eater* in December 1964. A first draft screenplay by the work's author, John Le Carré, was delivered, reworked and then resubmitted in August 1965. Clayton felt that the screenplay was still not entirely ready, and that another writer would be needed to make it more effective. He checked that Columbia were still interested in the project and, in October 1965, Columbia reaffirmed their intention to go ahead. At this point Clayton brought in Mordecai Richler for a rewrite and the revised screenplay, with which Clayton was satisfied, was completed in February 1966. (A copy in Clayton's file of a letter to

Nicolas Roeg, dated 30 March 1965, in which he enclosed a copy of the book, suggests Roeg was in Clayton's mind as a possible cameraman for the project.) However, Columbia wanted changes made to the Richler script which Clayton felt were unnecessary, so he withdrew. In a letter to John Le Carré (28 June 1966), Clayton explained what he thought were the reasons for Columbia's cancellation: 'They thought the subject was not exciting enough and had hoped for more of an adventure story.' He also thought Columbia might have been short of money after the cost of *Casino Royale*, and he added drily: 'There is the possibility that they had never read the book in the first place and were both surprised and shocked that it wasn't a kind of James Bond.' In fact, Columbia did eventually go ahead with the project, possibly encouraged by the success of the film version of Le Carré's *The Spy Who Came in from the Cold* (1965), but the film, released in 1969 and written and directed by Frank R. Pierson, flopped. The cast was headed by Christopher Jones, Pia Degermark (from *Elvira Madigan*, (1967)), Anthony Hopkins and Ralph Richardson.

Sweet Autumn (1966)

An original screenplay by Edna O'Brien. Clayton worked on it with the author between July and November 1966, but the film was never made.

The Walking Stick (1968)

Based on the novel by Winston Graham. Clayton initially expressed interest but the serious illness and subsequent death of his mother intervened. The film was made by Eric Till in 1970, starring David Hemmings and Samantha Eggar.

Mary, Queen of Scots (1968)

Clayton was tentatively approached by the legendary agent Peggy (Margaret) Ramsay about the possibility of doing this, with a screenplay by John Arden. But, Ramsay confided, Arden had already been approached by what she called 'the Mackendrick gang' – i.e. Alexander Mackendrick, who was also interested in the project – and 'he [Arden] thinks she is a lady that has been written about far too much'.[8] The film was made in 1971, directed by Charles Jarrott, starring Vanessa Redgrave and scripted by John Hale.

Zaharoff Pedlar of Death (1968)

Clayton was interested in making a film of the life and death of Sir Basil Zaharoff (1851–1936), possibly the richest man in the world in his time and a notorious munitions dealer. It was based on a highly acclaimed biography by Donald McCormick, published in 1965, and was to be produced by Universal Pictures. A publicity release set out the theme in lurid detail:

> In choosing the life story of Sir Basil Zaharoff for his next film subject, Producer-director Jack Clayton has set himself an unenviable task. Mystery-man Zaharoff's career, spanning over three-quarters of a century from the 1850s to the 1930s, ranged from brothel-touting on the Constantinople docks through the fields of munitions, intrigue and high espionage and took him into the Palaces, Parliaments and back alleyways of more than half the world. He peddled his wares and his wiles across the face of four Continents, and his bills were paid in blood by 'ignorant armies' clashing on battlefields as far apart as Paraguay, South Africa and Mons. Yet at the same time, he was involved in a love affair so poignant as to rival the great romances of history.
>
> Many of those who sought to thwart this man's fantastic ambition met with untimely ends – as did also those who probed too closely into his affairs. For as Zaharoff's power and influence grew, so did his passion for secrecy approach mania. All traces of his youth and origins, all personal papers and diaries, all possible witnesses, have been obliterated either by time or more sinister agents. Nor has the trail of violence ceased with his death. His grave was mysteriously broken into – for reasons and by persons still undiscovered. And two years later, the body of a young reporter who became too inquisitive, despite warnings of danger, was found floating in the Seine.
>
> The Zaharoff story is a new departure for Jack Clayton, whose

previous films – such as 'Room at the Top', 'The Innocents', 'The Pumpkin Eater' and 'Our Mother's House' – have had a uniquely English flavour. It will be made in association with Universal Pictures. Who, presumably, will be taking out some rather special insurance.

Clayton did an immense amount of research but the project was never given the go-ahead. He was still enquiring about the rights in 1978. In November 1990 he put forward a proposal for a feature film, *Zed Zed: The Extraordinary Life of Sir Basil Zaharoff*, with Roy Baird, David Conroy, Ben Kingsley and Hugh Whitemore. But it was never progressed.

The Tenant (1969 –75)

Based on a novel by Roland Topor, *The Tenant* was originally a Universal Pictures project, to be scripted by Edward Albee and directed by Clayton. It fell through when the relationship between Albee and Universal turned sour. In 1971 Paramount acquired it from Universal on Clayton's advice and a first rough-draft screenplay was completed by Christopher Hampton while Clayton was busy preparing *Gatsby*. By the time *Gatsby* was completed for delivery in March 1974, Clayton had learned from Robert Evans that Roman Polanski was interested in the project and wanted to play the leading role. It was then that things got complicated. After the exertions of shooting *Gatsby*, Clayton needed time to recover; moreover, he was heavily involved in the supervision of European dubbed versions of the film. But at no time, he claimed, was he specifically asked whether he was still interested, and at no time did he say 'no': indeed, he thought that this might be an ideal project for the first of his three-pictures deal with Paramount (which never materialised), as it seemed relatively inexpensive. Unfortunately the then head of Paramount, Barry Diller, thought Clayton had lost interest and began negotiations with Polanski. In a telephone conversation with Diller (15 September 1975), Clayton expressed his dismay that a project 'originally bought by Paramount for me ... was just transferred to someone else'. The project went to Polanski, who played the leading role alongside Isabelle

Adjani, Melvyn Douglas and Shelley Winters. Released in 1976, it was a quirky, claustrophobic film entirely characteristic of its director.

Unhappy that a project he had initiated with Paramount had been given to another director, Clayton had further arguments with the company over a Robert Bolt screenplay, *Guerany*, which he was also developing at this time.[9] The conflict culminated with Paramount's cancellation of *Something Wicked This Way Comes* in 1976 and it was at this point that an enraged Clayton threw a chair through Diller's window.

If You Could See Me Now (1977)

A personal project, in which Clayton wrote and developed a script based on the novel by Peter Straub, author of *Julia* (which had been filmed as *Full Circle* (1977)) and subsequently *Ghost Story*. He worked on a rough draft script with Jeanie Sims but eventually decided he did not want to direct it: 'having worked on the screenplay for roughly two years, I feel as though I had already made it ... it's basically a very good ghost-cum-murder story'.[10]

The Main (1979)

Based on the Trevanian novel, and to be made for David Merrick and scripted by Michael Cristofer, who had scripted *Silence* (see page 220). Financing had not been finalised when the offer of *Revelations* came from Paramount, so the project was postponed.

Revelations (1980–2)

Based on the novel by Phyllis Naylor. A first-draft screenplay by Waldo Salt was completed by December 1980, and after consultations and revisions suggested by Clayton, a second-draft screenplay by Salt and Lee Hutson was submitted in April 1981. It was originally to be made by Paramount but was postponed due to the writers' strike and the projected directors' strike. Further delay was caused by problems with the special effects on *Something*

Wicked. Clayton's choice for the leading role, Sally Field, backed out of the project in November 1982. Clayton was then interested in Sissy Spacek, who felt the role might be too close to the one she had recently played in *Raggedy Man* (1981), though as Jack said, by the time the film came out, no one would remember that. He had originally hoped to cast Vidal Peterson (from *Something Wicked*) in the role of the young boy but, as the delays dragged on, Peterson became too old for the role. The film was never made.

Hand-Me Downs (1981)

Clayton worked on a script adapted from the novel by Rhea Kohan. The film was never made.

The Bourne Identity (1983)

This was to have followed *Something Wicked*, a thriller based on the bestselling novel by Robert Ludlum. Clayton was not en-amoured of the novel, but may have been intrigued by the central situation of a hero who wakes up to find his memory completely gone – something that would have some personal resonance for Clayton after his stroke. He had met Burt Reynolds whilst dis-cussing *Revelations* with Reynolds's partner Sally Field, and felt he was a good actor whose potential had rarely been realised in the films he had chosen. Jeffrey Alan Fiskin delivered a screenplay in July 1983. But the production was postponed indefinitely due to location problems and Reynolds's other commitments.

We Have Always Lived in the Castle (1984)

Based on the novel by Shirley Jackson. A script development screenplay was prepared by Paul Thain between March and June 1984. It was to be called *Moon Shadows* and produced by Vista Films Inc., though in a letter to Herb Jaffe (27 June 1984), Clayton mentioned that one of the co-producers, Gabe Katzka, had indicated his dislike of anything with the word 'moon' in the title, so Clayton proposed some alternatives: *Love Patterns*, *A Silver Castle*,

A Private Place, A Sense of Guilt. The titles made no difference: the film was not made. Clayton's interest in the project remained, however, and another first-draft screenplay, this time by Donna Dewey, was prepared and submitted to him in September 1994.

One Last Glimpse (1985)

Screenplay by Evan Jones based on the novel by James Aldridge about the friendship between Ernest Hemingway and Scott and Zelda Fitzgerald. This was discussed as a possible project for Clayton with HandMade Films in June 1985. It is interesting that Clayton wished to return to this milieu even after the divided critical response to *Gatsby*. The film was not made.

The Enchantment (1985)

A short story by Jack Clayton (under the pseudonym of Alvarez Calderon) about the growing friendship between an embittered old man and a young boy. It was originally thought of as possible material for a short television film, but Jeanie Sims thought it had enough substance for a feature. A film treatment was developed by Paul Thain. (The short story is reproduced in the Appendices).

Hannah (1986)

Adapted by George MacDonald Fraser from the novel by Paul-Loup Sulitzer. Clayton felt it an interesting but difficult project for adaptation because of the length of the novel and the shortage of dramatically exciting incidents to progress the storyline. 'Unfortunately,' wrote Clayton in a memo in April 1986, 'despite all his endeavours George MacDonald Fraser, as we are all agreed, has not succeeded in overcoming these problems'.

The Last Enemy (1986–7)

Screenplay by Tony Stratton Smith, based on the book by Richard Hillary. It was to be made by Charisma Films Ltd, adapted by

Jeanie Sims and produced by Roy Baird and Tony Stratton Smith. It never happened.

Cold Spring Harbour (1988)

Based on a novel by Richard Yates. On submission of a first-draft screenplay in January 1989 the title was changed to *Tides of Summer*; then to *Bicycle Summer* when a screenplay by Wilham Harrison was submitted in June 1990; finally to *The Last Dance of Summer* when Harrison submitted a second draft of the screenplay in March 1994. The material had been brought to Clayton's attention by Donna Dewey in 1988 and obviously had a strong appeal.

The Stone Virgin (1988)

Screenplay by David Rudkin based on the novel by Barry Unsworth. Clayton's rough notes on a first reading are dated 12 May 1988. 'The whole thing should be like a knitting pattern,' Clayton wrote. 'Right now it's a tangled mess of wool.'

Augustus (1989)

Bio-pic of Augustus John from a screenplay by Robert Bolt. A memo from Jeanie Sims (5 June 1989) to Clayton identified huge potential in the material and thought it had a magnificent ending but felt that in its present form the construction was too chronological and sprawling. Also it was felt that the screenplay did not catch John's charisma: he was a male chauvinist pig, but why did women show him such devotion? In her comments, Jeanie Sims draws an interesting comparison between the character of Augustus John and that of John Huston, whom Sims and Clayton knew very well: 'a man of tremendous charm especially when it suited him to use it' and also 'quite ruthless' in relationships, who 'once having conquered invariably lost interest'. The fate of the screenplay is discussed in Adrian Turner's excellent biography of Bolt.[11]

Poe (The Dark Angel) **(1988–92)**

Original screenplay by Robert Blees. Katherine Ann Jones was invited to work on the script for Peer Oppenheimer Productions Inc. in July 1992 and delivered her screenplay in September of that year. It was not progressed.

The Cherry Orchard **(1990)**

Screenplay by Michael Luke and Monja Danischewsky based on the Chekhov play. There are detailed script notes about the screenplay by Jeanie Sims dated 25 October 1990. Originally submitted to Clayton in January 1989.

Revolutionary Road **(1992–4)**

Based on the novel by Richard Yates. Patrick O'Neal owned the rights and had written a screenplay. Donna Dewey submitted an 'unauthorised adaptation' of the Richard Yates and the Patrick O'Neal screenplay in April 1992, revised September 1993 and then again in May 1994. Not progressed.

Hay Fever **(1994)**

Screenplay by Robert McKee and Charles Crichton. A note from Fox (16 May 1994) seemed to confirm that Clayton was due to direct this.

If there is one phase in Clayton's career that was more difficult than any other it was the 1970s, particularly that traumatic period between the controversial reception of *Gatsby* and his stroke (Mordecai Richler was to suggest that there was a connection between them). During these years, Clayton tried and failed (or rather, so very nearly succeeded) in his attempt to bring to the screen three projects which, because of their themes, he felt passionately about.

Casualties of War (1970)

This was based on a true story by Daniel Lang that was published in the *New Yorker* on 18 October 1969.[12] The subject was owned by David Susskind and was going to be filmed by Warners. The topic was explosive: the court martial of four American soldiers in Vietnam who were accused of kidnapping, raping and then murdering a young Vietnamese woman. Charges had been brought at the instigation of one of the soldiers, who had refused to take part in the rape and had reported the incident to his senior officers. Clayton undertook a number of location-scouting missions between December 1969 and July 1970; and after an initial first-draft screenplay by Peter Hamill had been rejected, several suggestions were made to Clayton about possible replacements (including Reginald Rose, Lewis Carlino, William Goldman, Robert Anderson, John Milius, J. P. Miller and Paddy Chayefsky). A young screenwriter, David Giler, submitted a first-draft screenplay in August 1970 that was deemed to be magnificent. But the project never went ahead. It seems that the Pentagon stepped in and put a halt to it, clearly feeling that this kind of film about an already unpopular war might have a demoralising effect on morale and public opinion. It was not until the end of the 1970s with *The Deer Hunter* (1978) and *Apocalypse Now* (1979) that Hollywood felt able to deal in any serious or direct way with the subject of Vietnam. And it was not until the end of the following decade that *Casualties of War* (1989) was eventually made, directed by Brian De Palma from a screenplay by David Grabe, with Michael J. Fox giving his (as yet) finest screen performance as the conscience-stricken soldier.

Giler's screenplay grips from first to last. It begins as a tight, disturbing thriller and then moves into a suspenseful courtroom drama in which the themes of racism, justice and the brutalities of war are powerfully dramatised. The ending is particularly chilling. As the rapists are shown emerging from their terms of detention with captions that describe their being granted parole, we see the informer, Ericsson – in a virtuoso display of cross-cutting – arming himself in anticipation of the men coming for revenge. Boarding a bus, Ericsson finds himself sitting opposite a young Asian woman and he has a sudden nightmare vision of the young woman, Mao, whom the group had so brutally violated and killed. De Palma's 1989 film is one of his best, but one can only imagine the impact this film might have had if made, as planned, in 1970 or 1971. At that time, Hollywood's contribution to the Vietnam debate was about on the level of *The Green Berets* (1968).

Massacre at Fall Creek (1975)

This project was based on Jessamyn West's novel about the brutal murder of innocent, peaceful Indians, including women and children, by five white men and the trial that followed – the first occasion in history when white men were put on trial for murdering Indians. It was based on events that had taken place in 1824 and the narrative, to quote the publicity for the novel, 'centres on the killings, the trial of the murderers and the strangely moving aftermath'. Clayton worked on the development of the script with Larry McMurtry, who turned in a first-draft screenplay in January 1976. By this time there had been a detailed cost breakdown for the project, and Clayton had made copious notes about matters such as characterisation, costume, screenplay construction, and the basic intention of the movie. It was to be filmed by United Artists and David Merrick (for whom Clayton had made *Gatsby*). Somewhat lukewarm responses to the screenplay by two United Artists' readers, Marcia Nasatir and Mike Medavoy, drew a caustic response from Clayton who, in a letter to United Artists on 25 February 1976, complained about being given too little notice of their criticisms prior to a production conference, and accused them of lack of imagination, not reading the original novel, and not giving sufficient credit to the screenplay's many touches of improvement to the original in terms of structure and suspense. To the readers' suggestion that the massacre should be shown, Clayton retorts sardonically: 'If your Company ultimately decides that we should see the massacre, may I suggest that you engage Sam Peckinpah?'

One of the problems with the material was that there was no obvious hero: only (as in so many Clayton films) a lot of ordinary people some of whom behave heroically. It was an ensemble piece, running to over two hours in McMurtry's original draft. It foundered owing to United Artists' insistence on having five 'superstars' in the main roles, which could have wrecked the idea of an ensemble piece, and because United Artists and David Merrick fell out. It is a wordy screenplay, but as well as being full of tension, compassion, humour and horror, it has great wisdom and a tremendous, heart-wrenching ending. Clayton probably saw in it something of the qualities he had identified in *Casualties of War*: a work that shows the cruelty but also the complexity of prejudice and racism and where a court has to grapple with the issues of right and wrong, justice and pragmatism. Clayton had long wanted to do a Western (in interviews he had mentioned his love of the genre and his deep admiration for John Ford's *Stagecoach* (1939)). This film would have fitted into the revisionist mode of 1970s Westerns such as Arthur Penn's *Little Big Man* (1970), Robert Altman's *McCabe and Mrs Miller* (1971) and Robert Aldrich's *Ulzana's Raid* (1972). The failure of the project wounded Clayton deeply; worse was to come.

Silence (1977)

Based on the James Kennaway novel posthumously published in 1972, *Silence* was developed as a film project by Clayton working with screenwriter Michael Cristofer, who delivered a detailed draft of the screenplay in August 1977.[13] The story is about racial tension again, inflamed by an incident in which white men have run over a black youth in a slum area of Chicago. One of them, a doctor not directly involved in the incident but who finds himself being chased by black men out for vengeance, has to hide in a derelict block of flats. He stumbles into the room of 'Silence', a black woman who (for reasons we only learn about later) cannot or will not talk. An initially edgy relationship builds into one of trust and concern and will lead to a compelling finale. The film was to have been produced by Twentieth Century Fox and David Niven Jr, and Clayton was in the process of checking locations and casting (Jack Lemmon was said to have expressed interest in the main male role). About a fortnight before production was due to start, Fox suddenly cancelled the project. No reason was given at the time, but in Clayton's notes there is a comment that 'very soon afterwards Jay Kanter and Gareth Wigan, who had actually made the deal with David Niven Jr, left Fox and formed their own company'. By way of compensation Fox asked Clayton if he were interested in directing a property of theirs recently acquired, a horror story set in outer space, but Clayton turned down the opportunity to direct what later became *Alien* (1979), co-scripted by David Giler (who had written the brilliant screenplay for *Casualties of War*). A sad irony is that a few months after the cancellation of *Silence*, Clayton had a stroke which deprived him of speech; he had to learn to speak again with the devoted help of his wife, Haya Harareet, and the few friends who knew what had happened. Psychosomatic? 'I'm wary of psychosomatic diagnoses,' he told the *Observer* (19 April 1992), 'and I'm not saying that that cancellation caused it, but it may have been responsible for the area of my body affected ... I told nobody. I didn't want to be pitied. And I was frightened that if the truth got out I would never work again.'

Cristofer's screenplay for *Silence* is an extraordinary piece of work. Like the other two projects – *Casualties of War, Fall Creek* – it tackles head-on the themes of prejudice, violence and racial discrimination, offering no easy answers. Silence is a fascinating character, whose own silence is reflective of a distrust of words (shared by Clayton) and of a strategy to shut out a world too appalling to be borne. Again it is a suspenseful, claustrophobic drama, with, in this case, a moving relationship at its core: that between the disillusioned doctor and the silent woman. In the hospital where she is being treated for injuries but also being held as a murder suspect, she breaks her silence when the doctor sneaks in to see her, whispering the words 'magic ... hands' and pressing his hand on her throat (yet another image of the fascination with hands in Clayton's work). It is a moment before it dawns on him that she is asking for deliverance, giving him permission to kill her, and what follows may be the most moving 'murder' – or mercy – scene in the movies.

Whether *Casualties of War, Massacre at Fall Creek* or *Silence* would have been successful is impossible to say. None of them was obvious commercial material: they deal with harsh and uncompromising adult themes, but the impulses behind them are compassion and a desire to enrich human understanding. It is clear that the common themes of the three films – intolerance, ignorance, injustice – were themes that were exercising Clayton mightily at this time, and that, with any one of these works, he would have delivered an unequivocal statement: he could have it no other way. In the meantime, let me record that they are three of the finest screenplays it has been my privilege to read. Should they never be filmed, they should at least be published. The failure to bring them to the screen under the direction of an artist like Clayton is one of Hollywood's saddest stories of waste and missed opportunity.

Notes

1 *What's On and Where to Go*, 29 March 1983.
2 *Observer*, 19 April 1992.
3 Ephraim Katz, *International Film Encyclopedia* (London, Macmillan, 1994), p. 261.
4 Jerry Roberts, *Daily Breeze*, 30 December 1987.
5 The films were eventually to be made by other directors: *Sons and Lovers* (Jack Cardiff, 1960); *Saturday Night and Sunday Morning* (Karel Reisz, 1960); *The L-Shaped Room* (Bryan Forbes, 1962).
6 The originally assigned director, James Poe, who had also written the screenplay, was replaced by Sydney Pollack, and the film was made – to some critical acclaim – in 1969. Clayton was quite happy with the cast but, for the other reasons indicated, did not feel he could take on the film.
7 Even Kramer himself, who was not a man often given to self-doubt or self-reproach, had to admit in his autobiography that the film was a disappointment and that he should take some of the blame.
8 Letter from Peggy Ramsay to Jack Clayton, 19 June 1968.
9 This was the project later to be filmed as *The Mission* (Roland Joffe, 1986).
10 Letter to Stanley Kamen, 7 November 1980.
11 Adrian Turner, *Robert Bolt: Scenes from Two Lives* (London, Hutchinson, 1998).
12 It was published in book form by Secker & Warburg as *Incident on Hill 192* (1970), and later as a New English paperback in 1989 under the title of *Casualties of War* to tie in with the Brian De Palma film.

13 In his biography, *Joseph Losey: A Revenge on Life* (London, Faber & Faber, 1994), David Caute notes that Joseph Losey made an endeavour to interest writers and financiers in a film of *Silence* between 1978 and 1981 but nothing came of it. Losey's interest in the subject is also mentioned in Michel Ciment's *Conversations with Losey* (London, Methuen, 1985).

Conclusion

11

When I came out I had found that films could touch your life, that they could teach you how to live, and Simone Signoret was in my dreams forever. (Stephen Frears, on seeing *Room at the Top* at the age of 16 at the Elite, Nottingham)

It was such a moving experience to see Jack's films in the tranquil surroundings of a beautiful art gallery – far from the madding crowd, so to speak. I don't know whether it was the atmosphere of the place or the knowledge that Jack is no longer with us that made the films seem somehow different. There they were, on that big screen, making their own independent statements – yet every shot, every movement, every nuance unmistakably his, revealing more than anything else what he was really about. (Haya Harareet Clayton in a letter to Fred Zinnemann, 3 January 1996)

Jack Clayton died of a heart attack in the arms of his wife on 25 February 1995 in a hospital in Slough. He was a few days short of his seventy-fourth birthday; Haya believes it was on that same day seventeen years before that Jack suffered his stroke. In a letter to Haya a week after the death, Clayton's doctor, Roger Blackwood (who described his patient as a 'delightful man' and 'a remarkably pleasant and gentle soul'), wrote that 'sadly his heart was completely exhausted and even if he had survived the most recent onslaught upon it he could not have coped with things much longer'. Clayton had had a weak chest since being seriously ill with pneumonia at the age of 4. The nuns at the hospital then had given him up for dead, and he remembered that, as a last resort, one of them had given him a drop of brandy, which he always thought had saved him. It probably gave him a taste for brandy; it certainly gave him an appetite for life.

Later, in September 1995, a retrospective of his films was held at the National Gallery of Art in Washington, accompanied by a programme containing comments and tributes from, among others, Fred Zinnemann, François Truffaut, John Mortimer, Tennessee Williams, Dirk Bogarde, Deborah Kerr and Anne Bancroft. In February 1996 the National Film Theatre in London ran a complete season of his films. Above all, on the first anniversary of his death, there was a BAFTA ceremony in remembrance and celebration of his life and career.

In contrast to the lovefests favoured by the American Film Institute, the BAFTA ceremony was an always dignified and often delightful remembrance from people of various ages and backgrounds of a man whose life had deeply touched their own. Punctuated by a screening of *The Bespoke Overcoat*, affectionately introduced by David Kossoff, and a recording of the exquisite flute solo from Georges Delerue's score for *Something Wicked This Way Comes* (a favourite of Haya's), the tributes were delivered from a lectern at the front of the stage and included contributions from professional colleagues and close friends such as Sir John Woolf, Harold Pinter, Karel Reisz and Freddie Francis, Clayton's editor, Terry Rawlings, and his agent, Robert Shapiro. Sam Waterston spoke poetically about his experience on *The Great Gatsby* of working with a director who became 'completely a hero in my eyes, and I continue to think I saw him truly'. Another actor from *Gatsby*, Scott Wilson, read a letter from Jack to Haya's sister Rina, which he had requested should be passed on to her daughter Tamar when she felt she was old enough to understand it: it recounted Jack's rage and horror on a visit to Dachau at the way it had been reduced to a 'tourist spectacle', and he hoped the letter, passed on to the hands of the next generation, would ensure that all of us 'should never forget the outrage of the past and the outrageousness of the present'. On behalf of Maggie Smith, Zoë Wanamaker (who had appeared in *Memento Mori*) spoke of Jack's love of actors, his vision that avoided caricature, and his courtesy and patience, appreciated by all who performed under his guidance. Another actress from *Memento Mori*, Emma Richler, read an undated handwritten poem of Jack's, 'Obituary', which had been found amongst his possessions some weeks after he died. Her father, Mordecai Richler, who was one of Clayton's closest friends, evoked the 'troubled spirit' of a proud and compassionate man. In conclusion, the ceremony's host, Sir Sydney Samuelson, recalled the words of Nelson Riddle when he had accepted the Oscar for *The Great Gatsby*, paying tribute to his 'English director and his loyalty to my work when I most needed it'.

The appropriate seriousness of the occasion was, from time to time, lightened by a more personal or humorous anecdote. There was an unscheduled appearance by the irrepressible Mel Brooks, who spoke for himself and for his wife Anne Bancroft about this 'special man'. Jack in his role as deliciously wicked uncle was recalled by Terry Rawlings in a story of when, during a visit paid by the Rawlings family to Marlow in the 1960s, Jack explained away his possession of an Aston Martin by telling Rawlings's awestruck young sons that he 'was James Bond's best friend'. A similar picture was given by the sons and grandson of Karel Reisz, particularly in their recollection of watching the 1966 World Cup Final with Jack and being told by him that there would be no unseemly displays of nationalism and xenophobia, an instruction which Jack himself spectacularly forgot when Germany equalised in the last minute.

Stephen Redfern from the Marlow Pigeon Club recollected Jack's devoted enthusiasm for the sport of pigeon racing and his kindness towards his birds. Jack's interest had been stimulated by an end-of-film gift from the crew of *The Innocents* of two fantail doves that had performed so brilliantly at the first appearance of Quint's ghost. Thereafter the interest grew into a passion, particularly for racing pigeons and breeding champions, something that satisfied both the bird lover and the competitor in Jack. When he died, it was not only the film fraternity that mourned his passing: there was to be a touching obituary by a friend, Tony Cowan, in the magazine *The Racing Pigeon*, and a Jack Clayton Memorial Cup established in his honour.

Another facet of his character was revealed by Haya Clayton, when she told the story of Jack's unusual gift to a dear neighbour, Johnny, who was dying of cancer. During pre-production work on *The Massacre at Fall Creek*, Clayton had become fascinated with American Indian jewellery and began wearing a Navaho bracelet, also buying one for Johnny and insisting on telling him it had 'healing powers'. Haya thought it might seem a rather eccentric or flamboyant gift for someone who was a typical Englishman, but Jack had an intuition it was right. In the event Johnny was to wear the bracelet constantly, refusing to remove it even in the bath. He was wearing it the day he died, and it was to be buried with him.

A deeply sensitive man, Clayton was nevertheless not soft. If he had been, how could he have survived in a cut-throat world like the film industry? Karel Reisz talked of him as a true independent, oblivious to fashion, something of a hero to the English film-making community because of his fearlessness with the front office and his refusal to compromise. 'This is my set', he once told Sam Waterston with quiet firmness during the making of *The Great Gatsby*. 'No one gives directions to my crew on my set except me. No one.' But, as Reisz recognised, there was a price to be paid for such independence. The insistence on making films on his own terms undoubtedly hindered the continuity of his output; and the content of his material made the money men jittery. When the three important statements about prejudice and intolerance that Clayton wished to bring to the screen in the 1970s were, one by one, stalled then shelved, the effect on his career, then his health, was calamitous. It says much for his courage that he was able to recover from the ensuing stroke and make three more films of such fine quality – 'offbeat, beautifully crafted, emotionally complex', as Reisz justly defined them in the *Guardian* (25 March 1996).

Aaron Copland used to say, 'If it's in the music it's in the man.' Haya Clayton's epigraph at the beginning of this chapter suggests the reverse is equally true: that what was in the man came out unmistakably in that quantitatively slender but qualitatively substantial body of work. Amongst Clayton's possessions was a card from Haya which read, 'In a world where everything is a copy, you remain an original' – applicable both to the man and to the film-maker. Harold Pinter's professional tribute to Jack Clayton is Pinteresque in the sense that I understand the term – a model of pithiness and precision – and can perhaps stand as final testimony to Clayton's singular talent:

> Jack Clayton was a director of great sensitivity, intelligence and flair. He was a gentle man, with a quiet, wry sense of humour, but professionally he possessed the utmost rigour and a fierce determination. I wrote the screenplay of The Pumpkin Eater in 1963. It remains, in my view, a film of considerable power and, of course, absolute integrity.

Appendices: some writings of Jack Clayton

'You Can't Declare Peace' (1944–45); 'On The Prevention of War' (1946)

These two previously unpublished pieces were written when Clayton was in his earlier twenties and reflecting on his war-time experiences with the RAF. The first article, 'You Can't Declare Peace', is very much an elaboration of the ideas expressed in *Naples is a Battlefield* about the responsibilities of liberation, the rebuilding of Europe, and the laying of conditions (social and economic) to prevent another war. The second piece, 'On the Prevention of War', reflects on the nature of man and society that causes war, for 'nothing can ever be prevented unless you first study its cause'.

Although Clayton was never to make a war film the impact of World War II and the insight it gave him into human nature under stress had a powerful influence on his work. For this reason, as well as the intrinsic interest of the ideas, these documents are of value in understanding it.

'You Can't Declare Peace' (1944–45)

1. We in England have never had a true picture of the situation existing in Europe, either during the German occupation, or now after the liberation.

The information supplied to us has invariably suffered from a subjective viewpoint, which only dealt with a small corner of the whole situation. It has also been tainted with exaggeration, according to the popular trend of the moment. For instance, during the German occupation the trend of our information dealt mainly with the horror and brutality suffered by each country; whilst now, since the liberation of most of Western Europe, our information has swung to the opposite extreme, dealing with the gaiety and happiness of the population, the luxury commodities available, the amount of food obtainable in the black market, fashion parades, and the general feeling that everything is returning to normal again. Neither extreme presents a true picture of the situation existing for the whole population – if presented on its own. Physical suffering and persecution did exist under the Germans, but on the whole, only for a minority of the population. Equally on the other extreme, though most of the people were delirious with pleasure to be liberated, this hysteria lasted as is natural, only a short time, and luxury goods, black market food, fashion parades, etc., exists again only for a very small minority of the population. By this we can see that there is another side to each picture, and that we require a little knowledge of the whole picture before we can understand the true situation existing in Europe today.

2. If Great Britain plays the important role in future world affairs for which she may well be destined, her people, the ordinary men and women of Great Britain, will bear the ultimate responsibility for the decisions taken by the country. For this reason it is essential that her people do see the true situation in Europe.

3. To obtain a correct perspective on Europe today one has to understand a little of what has happened during the past few years.

Western Europe has been under the Nazi yoke for four years. The peoples of the different nations have received different treatment according to their countries' strategic, economic, and agricultural importance to the Third Reich, according to the resistance and sabotage in each country, the general behaviour of each population and dependent on the whims of those controlling the 'New Europe'.

Hitler promised that if he had to leave any of the occupied countries, he would destroy every single productive unit, try to exterminate the population, so that Europe would not survive richer than Germany. The amount of economic destruction differed in each country according to the amount of destructive time allowed the Germans by the speed of the Allied advance.

Despite these differences, it is possible to find a basic minimum point of suffering in both the human and economic spheres, which binds the different nations together; a common denominator which applies equally to all the occupied countries, which will serve as a basic starting point to examine and understand the mutual sufferings and problems arising from the occupation.

Two factors form the major part of this denominator:

A. The psychological effect of the swastika choking everything and the constant pressure of German propaganda. No liberty, continual uncertainty, fear for one's relations, family, and self, everything from the small social and cultural restrictions, to the actual persecution of individuals and whole families.

B. The majority of each population has been undernourished for four years. Every normal human being requires a minimum of 2,300 calories per day to ensure his health is not impaired. During the occupation the official ration was never more than 1,600 calories per day. The full effect of malnutrition will not be apparent for some time to come. Nevertheless the danger exists even if momentarily hidden beneath the surface.

4. These were the factors underlying the situation when the governments for each country and the appropriate Allied Mission took control after the liberation.

Their task is to effect immediate social and economic reconstruction in each country. To do this they have to solve certain problems which arise directly from the factors which we have just studied, they are:

A. Though in time the psychological effect of the occupation will die out, in the meanwhile its influence has promoted new problems.

Choked with restrictions and German propaganda, the population are out of touch with the latest developments in scientific, social and economic life, made by the rest of the world during the past four years. The effect of having freed the repressions suffered these four years necessitates the directing of these released feelings into new channels; and the effect of having removed the Germans, so long the object of the people's pent-up hatred, requires a substitute emotional outlet or target for the absorption of the as yet inexhausted mass feeling. For this very reason at the present moment, no matter how competent a government might be it would still receive considerable criticism from the people.

It would be of considerable advantage to supply the populations with work and food quickly, to help speed this transitional period.

This involves an immediate problem for the economic sphere.

B. To counter malnutrition it is necessary to produce and distribute at once large quantities of food or vitamin concentrates for the population. This again is dependent on the economic sphere.

C. The economic position in each country presents a vicious circle.

There is a great shortage of power in all the countries. Many of the electric generating plants have been destroyed. The production of coal for power etc. is part of the vicious circle. Production in the coal mines has decreased because the mine-workers are not properly fed. In order to provide more food it is necessary to run more trains to distribute it. More trains means more coal. Agriculture has declined because of insufficient heating for the farmers and lack of fuel for agricultural machinery. Again more coal is required.

Damaged industry requires raw materials for repair work; undamaged industry requires new materials to work with. Raw materials don't exist in these countries. Consequently most industry stands idle and there is large-scale unemployment.

The transport problem is the same. There is a great shortage of railway rolling stock and great damage to the railroad itself, due to German and Allied war destruction. A large number of bridges have been destroyed and most of the canal ways are blocked through damage or low-lying military bridges. Road transport for any sizeable form of distribution is impractical owing to a great shortage of road transports and petrol. Again the vicious circle.

To produce new rolling stock and reopen the railroads, or to build new bridges and clear the canal system, or to manufacture quantities of road transport, all require raw materials which don't exist.

Without coal to supply the power, industry to manufacture, and transport to distribute, it is impossible to supply work, food, clothes and other basic essentials to the people; and impossible to start any economic reconstruction in these countries.

5. We can see, therefore, that each country requires urgently certain economic commodities to cut this vicious circle and solve the bulk of its problems arising from this war. Until these problems are solved there can be no proper reconstruction; and no hope of prosperity in Europe. We know too that these countries cannot themselves supply the means to cut this vicious circle. The initial impulse to start life going again in Europe can only come from outside of Europe through imports. We can realise that it is the desire of each country to make

this initial impulse as small as possible. But who is to supply these commodities?

6. It is our moral responsibility in our battle against Nazism to assist those nations which have been ravaged by Nazism.

It is in our interest to ensure that these European countries, many of whom are our peacetime customers in world trade, regain their prosperity, and consequently their buying capacity quickly, for the safety of our own prosperity. No nation can alone stand prosperous, whilst those around it starve; because in order to enjoy prosperity every country, and Great Britain more than any other, is dependent on the prosperity of every nation as customers for export and import trade.

Through education and knowledge of the sciences we are daily losing our former dependence on nature. We are becoming increasingly able to control ourselves, our society, our world. But increasing control means increasing responsibilities. If things go wrong we can no longer blame nature. The fault lies at our door. The future is no longer dependent on natural forces against which we can do nothing; the future is what we choose to make it, and in this task every man has a part to play which he may not refuse.

It is our obligation to make sure no seeds are sown now which may develop later into another war. History can prove that when a nation or series of nations become economically frustrated, a war follows within a very short time. We cannot allow any situation to start now which will menace our own prosperity and future peace.

Many lives have been lost in this war, and all for the same basic reason; for the right of all nations to enjoy their own freedom and a good standard of living after the war. If we consider these lives, our own future, the future of our children, and the future of every citizen in this our world, we know we have no alternative but to give now the material economic aid needed by these European nations to build their share of freedom, prosperity and peace, and by so doing we shall ensure our own freedom and peace in this world.

Today Europe needs our aid, let us give it – because tomorrow we shall need the aid of Europe.

A. Calder-Marshall and Jack Clayton, *c.* 1944–45

'On the Prevention of War' (1946)

Mankind has the capacity to absorb unusual situations in his life and treat them, after a short period of inoculation, as quite normal: a part of his life, a part of the world, something perhaps unpleasant or dangerous but nevertheless something which is accepted. This acceptance is, in most cases, a kind of self-defence against circumstances – a defence springing from evolution, an ability continually to adapt to fresh circumstances in order to live.

This faculty, so advantageous and necessary to his life, has certain grave drawbacks unless intelligence is blended with nature's instinct. Because it is so easy, and so often the case, to accept a situation as inevitable and permanent, even after nature's initial demand has been satisfied and the necessity to accept no longer exists. This unfortunate happening occurs through lack of proper thought as to the true cause and effect of the situation in question. For perhaps it is only the cause or causes *behind* the effect that are inevitable or have any kind of permanence. So often when any great crisis occurs in our lives its very magnitude focuses it so prominently in our minds that the well from whence it springs – the real cause of the trouble – is obscured from our attention by its own shadow.

Man's mind, sensual and lazy, is too apt to seize on the obvious and create, out of what is probably only an effect, a complete case of both cause *and* effect and, having done this, exclaim, with a godlike sense of importance, that this particular situation is inevitable. Whereas the only thing which is inevitable is our own downward movement towards mental and physical ruin, until we can learn to cast aside our mental laziness, our own private ego's fear of the truth, our deliberate use of lies for our own personal gain, and examine each important occurrence critically and without personal bias or influence, for its true significance and perspective, by saying: What is the cause and what is the effect?

War is a typical example of this. Ten years ago, the word war struck into most of our hearts a horror and fear of this dread occurrence. And now? The word war has no such meaning. Used in every conversation for the past six years, the horror now has, by custom, lost much of its lustre, and if, for some, the horror still fully exists, it is coupled – by the necessity of accepting a situation in order to survive – with the belief that it is inevitable. For has it not existed since the beginning of all our history? The story of every nation is steeped in war, and the majority of people hide their laziness and stupidity behind this and like statements. But they forget that the same could be said for so many ordinary medical diseases a few years ago. And cannot be said today.

The science of medicine has proved that it can cure and, more importantly, prevent the majority of diseases. But to do this it has first to ascertain the causes of the illness. This is common sense. War can be compared to disease. It is, after all, a social illness. If science can prevent one disease by investigating its causes and then eliminating them or diverting them into new channels, why can't the same be done for another?

The San Francisco conference has been working for some time now to find a solution to this very question: how to eliminate war. By the success that has so far been enjoyed and by the means they are employing, it would appear that they have overlooked the necessity to investigate the causes and then try and work out some solution from their findings. They appear to be trying to tackle the situation in a sort of catch and carry process. The very most they can ever achieve by this means is a temporary cure.

Again, science has taught us that the only real mastery of a disease springs from its prevention. And I must repeat that nothing can ever be prevented unless you first study its cause. It is useless to make elaborate plans to stop a thing when you have no idea what starts it. Let us see, therefore, if we can help to tear aside this mysterious veil which surrounds war.

History, stripped of its national and emotional propaganda, shows us that, almost without exception, wars are fought for the personal gain of one or more tribes or communities or, in later years and developments, one or more nations. Whether this gain be in the form of prisoners for sacrifice, slaves for labour, new lands to cultivate, the elimination of another tribe or – the more modern interpretation – new lands for expansion, raw materials for industry or agricultural products, for strategic bases to protect an already founded Colonial empire or bases to be used as stepping-off points to secure an empire, they are all connected and are basically the same thing. They all represent personal gain to a community or nation at the expense of another.

There would appear to be three prime elements – but there may be many more – from which arises the state of war.

The first, for want of a more accurate term, we shall call the 'human' element. Into this all-embracing word, we compress all the mental and spiritual factors which dominate and control man's behaviour. And, as these are here, we include as well their parents and causes, heredity and environment – including the heredity and environment of generations back. This human element represents man as he stands before us, the product of countless generations whose blood, as it poured into his veins, gave him a myriad of cells, each one full of countless ties, of the majority of which he is never consciously aware.

The second, we shall call the social state. This means the conditions under which man lives on this earth. Everything, from the moral codes, social laws of states, religious environment and, most important, the financial or economic factor which, in the majority of men's lives, plays a very important role in modern times.

As can be plainly seen, element number one composes those factors from which man is composed and which dictate to a large extent man's behaviour. These factors individually, and the sum which together they compose, are as yet obscure even to science, although daily steps inch forward through the undergrowth towards a better understanding.

Element two is a subject far easier for us to understand. Because the social state is made by man. Though the causes behind the making of the many laws, etc. governing our social state may be a little obscure and may have sprung from our unconscious mind, they were at least consciously made, and this very factor gives us much more scope in our investigation.

The third element may appear at first strange and, indeed, non-existent. It is a combination of elements one and two. Man himself made certain laws to govern and control and simplify his life. These we have called element two. But these laws have far exceeded their original reason and have attained a new significance of their own. Gone is their original flavour: a rule or law made by man to regulate or assist him over certain circumstances or conditions, etc. No, our friend acceptance, whom we studied earlier, has entered the scene, and now these laws or rules have been accepted more or less as natural laws.

Few people stop today to consider how and why this or that law came into existence and, more important, whether it is really necessary at the present time. It has been accepted and, by virtue of this, its original intention has disappeared and it has attained a new significance of its own. Now this changed character of our human-made laws reacts back again on our human being and, by doing so, contributes our third element. It is like deciding to keep a dog, then realizing that it will be necessary, for our own convenience, to build a little house for the dog to sleep in at night. We do this and call it a kennel.

Years pass. We and the dog live quite happily. Then one day the dog dies. We still continue to live in our house but, in this interim period, we have married and had children. We realize that we require more bedrooms for our children, so we decide to build further rooms on our house. But we find that the only space available for this purpose is occupied by the dog kennel we built years ago. So what happens? We either decide not to build at all, or build in a quite unsuitable place, or move from the house altogether. We have forgotten that the original reason for the kennel was to house the dog and that, now the dog has died, the actual necessity for the kennel no longer exists. We see that the kennel has achieved, through our acceptance of matters, a new meaning quite different from the original intention. And we also see that this change of reason or purpose, in an object or law that we ourselves created, reacts back on us in quite a different way from that which was originally intended.

Jack Clayton, *c.* 1946

The *Queen* Interview (1960)

For its issue of 14 September 1960, *Queen* magazine invited a number of prominent people who seemed trendsetters in their particular field of expertise to give their thoughts on some of the leading issues of the day. Because of the success of *Room at the Top*, Clayton was one of the people invited, along with such personalities as songwriter Lionel Bart, interviewer John Freeman, conductor Colin Davis, racing driver Stirling Moss, singer and art critic George Melly, and an up-and-coming barrister by the name of Geoffrey Howe. Clayton's responses are an eloquent expression of his deep humanity.

How do you live with the threat of the bomb? As well as I have lived all my life with the threat of any other weapon of destruction. The choice of the weapon seems to me unimportant. I grant that the atomic bomb is more effective, as it virtually threatens to exterminate all life. However, this might be an advantage, as the enormity of the result may cause nations to think before going to war. Surely the real point of this question is not the increased threat of one weapon of death as opposed to another, but the absurdity that the threat of war can still exist in the world today.

What do you think is the right place for a woman in society? Any place that they desire, and having desired it are capable of achieving it.

Is the time ripe to give coloured people equal rights? What an extraordinary question. I had always understood that from an intellectual, religious or even humanistic point of view there had never been any doubts that all peoples shared equal rights. As apparently certain peoples and governments have chosen to ignore this fact, and by so doing have caused the emotional prejudices which so easily lead to bloodshed, the question is not 'Is the time ripe?' but how best can these normal human rights be given quickly and with the least possible suffering.

Should Britain become part of Europe? Obviously. If it is suggested that the British way of life might suffer if this happened, I cannot seriously believe that an Englishman could lose his characteristics so easily and – if he did, would this loss be so great?

Will communism eventually dominate the world? I find it diffcult today to understand what is meant by communism. There seem to be a number of different countries practising different versions of the same word. I have little doubt that the influence of these countries in the world will undoubtedly grow, as indeed it has been growing over the last twenty years. Particularly in the economic field, which has hitherto been considered the personal property of 'the Western world'. I think the individual nationalism which exists in these communist countries, just as much as any other nation, will in fact prevent a union complete enough to dominate the whole world. I hope that the only domination that the world may suffer is that of the individual and every individual, and then perhaps questions like these would never have to be asked, as they would already be archaic.

What has religion to offer present-day society? Belief in something – even if it is only in the virtue of a flea – is even more than a luxury to mankind – it is a necessity. If organised religion can help supply that belief, providing it is not one associated with tyranny, then it can only be offering something of value to society.

'Abstract on Vision' (1977)

Clayton wrote these notes while he was doing some preparatory work on a film, *If You Could See Me Now*, which was never finally made (see Chapter 10). It is evidence of the characteristically thoughtful way Clayton approached any project but it is of particular interest for its application to *The Innocents*: sixteen years on Clayton was still worrying over how you most effectively render the visualisation of ghosts on screen.

Abstract Note ('If You Could See Me Now') 12 April 1977

An abstract note which concerns vision – seeing. Eventually it may have some bearing on 'If You Could See Me Now', but nevertheless these are notes for their own sake.

In its very crudest sense, vision is based on patterns. From earliest life, a child is taught to identify different objects each of which fit into a certain pattern. We are basically taught what we see from an early age according to this pattern, in the same way that I personally believe we are taught beauty and ugliness by being informed what it is first.

As an example of this, if a child were totally isolated from the world and you presented it with a tree upside down, growing as it were from the sky, and told the child it was beautiful and that that was beauty, when that child emerged into the world and saw a tree growing as it does and you told it that was ugly, it is most likely that it would believe this. That's a very crude way of putting it, but one can in fact consider all the possibilities of that as far as colour is concerned and all kinds of shapes which we accept and pass on as being likeable and beautiful or dislikeable and ugly. In fact they may not be at all.

If my theory isn't true, why is it that beauty amongst different races and nations is so entirely different? Why, for instance, cannot we even tell one Chinese from another? Why is it that things in many different races which are considered most attractive are not so considered in others?

So: having imposed these patterns into the human mind, they remain always and become even more deeply embedded. Only a change of light, for instance, apart from the possibility of hallucinatory drugs, can in fact create out of a known shape something different which, of course, we later discover to be the old shape but that the light has changed.

Similarly, people with either highly developed imaginative vision or, perhaps one should say, a weak imaginative vision, can through light and shadow see things and place them into patterned shapes when they are not truly there. Hence, light, shadow or any kind of atmospheric visual change is, in fact, creating an illusion. Of course, it is almost always an illusion which has to fit into the conditioned pattern in our mind.

Vision, therefore, could very roughly be said to be seeing through shapes and light the patterns that we have been taught. So one could possibly draw a conclusion that we are not necessarily seeing what is really there; we are seeing a kind of mentally imposed blue-print onto whatever we are looking at.

Years ago I was able, by staring for a long period of time at a wall or any particular thing – perhaps because of the tiredness induced by staring – to see the actual thing I was looking at change. In other words, suppose I was looking at a wall with a picture on it, a radiator and a vase. That is what I know I am looking at, because that's what I'm told and have been brought up to believe I'm looking at. But at a certain moment the sight changes so that they become colours and shapes and the conception, as it were, of what one is seeing is changed.

It isn't really the eye getting tired that gives this new kind of vision, or different vision, it is the tiredness which breaks the old pattern. I am quite sure that meditation could probably have exactly the same effect.

I don't know anything about modern art or expressionist art, but I do feel that people like Picasso were using this kind of vision to express something in a different form – a form which, in fact, existed in that kind of sight but because it broke the old-fashioned pattern seemed so totally different and unlike the original, or their conception of what the original was.

I remember it was always my intention on 'The Innocents' to treat the ghosts, or particularly Quint, in this manner, but I was never able to really formulate how to do it and, to some extent, chickened out on the basis of making it more scary in the obvious way. I think now, looking back, it would have been more scary in this particular way.

Short Story: 'The Enchantment' (1985)

A short story can sometimes be more revealing of an artistic personality than a work of overt autobiography. This was Corin Redgrave's opinion of the novella *The Mountebank's Tale* by his father, Sir Michael Redgrave, a view expressed in a revealing talk he gave in the British Library in December 1998. The same might be true of Jack Clayton's short story 'The Enchantment'. He wrote it in 1985 and there was some discussion of developing it as a feature film (see Chapter 10). On a first impression, one notes the characteristic Clayton atmosphere and feel: the way it begins with place, the precise evocation of environment by which character is formed; the compassionate observation of ordinary people coping with their loneliness and of the plight of the abandoned vulnerable child; and a melancholy ending that reverberates in the mind. The central relationship that develops between an elderly widower and his mute nephew (whom he has temporarily to take care of after the death of his sister) corresponds to one of those idyllic periods that often occur in Clayton's films where the characters, as I described it in discussing *Our Mother's House*, 'create an intensely subjective world that becomes an idealised space in which they can momentarily live out their romantic dreams' (p. 142). Needless to say, reality will come crashing in but, briefly and magically, a perfect state of existence is achieved. I would characterise this as an expression of Clayton's romanticism, and what it reminds me of is T.S. Eliot's evocation of a similar idealism that he glimpsed in Henry James. 'His romanticism', Eliot said of James,

> implied no defect in observation of the things that he wanted to observe; it was not the romanticism of those who dream because they are too lazy or too fearful to face the fact; it issues, rather, from the imperative insistence of an ideal which tormented him. He was possessed by the vision of an ideal society; he *saw* (not fancied) the relations between the members of such a society. And no one, in the end, has ever been more aware – or with more benignity or less bitterness of the disparity between possibility and fact. (T. S. Eliot, *Vanity Fair*, February 1924)

I once applied that to the films of George Stevens: it seems to me equally applicable to Clayton's work.

Beneath all this lurks arguably an even more personal subtext. The leading character in 'The Enchantment', John Smith, is 57 years old, the age at which Clayton had his stroke. He has an elder sister, as did Clayton. Even his first name might have a certain significance, since Clayton was referred to as 'John Clayton' on his one and only school report. More particularly, the relationship he develops with the mute child seems not only a variation and revisiting of the situation of *Silence* (see Chapter Ten), but also relates to Clayton himself and to the stroke which temporarily deprived him of speech and compelled him to relearn language like a child. Clayton, then, identified closely with both characters; and it might be particularly significant that the relationship blossoms after a visit to Kew Gardens. Clayton loved flowers and plants and, as Haya Clayton told me, might have been a botanist if he had not gone into films, so he could well empathise with the revitalising effect a visit to Kew might have on both man and child. 'Each night', says the story, 'the child sat listening to every word, enchanted. And love, growing daily as he tried to soften a sordid life with happiness for the child, seized John and carried him in its wake towards the same enchantment. He began to see his own words as he offered them to the child, and each story became a world in which they both shared and lived.'

At this point we are almost in the world of *Our Mother's House* as seen from the point of view of Charlie Hook: for all his faults, Charlie does open the eyes of the children to the world outside and their fascination with his stories increases his own self-estimation. But the terrible desertion of the child by John, and its tragic aftermath, is more like the uncle's chilling indifference to the children in *The Innocents* and its consequences; it is also a reminder of the father whom Clayton never knew, and about whom, and to whom, he could never talk. Unlike these people, Clayton's hero takes on the guilt for what has happened. 'Only the darkness could see the tears which slipped down each cheek', the story says, in an image which recalls the silent tears Miles in *The Innocents* sheds at night when talking of an uncle who has no time for them and who symbolises, to this precociously sensitive child, an uncaring adult world. The ending of 'The Enchantment' is, on one level, tragic. But because of the hero's redemptive attempt to re-enter the enchanted world he and the child had created, the act of suicide is also an act of atonement. In this most beautiful of confessional stories, Clayton was, I believe, symbolically reaching towards a forgiveness of his father and an exorcising of childhood demons.

The Enchantment

John Smith lived on the fifth floor of the tenement building and the single window in his room peeped onto the backside of the city. Everything in sight, coated in years of grime, looked black and gave the feeling of an area no longer cared for or wanted.

The tenement was jammed between a mass of other buildings and their walls pressed tight around the window, so that the sun never shone inside the room. Far in the distance, over a maze of twisted roofs and broken chimney-pots, there was a faint glimpse of the river, but this, too, seemed dirty and was dark grey in colour. The window opened onto a fire-escape which had once linked each window with protective fingers but was now eaten with rusty age, threatened collapse, and served as a receptacle for the unwanted junk from each apartment and, on hot summer evenings, as a cooler refuge from the tiny, crowded rooms of the tenement. After winding around the building, the fire-escape sank down into the little courtyard below, which contained the evil-smelling tenement dustbins.

Opposite the tenement was a disused warehouse. On its tall, sloping roof, the lead guttering, long since broken loose, hung limp like some ineffective artificial limb, and at night the courtyard below echoed with a crash as the restless, sex-ridden cats dislodged the roof tiles.

All around, the windows were small and dirty and, on occasional ledges, a small plant thrust out a pallid bloom in search of the sun. Stretching across the area were endless parades of dingy, grey washing. The garments still heavy with water hung limp and still, whilst those already dry twitched and danced with each rustle of wind, as though mocking the bundles of neuroses they would shortly enfold. The atmosphere was thick with the sickly smoke from the factories and all the discordant clamour of the city beat heavily on the ear. Only when darkness obscured the slum did this chorus fade in a temporary armistice and the night was pierced solely by the intimate sounds inside the tenement.

The room was small and over-crowded. It had a sink, a cooking range that smoked and some old tin trunks pushed away in a corner. Next to the window stood the bed; it was brass and the knobs were peeling. The centre of the room was blocked by a table and two wooden chairs. By the fire was a worn easy-chair from which the stuffing peeped. The wall-paper had once been heavily patterned but age and damp had tarnished it and caused it to peel. The room was dun coloured and smelt of damp and stale tobacco smoke. Clustered on the mantel-shelf were the slender roots of his past: a miscellany of different objects with, as centre-piece, a faded family group.

John Smith was fifty-seven, grey-haired, and had the lonely habit of talking to himself.

He had been born in the slum, in a small house near the docks, the third child in a family of nine. His earliest remembrance was of lying in a cot, nursing a dull ache in his empty stomach and watching the sunlight twinkle on an old beer bottle standing on the window-sill. He had been swept into life to earn a bare living whilst still a child, and was still contriving to do so.

As a young man, he had never shown any great brilliance or tenacity and had found good jobs impossible to obtain and even bad ones difficult to hold. All his life, it seemed, he had been a failure. Nothing big and dramatic – just constant, nagging little failures.

As a result of a furtive moment stolen one night in an alley doorway, he got married, and spent the next few months searching for work whilst his wife's pregnancy drew to its climax.

One night, as he stood watching the gaslight flickering in the cold passage, his wife died squeezing from her loins a dead child. The sudden shock, and the malignant tongues of his wife's family, made him think that his unemployment and lack of money had caused her death, and gradually he grew to believe that he and his failures had murdered his wife and child.

From this moment, his fear of another failure was acute and he carefully avoided any test of responsibility and slowly backed away from reality. He cut away from his family and avoided his friends, and was idly floating – but only just floating – in a backwater of obscurity. For the past eleven years he had lived, and worked as caretaker, in the tenement and paid no rent for his room. And each morning he arose at six and looked out at the view.

One day, as he was laying the table for his tea, there was a knock at his door. Without turning, he called out, 'Come in.'

The door opened, and a powerfully-built woman stood on the threshold. 'Mr. Smith?' she enquired.

'Yes.'

'Good, I don't know how many stairs I've been up and down looking for you. These tenements are all the same – rabbit warrens, that's what they are. Give me a house every time. Then you know where you are.'

She wheezed as she spoke and, seeing the look of enquiry on his face, declared abruptly, 'I'm Agnes Mills, and I've brought you a message from your sister.'

'My sister?' He looked at her blankly.

'Well, you are John Smith, aren't you, and you have got a sister, haven't you?' she replied crossly.

He nodded.

'Well, I've just laid her out,' she carried on without a pause. 'She sent you along this,' and she pulled from outside the door a small child. 'His name's David.'

'Laid her out ... You mean she's dead?'

'Your sister? Oh, yes. I was saying to Mrs Lettish – she lives next door to me – I said '"Mrs Lettish, I don't give her another twenty-four hours, she's that pinched and worn out. You mark my words, she'll be a goner before the night's out." And she was. I seldom make a mistake with a corpse. In my business you can't afford to.' And Agnes stood looking rather triumphant.

John stared at her. A host of memory fragments broke in front of him. He tried to picture his sister and couldn't. She had lain tucked in the past for twenty years. He glanced at the family group on the mantel-shelf and tried to recall her features. Suddenly realising, for the first time, the presence of the child, he turned sharply to Agnes.

'Is this her child?'

'Of course it is.' And she patted the little boy on the head and said cheerfully, 'Aren't you, David?'

The child gave no sign of having heard. His dark eyes were fixed on John.

Agnes continued: 'That's why I brought him to you.' She broke off, as her tongue searched for and sought to free a fragment of food caught between her discoloured teeth. 'She said, "Take my boy to my brother. I'll not have him brought up in a pauper's orphanage. Tell him to look after David." She said you'd understand.'

John sank slowly into a chair. 'But how can I look after a child? I'm getting old and ...' His voice trailed off as he gazed around the room.

Agnes looked indignant and said sharply, 'Your sister asked me to bring the child here and give you her message. That I've done. What you do now is your affair. If you don't want it, take it around to the welfare people yourself. At least I've done my duty.' She stood looking very complacent. 'Well, I can't afford to stand here all day. Here's the child, and I'll bid you good-day.'

She pushed the child into the room and swept out. The door slammed loudly and the room was left in silence.

John sat in the chair not knowing what to do. His eyes caught the child silently watching him. He coughed nervously and, in a voice that was too loud for the room, said, 'Well, David, I'm your Uncle John. Do you want to say here with me?'

David didn't reply. John tried again. 'I'm sorry about your mother – my sister – I was very fond of her and I'm sure you were too.'

The two dark eyes of the child stared hard at him, as though seeing the twenty years that he had forgotten his sister.

John bent down and, for the first time, noticed how thin the child was and how his arms, clothed in a worn jersey, clutched a cardboard valise. He said softly, 'Put your case down, David ... That's better. Now tell me, would you like to live here with your Uncle —.'

He broke off as, with a crash, the door was flung open and the head of Agnes popped around. She looked hot and red and as she spoke each word was punctuated with a wheeze. 'I forgot to tell you ... These stairs would kill me ... He won't answer you, never ... He's mute, 'as been ever since he came into the world ... Dumb. He'll never answer you.'

Shaking her head and coughing, she disappeared around the door as it closed. John sat looking at the child for a moment and then quietly got up and placed the kettle on the stove.

As John drew the curtains, he saw a watery sun trying to soften the view. Opening the window, he climbed out on the fire-escape and settled himself in an old basket-chair. Placing his feet up on the rail, he let himself slip into the comfortable atmosphere of a Sunday morning. John liked Sundays. He could remember as a child some-one had told him that 'God had given Sunday to all the people for their very own day'. But, funny, he could never remember who had told him. Anyway, it didn't matter, he liked the words: 'their very own day'. He liked the quieter, more friendly noise; the feeling of people, tired out with a week of work, lying in bed not having to watch the alarm-clock, and he liked the more relaxed expressions on people's faces. Most of all, he liked to sit, read his Sunday paper, and be left alone.

There was a sound behind him, and the child came out to him with the paper clutched tightly in his hand. John took it and scanned it idly for his favourite items. A travel story attracted his attention, when he became aware of the child.

The boy was sitting beside him, staring through the bars of the escape. He was quite still and, somehow, this immobility was strangely disturbing. Peering from behind the paper, John reflected for the hundredth time since his arrival that this was a most unsuitable life for a little boy. But what to do? That was the question. How could a man of his age, who had lived alone for twenty years, suddenly start looking after a child? Especially as the money that he drew each week, with habitual care, barely covered his own needs. In addition, he was not really a suitable person to look after a child. It needed a woman's care and entailed a lot of knowledge and responsibility ... a lot of responsibility.

Oh, if only that awful woman hadn't brought the child to him. Suppose she hadn't found him, then what would have happened? It would have been sent to a home. But the woman had found him, and what about his sister? It was her wish, her dying wish, that he should look after the boy, if he could believe that terrible woman. Didn't he owe it to her, after his neglect of the past years, to do this little thing ... ? But what right had she to send him this, her child? It couldn't even speak; couldn't tell him when it was hungry or when it wanted to go to the lavatory. Nothing. It was ridiculous. He felt cross, and his Sunday morning bubble was pricked.

He threw the paper down and went inside the room to shave. The child followed him. He had just started when, reflected in the mirror, he saw the child was watching him intently. His hand slipped, and the white lather was stained red. He turned on the child, sharply.

'Don't stand there watching me. It makes me nervous, and see what you've done!' He pointed at the red mark on his face. 'Don't stand around here. Why don't you go out on a nice day like this? Fresh air, that's what you need. Go and ...' He faltered, then suddenly got the obvious idea. 'Go and play with the other children. Go on.'

A feeling of relief passed over him as he saw the child quietly leave the room, and he finished his shave without interruption. Feeling much better, he started to think about Sunday again. A church service was playing on the next door radio. Yes, it was a good day.

He went out on the escape and, with a prolonged grunt of satisfaction, settled himself in the chair and picked up the paper. As he did so, a large drop of rain splodged over the front page. With absolute fury, he stamped inside and slammed the window. This settled it. His mind was made up.

During his lunch-hour next day, he set off for the Welfare Centre. Despite his decision of the previous morning, he was troubled and muttered to himself as he walked, 'How can a little kid grow up properly with an old, selfish man? You must do the right thing for the child. You have neither the money, the patience, nor the knowledge. It will just stagnate in dirty slums, like you have all your life. My sister didn't realise – couldn't have realised – what she was asking. Perhaps she was delirious or something – she never was very strong. Why, it might ruin the child for ever.' But, to his irritation, another voice inside him seemed to answer, 'Your sister knew only that you were flesh and blood of the child and that better than all the efficient care of an orphanage was the warmth and love of blood. Remember, John, don't fail again. Don't destroy this child as well. Remember, John, what happened. You mustn't let go this time, for it may be your last chance. Ever.'

At the Welfare Office, after a few moments, he was seated before a desk, explaining the situation to a small, grey-haired woman whose stature and gentle charm belied the firm mind which nestled beneath.

'Yes, Mr Smith, you have done the right thing in coming to us. You see, a child needs not only specialised care and attention but the companionship of other children. I'm quite sure your sister gave the child to your care because she knew you would take the sensible course and not listen to foolish sentiment.'

She spoke with such obvious knowledge and sincerity that any doubts in John's mind were being swiftly, and willingly, dispelled.

'There is another thing. How would you educate him? No, I don't mean the ordinary schooling that would be available, of course. No, I mean the out-of-school education. The encouragement and moulding which is so necessary for the proper cultivation of a healthy young mind. And, frankly, Mr Smith, if you will pardon me for saying this, I don't think your age or background would be entirely suitable to undertake this satisfactorily. And, I repeat, what we can best give the child is a natural relationship with other children. It is so important.'

The interview ended with John's ready promise to bring the child to the Centre in two weeks' time. He parted from the grey-haired lady with an easier mind.

On his way home, he called at the newsagent on the corner to buy his weekly ounce of tobacco. As he was leaving the shop, his eye was caught by a large and dusty bottle whose multicoloured contents were described on the label as 'Jelly Babies'. He left the shop with a small paper bag in his hand.

As he entered the room, he could see, through the window, the child sitting on the escape. He crossed the floor and stood by the window. David hadn't heard him and sat quite still, his head resting on the rusty support of the hand-rail and his eyes fixed on the court-yard below.

John watched, wondering what strange quality possessed this wisp of a child that seemed to isolate him from everything. He called softly. Realising his presence, David turned with a start. John sat down and called the boy again. He came and stood next to the chair.

'David, I've got a little surprise for you. A present.' John took the paper bag from his pocket and showed it to the child. 'Now, guess what's inside … Go on, look for yourself.'

Shyly, the child took the paper bag and, carefully unravelling the top, looked inside.

John said, 'Do you like them? They're called Jelly Babies. Jelly Babies.' He liked the sound of the name. 'Well, aren't you going to try one? Here now.' He took one from the bag and popped it into David's mouth.

Filling his pipe, John watched the child eat the sweet with care, as though it were something delicate and precious. Taking the paper bag, John tucked it into the pocket of the child's jersey. 'You keep them there, then they'll be nice and handy whenever you fancy one.' He picked the child up and sat him on his lap. 'There's not very much of you, is there?' he said, bouncing the boy on his knee. 'Why, there'd only have to be the tiniest wind and you'd be blown away. You had better eat up all those sweets quickly, then you'll be much heavier.'

He saw something that was almost a smile flit across the child's face. Funny, he thought, that's the first time he's smiled. Must be the sweets. Funny what sweets will do with a child.

John's irritation of the previous day, his anger at having to face up to a problem, had vanished after the simple solution arrived at with the grey-haired woman at the Welfare Centre. His conscience was at ease and he felt quite expansive.

'You know, David, I've been thinking about you. You can't sit here alone all day. It's not good for you, all on your own. So I saw a lady this morning – Mrs Milligan, she lives on the next floor – and I told her about you and she said that you could go and play with her children whenever you liked. She's got seven so there will be plenty for you to choose from. Now, I've got to get on with my work this afternoon, otherwise there will be complaints from downstairs, so I'll take you to Mrs Milligan, then you can come back and have tea here later on. How's that?'

The child paused for a second, then nodded. Taking the boy by the hand, he went down the stairs to the floor below. They stopped at number eleven and knocked. The door was opened by an enormous woman, who seemed to exude a sweaty friendliness as her room at that moment exuded children.

'Why, hello, Mr Smith, I see you've brought him along, good.' And, turning to the brood of children littered about the doorway, she poked her thumb at David and said, 'This is David. He's staying with Mr Smith here for a few days and he's come to play with you.'

The children eyed the boy with suspicion and David stood tight against John's leg, not looking at them. Mrs Milligan leaned towards John and, in an exaggerated, confidential voice which could be plainly heard on the floor below, whispered, 'It's all right, I've explained to them about his affliction. My eldest 'll look after him. Well, out you go, the lot of you.'

David was caught in the surge as the children rushed down the stairs, and disappeared amongst the screams and yells of the others. Mrs Milligan shouted after them, 'You take good care of him, Effie, and don't get into no mischief and, Jimmy, if you ruin your best trousers I'll knock your bloody head off, straight I will.' Without a pause, she turned to John. 'Now we got rid of them, how about joining me in a nice cup of tea? I've got the kettle on.'

John excused himself, saying that he was behind with his work already, due to the child, and he daren't risk any more complaints. He made his escape, and spent the afternoon cleaning the ground-floor passage and fixing a leaking tap in the basement.

At five o'clock, he returned to his room and put the kettle on. Remembering the washing hanging on the line, he went out onto the escape. The washing was dry but covered in tiny black soot marks. Taking it off the line, he was just entering the room when he saw something move in the courtyard below. Looking down, he saw it was the child, sitting on the lowest step, alone. John called him and the child looked up and started to mount the stairs.

John was filling the teapot when the child entered and stood leaning against the window. 'Come and sit down and have your tea,' said John. 'I expect you're hungry after the fresh air. Did you like the children? Did you play some nice games? Come on, you sit down there, that's it ... There's your tea. It must have been nice for you to have some children to play with. A child must have its youth ... whilst it can. You'll realise that when you're my age.' He was talking to the child but also to himself. 'Yes, have your fun whilst you can ... and you can't find much fun in being alone with an old fogey like me all the time. Go on, help yourself to bread and butter. Yes ... and you'd grow old, very old, if you only had me to talk to all the ...'

He stopped short, realising what he'd said, then continued quickly, too quickly: 'Aren't you going to have some honey? There's some at the bottom of the jar. Scrape it out with this knife, that's it. Like a little bee you are, that's what they do, scrape out the flowers and bring back the honey to the hive each night. And they're clever, oh yes, they never go to the wrong hive. They know what belongs to them.'

He saw that David was hanging onto every word, with a pathetically eager expression on his face. John felt pleased with himself. 'So you'd like to be a bee, eh?' The child nodded. 'Well, one day, if you're a good boy, I'll tell you a nice story all about them. They're much nicer than a lot of people I know. They stick together, they do. No arguments, just like a big family they are. All working together and living together. Bees aren't lonely, like some people. They got companionship ... life's fun to them.' He was thinking of the words of the little grey-haired woman and seeing a great bunch of children, clean and bright, laughing and playing together in a courtyard. 'They're like a lot of children playing together. Companionship, that's what they got. How would you like to live with a lot of other children in a great big house, just like a beehive? ... David, suppose I could arrange for you to go to a nice place like that ... with nurses to look after you, and a nice new suit ...' he glanced at the boy's ragged little jersey, 'and lots of children all laughing and singing. You'd like that, wouldn't you?'

He saw that the excitement had gone from the child's face and his eyes were fixed on the plate as he ate. John was disappointed and his voice was almost pleading as he repeated, 'You would like that, wouldn't you?'

The child nodded slowly. 'Good', said John, feeling pleased. 'Good, I knew you would. Yes, I knew it. Well, I shall have to see what I can do. Go and see some people, try and fix it for you.' He got up and took his mackintosh from the peg by the door. 'Well, I've got to go out now, got to see a friend about something. You must put yourself to bed like a good boy.'

He opened the door and was half out when he turned and said, 'On my way out, I'll have a word with Mrs Milligan and see if you can play with her children again tomorrow. All day. Goodnight, dear.' And, without knowing why, he bent down and, rather awkwardly, kissed the child on its head. Then he went out quickly.

John got up at six, drew the curtains and looked at the view. The child was still asleep, in the little bed they had installed on the other side of the window. Moving quietly, John dressed and hurried out to start his round of duties. Today was his half-day and it was always a rush to cram his work into the morning.

At nine o'clock, he took the child to Mrs Milligan and left him there for the day. And Mrs Milligan heartily assured him that her 'Effie' would look after the boy all right.

As he scrubbed the stairs and passage of the second floor, he was inwardly thinking of the quiet, peaceful afternoon ahead, with his pipe and his newspaper. Suddenly, a voice cut through his dreaming. A harsh, nasty voice. He recognised it as that of Mrs Pope, raised in complaint. Indeed, John had never heard it otherwise.

Mrs Pope lived at number nineteen on the second floor. Her husband lived there too. Secretly, John was scared of her and now, hearing his name mentioned, he peeked cautiously around the stairs. Mrs Pope stood outside her door, complaining to her friend and neighbour, an amorphous spinster by the name of Miss Earl. Mr Pope, a small, smug little man who always wore a stiff collar and was addressed by his wife as 'Mr Pope', stood with them.

'It's a disgrace, that's what it is,' shouted Mrs Pope. 'I pay my rent each week and what do I get? Dirt. No one ever cleans the place and the pipes all leak. It's bad enough for Mr Pope, in his position, to live in such a place, but when it's filthy as well ... It's not healthy to live here, that's what I told the landlord. But all he says is, "We supply your flats" – flats indeed – "with a caretaker, you must speak to him." Speak to him, that lazy old bastard. Never does anything but laze about and cheek people. Do you know, he was even rude to Mr. Pope the other day. Mr Pope, mark you, in his position, hard-working and respected.'

The three of them were walking along the passage towards John. He pressed himself against the wall.

'He's the trouble in this place, never done a stroke of work in his life. You mark my words, he's a real bad lot. That's what I says to Mr Pope, the first day we arrived here twelve years ago. "Mark it," I said, "he's a bad lot".'

They were just approaching John when he saw Miss Earl lean over and whisper in Mrs Pope's ear, 'I've heard tell that he killed his wife, but there was no proof.'

Mrs Pope nodded knowingly: 'And I'd like to know where that child of his comes from.'

Miss Earl said quickly, 'He says it's his sister's. You don't think ...'

'Sister indeed,' rejoined Mrs Pope, 'I bet he knows more about it than he says. Why do you suppose it's dumb? There are some as says that God punishes the wicked in His own way.'

Mr Pope entered the conversation in a rather genteel voice. 'What I don't understand about the man is that he's got no self-respect. Can't even look after the kid proper.' He straightened his tie. 'Leaving it every day with that common Irish-woman.'

Mrs Pope plunged on again. 'And I hear it's such a nasty brat that even the Milligan children won't play with it.'

Miss Earl cut in. 'Oh, I heard they wouldn't play with it because it's dumb. He just sits there and won't play with the others. I always say ...'

'It's not because it's dumb,' said Mrs Pope. 'You mark my words, it's a punishment. God has strange ways, but He don't forget none ...' The voice died away as the trio vanished down the passage.

John straightened and the mop slipped from his fingers. His anger at Mrs Pope's words was dead. A new and awful thought had entered his head.

Rushing the mop and pail hurriedly into a cupboard, he ran out of the building. In the street, the sun was shining, but he didn't see it. In the distance, he saw a group of children playing. Half-running, he approached them, searching each face for that of David.

There were children everywhere – big children, little children, some playing hopscotch or skipping or playing marbles or tag – but no David.

He walked around the block, searching each group of children that he passed. He crossed the road and approached the tenement from the rear. On the left was the scarred waste of a bombed house and, hearing children's voices, he hurried over to it. In a cellar, gauged open by bomb blast, he found three of the Milligan children playing. Leaning over the wall, he called out, 'Jimmy, where's David?'

The game stopped. Jimmy, a square, healthy-looking boy, looked up. 'He's gone home ...' He kicked a loose stone. 'Said he didn't want to play any more ...' There was something sheepish in the way he spoke and in the manner of the other children.

John turned and walked back to the tenement. Opening the court-yard door, he was about to climb the escape when he heard a faint sound. He turned, and saw David.

A shaft of sunlight cut through the gloom of the yard and bathed the far wall with yellow light. The child sat amongst the overflowing dustbins. From these, he had salvaged some dead flowers and an old bottle, wrapped in dirty paper. He had arranged them in his lap and was playing some mysterious game all of his own. In his hand was clutched a pink jelly baby and the sun, finding it, made it leap and twinkle with red and pink diamonds.

John watched him and was just about to interrupt when, with a pain that pierced through him, he saw the child's mouth open and a myriad of soundless words tumble over the sticky sweet in his hand.

That afternoon, the child walked along the crowded high street, his hand firmly clasped in John's. Dodging in and out between the hurried shoppers, they finally boarded a bus and scrambled on top.

'Fares please,' demanded the Conductor. John, easing the collar on his perspiring neck, thought for one instant of the way he had planned to spend his free afternoon, said: 'One and a half to Kew Gardens, please.' His voice sounded strangely firm. He handed the tickets to the child with a little smile. Wait, just wait, till he sees real flowers ... He sat back in his seat, watching the child, and waited.

It was in a kingdom of green that they walked together. The vivid flashes of colour from the flowers and the cool stonework of the buildings seemed to accentuate the green in which they were set. And everywhere hung that mellow softness that age bestows on the things it loves.

To the child's eyes, accustomed to a world of colourless etchings, it was a strange and wondrous place. And John, walking at his side, discovered a new child. Slowly, as they penetrated deeper into the grounds, he saw David's shyness evaporate. He scampered from one flower-bed to the next, his face flushed and animated. No flower was too small or too delicate to escape his attention, and each separate bloom seemed more exciting than the last. He ran ahead of John, dashed back, pointed, waved and danced with delight. Nothing escaped his inquisitive eye and, each time he discovered a fresh treasure, John was dragged over to share in its delight.

Watching the child as it mutely tendered each new miracle for his approval, a strange thing happened to John. He began to see the flowers, the trees and the grass as though for the first time. The beds of flowers were no longer blobs of colour, known and seen by the collective name of the species. Each one now seemed different, special, and a very miracle of form and colour. He saw the gardens with eyes unfettered by age or habit. He saw through the eyes of the child.

They walked together along spacious paths, flanked with elegant borders, and came to the lake. The bright reflected blue of the sky and the mysterious green of its depths met suddenly on the surface. Around it, trailing their silver fronds in the water, were a long row of willow trees. The smoothness of the water was rippled only by the majesty of a lone black swan.

The child gasped and ran to the water's edge. They sat down on the bank and the child, leaning over the twisted root of a willow, gazed at his reflection, mirrored in the shallow water. His hand stole softly into the water, changing colour as it neared the bottom and the reflection vanished. As he withdrew his hand, John watched small crystal globules run down the boy's arm and fall softly on the emerald moss.

They sat there for a little while and neither spoke. Eventually, John led the child towards the tropical greenhouse, which, reflecting the sun, seemed to float in the haze and glittered like some jewelled temple.

Inside, the moist heat was oppressive and the vast hall was deserted. Walking down the centre aisle, they both gazed with awe at the palm trees towering over their heads. Their footfalls echoed strangely from the glass walls and, when they stood still, there was a heavy silence. No noise or wind could penetrate the giant transparent sheath; yet there was a strange feeling that each fat leaf, each snaking vine, had moved just before their eyes had fixed it. It was as though, through their skins, they felt the unseen, unheard movement of each plant as it grew and twined and wound about its neighbour. A thick, dreamy scent hung over the lascivious, green undergrowth.

John glanced at the child and noticed that he, too, was uneasy in this forced atmosphere. They left, and stood outside in the cool air once more, then wandered off together through the lovely gardens.

That night, he put the child to bed himself and, after he had tucked it up, sat thinking of their afternoon. He suddenly realised with surprise that he had enjoyed himself. He heard the child turn over restlessly. Softly, he got up and drew the curtains and, in the pale light from the moon, saw that the child lay with its eyes fixed on the ceiling, a little smile on its lips.

He sat on the bed and whispered, 'Are you still thinking of the garden, David?' David nodded. 'We'll go there again together before ...' He stopped. 'It would be wonderful to live somewhere like that garden. You know, David, when I was a boy I used to want to get away. But somehow I never seemed to get very far. I suppose I was looking for a garden like that ... It would be wonderful to have a garden like that of your own.'

He sat there, thinking, and the child didn't move. 'Perhaps one day we will ... yes, perhaps.' He started to undress and got into his bed. 'You'd better go to sleep now. Close your eyes and think of today. Where we've been and everything we've seen. You'll sleep.'

John lay there and heard his alarm clock slowly tick away the seconds to six o'clock. Fancy enjoying this afternoon, he thought to himself. Perhaps it's the first time you've ever made any person happy. Yes, that must be why; it is the first time. And he was happy too. I've never seen anything like it, scampering and jumping ... He should have somewhere nice like that to grow up in – not the dirty, cruel slum that you've had around you all the time. But he'll be all right in the home; they'll look after him ... But will he? Will he be as happy as he was today? You made him happy today – will they? ... Don't be silly – remember what the grey-haired woman said, 'no foolish sentiment' ... Now, go to sleep and don't be silly ... But fancy you making someone happy ... And he slipped away into sleep.

The alarm went at six o'clock. He got up and looked at the view. All that day, as he worked, he thought of the previous day and smiled at himself for having enjoyed it. Must be going back to second childhood, he thought.

But the day passed quickly, and he was pleased to go back to his room at five o'clock. The child was waiting and, as he opened the door, it ran to greet him, smiling.

They had tea and, afterwards, he sat on the escape in his old basket-chair with the child beside him. 'You know, David, I've been thinking all day about that wonderful garden. Have you been thinking about it, too? Yes, I thought you would. Well, I've been thinking ... why shouldn't you have a garden like that? No, I'm serious. A garden of our own. A little one, like this.' And he picked up from the rubbish by the chair an old wooden box. 'It would only be very small, of course, but at least we could make it ourselves, and it would really be ours, wouldn't it? I remember seeing one in a big shop, years ago. We could have flowers and little paths – just like the ones we saw yesterday. Why, we might even have a lake in it ...' The child clapped its hands as he said this. 'And we could work together on it each evening, and I could tell you all kinds of stories about the fairies and goblins who'd come to live in it ... Why, we'd have all the fairies in the slum coming and asking us if they might live here. What do you say?'

The child was so wildly excited, jumping up and down, that John felt a queer lump grow in his throat. He wondered why. 'Well, we'll start tonight,' he said. 'Go and get the box of tools from the dresser, and in no time our garden will be ready.'

They sat together on the balcony, working on their garden, until it was late.

Each morning, John arose at six and, each morning, he looked at the view. And each day, he rushed through his work to get back to his room and the little garden.

And the garden grew. They packed the old box with earth from the bomb site, and the child spent hours selecting the small plants which together they pressed into the soil. There were little paths made of sand, and a piece of broken mirror formed a lake.

Each night, he told the child stories about their little garden. Stories about fairies and goblins who lived a lonely, sad life in the dirty slum but now, sheltered beneath the little flowers in the box, were happy and gay.

At first, the stories were brief remembrances from his childhood, but, as the gossamer threads of love for the child grew stronger day by day, so his imagination became fertile. And so the stories grew larger in scope until, bursting from the little orange-box, they were scattered over the view from the window. His imagination transformed the dingy view into a garden of molten colours. The disused warehouse opposite dissolved into the greenest of lawns and was endless; the broken guttering, hanging limp, became a tree – a special tree which enclosed the heart of an old man, and, on windy days, the branches of silvery leaves waved as once did his hair. The broken tiles on the adjoining roof were seen as little steps up to the sky – steps to a little palace standing on a blue mound of sky. All around were beautiful trees with slender, winding roots and, growing from the moss at their feet, hundreds of vivid, waving flowers. In the centre of the lawn was a deep well, with a single blood-red lily growing in the surface.

Each night, the child sat listening to every word, enchanted. And love, growing daily as he tried to soften a sordid life with happiness for the child, seized John and carried him in its wake towards the same enchantment. He began to see his own words as he offered them to the child, and each story became a world in which they both shared and lived.

Each day, he hurried through the passages, washing, swabbing and dusting, unaware of what he was doing. For, to John, this was no longer reality. He heard the cheery shout of Mrs Milligan as she wished him good morning; he heard the continual words of abuse from Mrs Pope; he heard the early morning bustle of the building and the sigh of the tenement at night. But he was unaware of what the voices said. He floated as though through a dream, hearing, seeing, but knowing that they were but whispers in a dream. His reality was in the garden. It started always as he shut the door and looked around the room. There was the child, waiting, and together they would sit beneath the trees and amidst the flowers and gaze out at their own world.

Day by day, this world became more acidly sharp as, day by day, time lapped at the fringe of the garden, bringing the hour of the child's departure ever closer. And John could not bring himself to tell the boy that soon he must leave the garden and live in an orphanage.

On Tuesday, John awoke, stretched, and then remembered. This was the day. He glanced over at the child, sleeping peacefully on the little bed. He got up and drew the curtains. On the cracked window-pane, a spider was completing its web, which glistened with the early frost. A morning sun, gold and red, was sweeping the mist from the sky. The garden, hiding behind shrouds of mist, was very quiet. He stood and looked ... then he started the fire, shaved and prepared breakfast.

Bending over the child's bed, he watched his dreaming slumber for a moment before waking him.

David dressed and sat down at the table. John poured out the tea and, as he handed the child a cup, he glanced at David's face. He knows. Yes, thought John, he knows.

Breakfast passed without a word. But the moment came. John tried to make a little joke as they packed and tied the child's valise with thick twine, but his eyes were so misty that he couldn't see if the boy had smiled.

John opened the door, and the child walked past him into the passage. As he shut the door, John glanced back at the window, and saw that the mist was gone and the garden shone like gold in the sunlight.

Outside, the streets were empty. They walked along, the child's hand clutched tightly in his. Their footsteps sounded loud and metallic on the paving stones, still traced with frost. As they drew near the Welfare Centre, their footsteps became drowned beneath the boom of early traffic. John's eyes were fixed ahead, neither glancing to the right nor left, and never down to the child.

At the foot of the steps, he paused for a second, then marched inside the building. They were shown into a bare waiting room. It was cold and smelt of disinfectant, which a charwoman was liberally sluicing over the floor.

They sat down. John was silent and listened to the steady splashing of the mop. Suddenly he turned to the child. 'David, I know that you are going to be happy here with the other children. It's your only chance to grow up and be somebody ... and ... and to get out of this slum. You must try and understand what I'm telling you. And there'll be a garden, too, a proper garden ...'

The charwoman had stopped work and was watching them. 'You leaving him here?' she asked. John nodded. She sniffed. 'I got nine of them.' She lost interest and continued with her mopping.

John turned to the child, smiled thinly and wondered what to say. The door opened and the little grey-haired woman strode over to them, briskly. David got down from his chair and stood close to John.

'Good morning, Mr Smith. You are bright and early this morning. I see you've brought David. How are you, my dear? You're coming to stay with us. We'll take care of you and you'll have lots of fun.'

As she spoke, John watched the film of water from the char-woman's mop creep slowly across the floor. It was flecked with bubbles of disinfectant and a cigarette butt, sodden, floated on it. He saw the shoes of the little grey-haired woman: they were brown and practical and reminded him of red apples.

The child's hand was twisting and turning a loose thread on the arm of John's overcoat. '... Well, Mr. Smith, I expect you'd like to say goodbye to David. Not goodbye, au revoir. Until you meet again.' She smiled kindly down at the child. The charwoman stopped work and gazed at them with a vacant but interested stare. John coughed. The child stood looking at him, still twisting the thread on his sleeve.

'Goodbye, David .. I'll ... Goodbye.' His voice died to a whisper. The woman took the child's hand and led him to the door, saying, 'Now, first, my dear, we'll have to see what's in that suitcase of yours, and then we'll give you a nice, new suit ...'

As they left the room, John wanted to call out: 'David, I'll keep the garden for you ... wait till you come back ...' But no sound came from his throat. He turned and ran out of the building, and bumped into the postman as he ran down the steps.

It was a fine day, with just that tang in the air which spoke of approaching autumn. All the bustle of the morning traffic had polished away the frost. Standing on the kerb, John was jostled by pedestrians, moving with purpose to a set destination. Aimlessly, he crossed the road, and was met by a fresh stream of people as they were disgorged by a tube entrance. He turned in the direction of the tenement – and became aware of some commotion on the opposite pavement.

On the steps of the Welfare Centre, a group of people had gathered, and John noticed the little grey-haired woman was waving and shouting at him. He felt suddenly frightened and started to hurry across when, in a sudden flash, he saw the child.

David was running breathlessly across the road, his valise clutched to his chest. In one brief second, John saw the expression on the child's face, caught a glimpse of one unbuttoned shoe, and heard the little grey-haired woman shouting, 'For God's sake, stop him!' He noticed the curious expressions on the faces of the passers-by suddenly freeze ... And he saw the frightened eyes of the bus driver as he swung the wheel and jammed on the brakes, which seared on the tarmac, screaming, as the bus engulfed the child.

The scream died, and everything stood petrified. The only movement was from the child's valise, which, rolling in the gutter, spilled its contents over the road. It came to rest, crushed and empty.

The crowd surged forward, until the shining vermilion of the bus was obscured from John's sight. He walked slowly through the stationary traffic to the centre of the crowd ...

The room was leaden with the half-light of approaching dusk when John returned. He closed the door and heard the latch click. He walked across to the window and climbed out onto the escape.

The last glint of the sunset was still in the sky and made the buildings stand out like harsh caricatures. He seemed to feel time eating and disintegrating everything, as it had rusted the handrail, rough beneath his hand. There was nowhere a hint of green, a shoot, a petalled flower. The garden, like the child, was gone.

He stood staring, and then came back into the room, where only the darkness could see the tears which slipped down each cheek. He sat there, his fingers twisting the loose thread on his coat-sleeve, whilst the emotion drained slowly from his body.

Suddenly, he sat forward in his chair. He heard a noise. Someone had called him. Without realising what he was doing, he sprang to the window. And saw the child.

Right in the far distance, moving through great fields of flowers, the child was running towards him. He saw the expression on the boy's face, and saw that one shoe was unbuttoned. And then he saw that David's lips were moving. And, clear in the night air, he heard: 'Uncle John ... Uncle John ...'

With a bound, John was through the window and running up in the cool darkness to meet him.

Sharp at seven a.m., the dustman opened the area door, and found the body of John Smith. It lay, crushed, in the centre of the yard. One arm was stretched out awkwardly, the hand clutching a dead flower, at the base of the dustbins. The yard was still and quiet and, next to the body, was a broken tile, dislodged the previous night by the restless, marauding cats.

Filmography

Jack Clayton's film career began in 1935 when he was employed by Alexander Korda's London Films as a third assistant director, a job he defined as 'one who runs messages for everybody, calls the actors and acts as general dogsbody'. His route to direction involved a long apprenticeship in less exciting aspects of the profession. The lesson he was to draw from this and the advice he was to pass on to younger aspirants in any walk of life, was: 'Never be good at something you don't enjoy doing.'

Third assistant director

The Conquest of the Air, 1936. Dir. Zoltan Korda, and others. Documentary. With Laurence Oliver, Hay Petrie.

Men Are Not Gods, 1936. Dir. Walter Reisch. Leading players: Miriam Hopkins, Sebastian Shaw, Rex Harrison.

Wings of the Morning, 1936. Dir. Harold Schuster. Leading players: Henry Fonda, Anabella, John McCormack. (Britain's first Technicolor film.)

Under the Red Robe, 1937. Dir. Victor Seastrom. Leading players: Conrad Veidt, Raymond Massey.

Over the Moon, 1937. Dirs. Thornton Freeland, William K. Howard. Leading players: Merle Oberon, Rex Harrison.

The Divorce of Lady X, 1938. Dir. Tim Whelan. Leading players: Laurence Olivier, Merle Oberon.

Prison Without Bars, 1938. Dir. Brian Desmond Hurst. Leading players: Edna Best, Martita Hunt, Glynis Johns.

Q. Planes (US title: *Clouds Over Europe*), 1939. Dir. Tim Whelan. Leading players: Ralph Richardson, Laurence Olivier.

The Spy in Black (US title: *U-Boat 29*), 1939. Dir. Michael Powell. Leading players: Conrad Veidt, Valerie Hobson.

The Thief of Bagdad, 1940. Dirs. Ludwig Berger, Michael Powell, Tim Whelan. Leading players: Sabu, Conrad Veidt. (Clayton was the co-ordinating second assistant director for all three shooting units.)

Major Barbara, 1941. Dir. Gabriel Pascal. Leading players: Wendy Hiller, Rex Harrison, Deborah Kerr.

Atlantic Ferry (US title: *Sons of the Sea*), 1941. Dir. Walter Forde. Leading players: Michael Redgrave, Valerie Hobson.

Assistant director

While the Sun Shines, 1946. Dir. Anthony Asquith. Scr. Terence Rattigan. Ph. Jack Hildyard. Leading players: Brenda Bruce, Ronald Howard, Barbara White.

Production manager

An Ideal Husband, 1947. Dir. Alexander Korda. Scr. Lajos Biro. From the play by Oscar Wilde. Ph. Georges Perinal. Mu. Arthur Benjamin. Leading players: Paulette Goddard, Hugh Williams, Michael Wilding.

Second unit director

Bond Street, 1948. Dir. Gordon Parry. Scr. Anatole de Grunwald. Ph: Otto Heller. Mu. Benjamin Frankel. Leading players: Roland Young, Jean Kent.

Associate producer

The Queen of Spades, 1948. Dir. Thorold Dickinson. Scr. Rodney Ackland, Arthur Boys. From the story by Alexander Pushkin. Ph. Otto Heller. Mu. Georges Auric. Leading players: Anton Walbrook, Edith Evans, Yvonne Mitchell.

Flesh and Blood, 1951. Dir. Anthony Kimmins. Scr. Anatole de Grunwald. From the play 'A Sleeping Clergyman' by James Bridie. Ph. Otto Heller. Mu. Charles Williams. Leading players: Richard Todd, Glynis Johns.

Moulin Rouge, 1952. Dir. John Huston. Scr. John Huston, Anthony Veiller. From the novel by Pierre La Mure. Ph. Oswald Morris. Mu. Georges Auric. Leading players: José Ferrer, Zsa Zsa Gabor, Katherine Kath, Colette Marchand, Suzanne Flon.

Beat the Devil, 1954. Dir. John Huston. Scr. John Huston, Truman Capote. From the novel by James Helvick (pseudonym of Claud Cockburn). Ph. Oswald Morris. Mu. Franco Mannino. Leading players: Humphrey Bogart, Jennifer Jones, Gina Lollobrigida, Robert Morley, Peter Lorre, Edward Underdown, Ivor Barnard, Bernard Lee.

The Good Die Young, 1954. Dir. Lewis Gilbert. Scr. Lewis Gilbert, Vernon Harris. Ph. Jack Asher. Mu. Georges Auric. Leading players: Laurence Harvey, Margaret Leighton, Gloria Grahame, Richard Basehart, Joan Collins, John Ireland, Stanley Baker, Robert Morley.

I Am A Camera, 1955. Dir. Henry Cornelius. Scr. John Collier. From the Berlin stories of Christopher Isherwood and the play by John Van Druten. Ph. Guy Green. Mu. Malcolm Arnold. Leading players: Julie Harris, Laurence Harvey, Shelley Winters, Patrick McGoohan.

The Story of Esther Costello, 1957. Dir. David Miller. Scr. Charles Kaufman. From the novel by Nicholas Monsarrat. Ph. Robert Krasker. Mu. Georges Auric. Leading players: Joan Crawford, Heather Sears, Rossano Brazzi. (Clayton also directed the second unit.)

Producer

Sailor Beware (US title: *Panic in the Parlour*), 1956. Dir. Gordon Parry. Scr. Philip King, Falkland L. Cary. From their play. Ph. Douglas Slocombe. Mu. Peter Akister. Leading players: Peggy Mount, Ronald Lewis, Shirley Eaton, Esma Cannon, Cyril Smith.

Dry Rot, 1956. Dir. Maurice Elvey. Scr. John Chapman. From his play. Ph. Arthur Grant. Mu. Peter Akister. Leading players: Ronald Shiner, Brian Rix, Sid James, Joan Sims, Heather Sears, Peggy Mount.

Three Men in Boat, 1956. Dir. Ken Annakin. Scr. Hubert Gregg, Vernon Harris. From the novel by Jerome K. Jerome. Ph. Eric Cross. Mu.

John Addison. Leading players: David Tomlinson, Jimmy Edwards, Laurence Harvey, Shirley Eaton, Martita Hunt, A.E. Matthews.

The Whole Truth, 1958. Dir. John Guillermin. Scr. Jonathan Latimer. From the play by Philip Mackie. Ph. Wilkie Cooper. Mu. Mischa Spoliansky. Leading players: Stewart Granger, George Sanders, Donna Reed.

Director

Naples is a Battlefield, 1944, 13 mins., b/w (uncredited)

'As I arrived in Naples when it was liberated, I wrote the original idea and shot a good seventy-five per cent of the material in this film, which was put together and edited in England by Peter Baylis – also of the RAF Film Unit – and subsequently released as a Ministry of Information film.' (Jack Clayton)

The Bespoke Overcoat, 1955, 37 mins., b/w

Production company: Remus (John and James Woolf)
Producer: Jack Clayton
Screenplay: Wolf Mankowitz
Photography: Wolfgang Suschitzky
Music: Georges Auric
Art direction: Anthony Masters
Editing: Stanley Hawkes
Leading players: David Kossoff (Morry), Alfie Bass (Fender), Alan Tilvern (Mr Ranting), Alf Dean (The Gravedigger)
• British Academy Award, 1955 (Best Specialised Film)
• Venice Film Festival, 1955 (Best Short Film)
• Hollywood Academy Award, 1956 (Best Short Subject, two-reel)

Room at the Top, 1959, 117 mins., b/w

Distributor: Independent/British Lion
Production company: Remus
Producers: John and James Woolf
Screenplay: Neil Paterson, from the novel by John Braine
Photography: Freddie Francis

Editing: Ralph Kemplen
Art direction: Ralph Brinton
Music: Mario Nascimbene
Sound direction: John Cox
Sound recorder: Peter Handford
Leading players: Laurence Harvey (Joe Lampton), Simone Signoret (Alice Aisgill), Heather Sears (Susan Brown), Donald Wolfit (Mr Brown), Ambrosine Phillpotts (Mrs Brown), Donald Houston (Charles Soames), Raymond Huntley (Mr. Hoylake), John Westbrook (Jack Wales), Allan Cuthbertson (George Aisgill), Mary Peach (June Samson), Hermione Baddeley (Elspeth), Beatrice Varley (Aunt Emily) and Wilfrid Lawson (Uncle). Also featuring: Prunella Scales, Wendy Craig, Richard Pasco, Ian Hendry, Jack Hedley, Darren Nesbitt
- Hollywood Academy Awards: Best Actress (Simone Signoret), Best Adapted Screenplay (Neil Paterson)
- Hollywood Academy Award Nominations: Best Film, Best Actor (Laurence Harvey), Best Supporting Actress (Hermione Baddeley), Best Director (Jack Clayton)
- British Film Academy Awards: Best Film from any Source, Best British Film, Best Foreign Actress (Simone Signoret)
- Cannes Film Festival: Best Actress (Simone Signoret)
- Samuel Goldwyn International Film Award: Best Foreign Film
- Acapulco Film Festival: Best Film
- Prague Film Festival: First Prize and Diploma

The Innocents, 1961, 99 mins., b/w, Cinemascope

Production company: Achilles Productions, Twentieth Century Fox
Executive producer: Albert Fennell
Producer: Jack Clayton
Screenplay: William Archibald, Truman Capote, based on the novella *The Turn of the Screw* by Henry James. Additional scenes and dialogue by John Mortimer
Photography: Freddie Francis
Music: Georges Auric
Music director: W. Lambert Williamson
Lyric: 'O Willow Waly' by Paul Dehn
Art direction: Wilfred Shingleton
Editing: James Clark

Sound recording: John Cox, A. G. (Buster) Ambler
Camera operator: Ronnie Taylor
Costumes: Sophie Devine
Leading players: Deborah Kerr (Miss Giddens), Michael Redgrave (The Uncle), Martin Stephens (Miles), Pamela Franklin (Flora), Megs Jenkins (Mrs Grose), Peter Wyngarde (Quint), Clytie Jessop (Miss Jessel), Isla Cameron (Anna), Eric Woodburn (Coachman)

The Pumpkin Eater, 1964, 110 mins., b/w

Production company: Romulus/Jack Clayton for Columbia Pictures release
Producer: James Woolf
Screenplay: Harold Pinter, based on the novel by Penelope Mortimer
Photography: Oswald Morris
Editing: James Clark
Art direction: Edward Marshall
Music: Georges Delerue
Sound recordists: Peter Handford, John Aldred
Costumes: Motley
Associate producer: James Ware
Leading players: Anne Bancroft (Jo Armitage), Peter Finch (Jake Armitage), James Mason (Bob Conway), Janine Gray (Beth Conway), Cedric Hardwicke (Jo's father), Rosalind Atkinson (Jo's mother), Alan Webb (Jake's father), Richard Johnson (Giles), Maggie Smith (Philpot), Eric Porter (Psychiatrist), Cyril Luckham (Doctor), Anthony Nicholls (Surgeon), John Junkin (Undertaker), Yootha Joyce (Woman in Hairdresser's), Leslie Nunnerley (Waitress at Zoo), Frank Singuinea ('King of Israel'), Gerald Sim (Man at Party). The children: Gregory Phillips/Rupert Osborn (Pete), Michael Ridgeway/Martin Norton (Jack), Frances White/Kate Nicholls (Dinah), Fergus McLelland/Christopher Ellis (Fergus), Elizabeth Dear/Sarah Nicholls (Elizabeth), Sharon Maxwell/Mimosa Annis (Sharon), Kash Dewar (Mark)
- Hollywood Academy Award Nomination: Best Actress (Anne Bancroft)
- British Academy Awards: Best Foreign Actress (Anne Bancroft), Best Screenplay (Harold Pinter), Best Cinematography, black and white (Oswald Morris), Best Costume Design, black and white (Motley)

- Golden Globe Award: Best Actress – Drama (Anne Bancroft)
- Cannes Film Festival Award: Best Actress (Anne Bancroft)

Our Mother's House, 1967, 105 mins., col.

Production company: Heron Film Productions/Filmways for MGM
   distributors
Executive producer: Martin Ransohoff
Producer: Jack Clayton
Screenplay: Jeremy Brooks and Haya Harareet, from the novel by
   Julian Gloag
Photography (Metrocolor): Larry Pizer
Editing: Tom Priestley
Art direction: Reece Pemberton
Music: Georges Delerue
Sound director: Terry Rawlings
Sound recordist: Ken Richie
Costumes: Sue Yelland
Leading players: Dirk Bogarde (Charlie Hook), Margaret Brooks
   (Elsa), Pamela Franklin (Diana), Louis Sheldon Williams (Hubert),
   John Gugolka (Dunstan), Mark Lester (Jiminee), Sarah Nicholls
   (Gerry), Gustav Henry (Willy), Parnham Wallace (Louis), Yootha
   Joyce (Mrs Quayle), Claire Davidson (Miss Bailey), Anthony
   Nicholls (Mr Halbert), Annette Carell (Mother), Gerald Sim (Bank
   Clerk), Edina Ronay (Doreen), Diana Ashley (Girlfriend), Garfield
   Morgan (Mr Moley), Faith Kent (Woman Client), John Arnatt
   (Man Client), Jack Silk (Motorcyclist)

The Great Gatsby, 1974, 140 mins., col.

Production company: Paramount
Producer: David Merrick
Screenplay: Francis Ford Coppola, based on the novel by F. Scott
   Fitzgerald
Photography (Eastman Color): Douglas Slocombe
Editing: Tom Priestley
Production designer: John Box
Art direction: Eugene Rudolf, Robert Laing
Costumes: Theoni V. Aldredge
Sound recording: Ken Barker

Musical supervisor and additional music: Nelson Riddle

Music / song: 'What'll I Do' by Irving Berlin, sung by Bill Atherton; 'The Sheikh of Araby' by H. B. Smith, F. Wheller and P. Snyder; 'Five Foot Two, Eyes of Blue' by S. Lewis, J. Young and R. Henderson, sung by Nick Lucas; 'Who?' by O. Harbuch, Oscar Hammerstein II and Jerome Kern; 'I'm Gonna Charleston Back to Charleston' by R. Turk, L. Handman, sung by Nick Lucas; 'Yes, Sir, That's My Baby' by G. Kahn and W. Donaldson; 'We've Met Before' by Irving Berlin and Nelson Riddle; 'Whispering' by J. Schonberger, R. Coburn and V. Rose; 'Charleston' by C. Mack and J. Johnson; 'It Had To Be You' by G. Kahn and T. Jones; 'When You and I Were Seventeen' by G. Kahn and C. Rosoff, sung by Nick Lucas; 'Alice Blue Gown' by J. McCarthy and H. Tierney; 'My Favourite Beau' by Irving Berlin and Nelson Riddle; 'Kitten on the Keys' by Z. Confrey; 'Beale Street Blues' by W. C. Handy, piano solo by Jess Stacy; 'Ain't We Got Fun' by G. Kahn, R. Egan and R. Whiting.

Leading players: Robert Redford (Jay Gatsby), Mia Farrow (Daisy Buchanan), Bruce Dern (Tom Buchanan), Karen Black (Myrtle Wilson), Scott Wilson (George Wilson), Sam Waterston (Nick Carraway), Lois Chiles (Jordan Baker), Howard Da Silva (Meyer Wolfsheim), Roberts Blossom (Mr Gatz), Edward Herrmann (Klipspringer), Elliot Sullivan (Wilson's Friend), Arthur Hughes (Dog Vendor), Kathryn Leigh Scott (Catherine), Beth Porter (Mrs McKee), Paul Tamarin (Mr McKee), John Devlin (Gatsby's Body-guard), Patsy Kensit (Pamela Buchanan), Marjorie Wildes (Pamela's Nurse), Blain Fairman (Policeman), Bob Sherman and Norman Chauncer (Detectives at Pool), Regina Baff (Max Baedeker), Janet Arters and Louise Arters (Twins), Sammy Smith (Comic)

- Hollywood Academy Awards: Best Music Scoring (Nelson Riddle), Best Costume Design (Theoni V. Aldredge)
- British Academy Awards: Best Cinematography (Douglas Slocombe), Best Art direction (John Box), Best Costume Design (Theoni V. Aldredge)

Something Wicked This Way Comes, 1983, 94 mins., col.

Production company: Buena Vista
Producer: Peter Vincent Douglas
Screenplay: Ray Bradbury, based on his novel

Photography: Stephen H. Burum
Editing: Argyle Nelson, Barry Mark Gordon
Production designer: Richard MacDonald
Art direction: Richard B. Mansbridge, Richard James Lawrence
Music: James Horner
Special visual effects: Lee Dyer
Costumes: Ruth Myers
Sound supervisor: Bob Hathaway
Leading players: Jason Robards (Charles Halloway), Jonathan Pryce (Mr Dark), Diane Ladd (Mrs Nightshade), Pam Grier (Dust Witch), Royal Dano (Tom Fury), Vidal Peterson (Will Halloway), Shawn Carson (Jim Nightshade), Tony Christopher (Young Ed), Sharon Lea (Young Miss Foley), Mary Grace Canfield (Miss Foley), Richard Davalos (Mr Crosetti), Jack Dengel (Mr Tetley), Jack Dodson (Mr Douglas), Bruce M. Fisher (Mr Cooger), Ellen Geer (Mrs Halloway), Brendan Klinger (Cooger as a child), James Stacy (Ed, the bartender), Arthur Hill (Narrator)

The Lonely Passion of Judith Hearne, 1987, 116 mins., col.

Production company: HandMade Films / United British Artists
Executive producers: George Harrison, Denis O'Brien
Producers: Peter Nelson, Richard Johnson
Production associate: Elton John
Screenplay: Peter Nelson, based on the novel by Brian Moore
Photography: Peter Hannan
Editing: Terry Rawlings
Production design: Michael Pickwood
Art direction: Henry Harris
Music: Georges Delerue
Musical arrangement: Rick Wentworth: 'Prelude No. 4 in E. Minor' by Chopin
Costumes: Elizabeth Waller
Sound recording: Alistair Crocker
Leading players: Maggie Smith (Judith Hearne), Bob Hoskins (James Madden), Wendy Hiller (Aunt D'Arcy), Marie Kean (Mrs Rice), Ian McNeice (Bernard Rice), Alan Devlin (Father Quigley), Rudi Davies (Mary), Prunella Scales (Moira O'Neill), Aine Ni Mhuiri (Edie Marinan), Sheila Reid (Miss Friel), Niall Buggy (Mr Lenehan), Kate Binchy (Sister Ignatius), Martina Stanley (Sister Mary-Paul),

Veronica Quilligan (Mrs Mullen), Frank Egerton (The Major), Leonard McGuire (Doctor Bowe), Kevin Flood (Owen O'Neill), Catherine Cusack (Una O'Neill), Peter Gilmore (Kevin O'Neill), James Holland (Shaun O'Neill), Aidan Murphy (Youth at Liquor Store), Emma Jane Lavin (Young Judith), Dick Sullivan (Priest), Alan Radcliffe (Young Priest), Seamus Newham and Paul Boyle (Taxi Drivers), Isolde Cazelet and Marjorie Hogan (Old Women), Gerard O'Hagan (Water), Anna Murphy and Gemma Murphy (Girl Gigglers), Paddy Joyce (Drunk in Pub), Richard Taylor (Tin Whistle Player), Sue Hampson (Cellist at Aunt D'Arcy's), Mike Rennie (Violinist at Aunt D'Arcy's)

- British Academy Award: Best Actress (Maggie Smith)

Memento Mori, 1992, 100 mins., col.

Production company: BBC TV – Screen 2 in association with WGBH, Boston
Producer: Louis Marks
Screenplay: Alan Kelley, Jeanie Sims, Jack Clayton, from the novel by Muriel Spark
Photography: Remi Adefarasin
Editing: Mark Day
Production designer: Oliver Bayldon
Music: Georges Delerue (piano soloist: Peter Katin)
Costumes: Les Lansdown
Sound recording: John Pritchard, Aad Wirtz
Sound editing: Julia Buckland, Bronwen Jenkins
Casting: Irene Lamb
Leading players: Maggie Smith (Mrs Mabel Pettigrew), Michael Hordern (Godfrey Colston), Renée Asherson (Charmian Colston), Stephanie Cole (Dame Lettie Colston), Thora Hird (Jean Taylor), Maurice Denham (Guy Leet), John Wood (Inspector Henry Mortimer), Zoë Wanamaker (Olive Mannering), Peter Eyre (Eric Colston), Cyril Cusack (Peter Mannering), Jacqueline Leonard (Gwen), Elizabeth Bradley (Mrs Anthony), Margery Withers (Grannie Barnacle), Robert Flemyng (Ronald Sidebottome), Barbara Hicks (Tempest Sidebottome), Muriel Pavlow (Grannie Valvona), Damaris Hayman (Miss Lottinville), Anna Cropper (Mrs Mortimer), Paul Opacic (Jeff), Mary Healey (Ward Sister), Preston Lockwood (Deaf Old Man), Arthur Hewlett (Ancient Man), John

Baskcomb (Fat Old Man), Jan Carey (Tea Shop Manageress), Leonard Maguire (Mr Willoughby), Martina Stanley (Nurse Lucy), Richard Lawry (Photographer), Dominic Taylor (Young Journalist), Terence Soall (Publisher), Walter Sparrow (Small-holder), Andrew Charleson (Policeman), Frank Shelley (The Stranger), Aimee Delamain (Ambulatory Grannie), Emma Richler (Young Nurse), Alan Leith (Detective), Hilda Sachs, Brenda Cullity, Brigitte Loesser (Tea Room Trio)

Select bibliography

Aldgate, Anthony, *Censorship and the Permissive Society: British Cinema and Theatre, 1955–1965*, Oxford, Clarendon Press, 1995.

Allen, Jeannie Thomas, '"The Turn of the Screw" and *The Innocents*: Two Types of Ambiguity', in *The Classic American Novel and the Movies*, ed. Gerald Peary and R. Shatzkin, New York, Ungar, 1971, pp. 132–42.

Andrew, Dudley, *Concepts in Film Theory*, Oxford, Oxford University Press, 1984.

Archibald, William, *The Innocents*, New York, Samuel French Publishers, 1950.

Armes, Roy, *A Critical History of British Cinema*, London, Secker & Warburg, 1978.

Atkins, Irene Kahn, 'In Search of the Greatest Gatsby', *Literature/Film Quarterly*, Vol. 21, No. 3, Summer 1974, pp. 216–28.

Betts, Ernest, *The Film Business*, London, George Allen & Unwin, 1973.

Billington, Michael, *The Life and Work of Harold Pinter*, London, Faber, 1996.

Bogarde, Dirk, *Snakes and Ladders*, London, Chatto & Windus, 1978.

Bordwell, David, 'The Art Cinema as a Mode of Film Practice', in *Film Criticism*, Vol. 4, No. 1, Fall 1979. Repr. *Film Theory and Criticism: Fifth Edition*, ed. Leo Braudy and Marshall Cohen, Oxford, Oxford University Press, 1999.

Bradbury, Ray, *Something Wicked This Way Comes*, London, Hart Davis, MacGibbon, 1963.

Braine, John, *Room at the Top*, London, Eyre & Spottiswoode, 1957.

Braun, Eric, 'The Decade of Change', *Films and Filming*, December 1973, pp. 28–40.

Butler, Ivan, *The Making of Feature Films – A Guide*, Harmondsworth, Penguin, 1971.

Cameron, Ian, *Movie Reader*, London, November Books, 1970.

Clarke, Jeremy, 'Jack Clayton Back on Track', *Films and Filming*, November–December 1988, pp. 9–11.

Cowie, Peter, 'Clayton's Progress', *Motion*, No. 3, Spring 1962, pp. 34–40.

Crist, Judith, *The Private Eye, the Cowboy and the Very Naked Girl*, New York, Holt, Rinehart & Winston Inc., 1970.

Durgnat, Raymond, *A Mirror for England*, London, Faber & Faber, 1970.

Fitzgerald, F. Scott, *The Great Gatsby*, New York, Scribner's, 1925.

Gaston, G. M. A., *Jack Clayton: A Guide to Reference and Resources*, Boston, G. K. Hall, 1981.

Giannetti, Louis D., 'The Gatsby Flap', *Literature/Film Quarterly*, Vol. 3, No. 1, Winter 1975, pp. 13–22.

Gloag, Julian, *Our Mother's House*, London, Secker & Warburg, 1963.

Gow, Gordon, 'The Way Things Are: An Interview with Jack Clayton', *Films and Filming*, April 1974, pp. 10–14.

—— 'The Great Gatsby', *Films and Filming*, June 1974, pp. 45–7.

Grobel, Lawrence, *The Hustons*, London, Bloomsbury, 1990.

Hall, Stuart and Whannel, Paddy, *The Popular Arts*, London, Hutchinson, 1964.

Harcourt, Peter, *Movies and Mythologies*, Toronto, Canadian Broadcasting Corporation, 1977.

Higson, Andrew, 'Interview with Jack Clayton', partly transl. Evelyn Piellier as 'Fantomes à Louer', *Magazine Littéraire*, Vol. 22, No. 2, 1985, pp. 38–9.

—— 'Gothic Fantasy as Art Cinema: the Secret of Female Desire in *The Innocents*', in *Gothick Origins and Innovations*, ed. Allan Lloyd Smith and Victor Sage, Amsterdam, Rodopi, 1994, pp. 204–17.

Hill, John, *Sex, Class and Realism: British Cinema, 1956–1963*, London, British Film Institute, 1986.

Hill, John and Gibson, Pamela (eds), *The Oxford Guide to Film Studies*, New York and Oxford, Oxford University Press, 1998.

Houston, Penelope, 'Room at the Top?' *Sight and Sound*, Spring 1959, pp. 56–9.

—— 'The Innocents', *Sight and Sound*, Summer 1961, pp. 14–15.

—— *The Contemporary Cinema*, London, Penguin, 1963.

—— 'Keeping Up With the Antonionis', *Sight and Sound*, Autumn 1964, pp. 163–7.

—— 'Gatsby', *Sight and Sound*, Spring 1974, pp. 38–9.

Hudson, Roger, 'Putting the Magic in It: Two Editors, James Clark and Anthony Harvey, Discuss their Work', *Sight and Sound*, Spring 1966, pp. 78–83.

Huston, John, *An Open Book*, London, Macmillan, 1981.

James, Henry, *The Turn of the Screw*, London, Heinemann, 1898.

—— *The Art of the Novel: Critical Prefaces*, intro R. P. Blackmur, New York, Charles Scribner's Sons, 1962.

Jarvie, I. C., *Towards a Sociology of the Cinema*, London, Routledge & Kegan Paul, 1970.

Kael, Pauline, *I Lost it at the Movies*, Boston and Toronto, Little Brown & Co., 1965.

—— *Kiss Kiss Bang Bang*, New York, Bantam, 1969.

—— *Hooked*, London and New York, Marion Boyars, 1990.

Kennaway, James, *Silence*, London, Jonathan Cape, 1972.

Laing, Stuart, '*Room at the Top*: The Morality of Affluence', in *Popular Fiction and Social Change*, ed. Christopher Pawling, Basingstoke, Macmillan, 1984, pp. 159–84.

Landy, Marcia, *British Genres: Cinema and Society 1930–1960*, Princeton, NJ, Princeton University Press, 1991.

Lang, David, *Casualties of War*, London, Hodder & Stoughton, 1989. First pub. *New Yorker*, 18 October 1969, pp. 61–146.

Lorentz, Janet E., '*The Lonely Passion of Judith Hearne*' in *Magills Cinema Annual 1988*, ed. Frank N. Magill, Pasadena, CA, Salem Press, pp. 219–22.

Lovell, Alan, 'The British Cinema: the Unknown Cinema', London, British Film Institute Education Department seminar paper, 1969.

Marwick, Arthur '*Room at the Top, Saturday Night and Sunday Morning* and the Cultural Revolution in Britain', *Journal of Contemporary History*, Vol. 19, No. 1, January 1984, pp. 127–51.

—— (ed.), *The Arts, Literature and Society*, London, Routledge, 1990.

Maslin, Janet, 'Ballantine's Scotch, Glemby Haircuts, White Suits and White Teflon, Gatsby 1974', in *The Classic American Novel and the Movies*, ed. Gerald Peary and Roger Shelzin, New York, Ungar, 1977, pp. 261–7.

McFarlane, Brian, *An Autobiography of British Cinema*, London, Methuen, 1997.

McIlroy, Brian 'Tackling Aloneness: Jack Clayton's *The Lonely Passion of Judith Hearne*', *Literature/Film Quarterly*, Vol. 21, No. 1, 1993, pp. 33–7.

McVay, Douglas, 'The House that Jack Built', *Films and Filming*, October 1967, pp. 5–11.

Monaco, James, *American Film Now*, New York, Plume, 1979.

Moore, Brian, *The Lonely Passion of Judith Hearne*, London, André Deutsch, 1955.

Mortimer, Penelope, *The Pumpkin Eater*, London, Hutchinson, 1962.

—— *About Time Too*, London, Weindenfeld & Nicholson, 1993.

Munson, Brad, '*Something Wicked This Way Comes*: Adding the Magic', *Cinefex*, No. 12, April 1983, pp. 6–27.

Murphy, Robert, *Sixties British Cinema*, London, British Film Institute, 1992.

Oakley, Charles, *Where We Came In*, London, George Allen & Unwin, 1964.

Palmer, Barton R., 'What was New in the British New Wave? Re-Viewing *Room at the Top*', *Journal of Popular Film and Television*, Vol. 14, No. 3, Fall 1986, pp. 125–35.

Palmer, James W., 'Cinematic Ambiguity: James's *The Turn of the Screw* and Clayton's *The Innocents*'; *Literature/Film Quarterly*, Vol. 5, No. 3, 1977, pp. 198–215.

Perkins, V. F., 'The British Cinema', *Movie*, No. 1, May 1962, pp. 3–7.

—— 'Censorship', *Movie*, No. 6, December 1962, pp. 16–22.

Perry, George, *The Great British Picture Show*, London, Paladin, 1975.

Petrie, Duncan J., *Creativity and Constraint in the British Film Industry*, Basingstoke, Macmillan, 1991.

Pinter, Harold, *Five Screenplays*, London, Methuen, 1971.

Pirie, David, *A Heritage of Horror: the English Gothic Cinema, 1946–1972*, New York, Avon, 1973.

Plaschkes, Otto, 'Jack Clayton Remembered', *Direct*, Summer 1995, p. 15.

Plimpton, George, *Truman Capote*, London, Picador, 1998.

Rebello, Stephen, '*Something Wicked This Way Comes*', *Cinefantastique*, Vol. 13, No. 5, 1983, pp. 28–49.

—— 'Jack Clayton's *The Innocents*', *Cinefantastique*, Vol. 13, No. 5, 1983, pp. 51–5.

Recchia, Edward, 'An Eye for an I: Adapting Henry James's *The Turn of the Screw* to the Screen', *Literature/Film Quarterly*, Vol. 15, No. 1, 1987, pp. 28–35.

Reisz, Karel, 'Big Budget Game Hunter', *Guardian*, 25 March 1995, p. 19.

Richards, Jeffrey and Aldgate, Anthony, *Best of British Cinema and Society, 1930–1970*, Oxford, Basil Blackwell, 1983.

Rosen, Marjorie, 'Francis Ford Coppola Interviewed' and 'Jack Clayton – I'm Proud of that Film', *Film Comment*, Vol. 10, No. 4, July–August 1974, pp. 43–52.

Sarris, Andrew, *The American Cinema: Directors and Directions, 1929–1968*, New York, Dutton, 1968.

Signoret, Simone, *Nostalgia Isn't What It Used To Be*, London, Weidenfeld & Nicholson, 1978.

Sinyard, Neil, 'Directors of the Decade: Jack Clayton', *Films and Filming*, September 1983, pp. 26–9.

—— *Filming Literature: The Art of Screen Adaptation*, London, Croom Helm, 1986.

—— *Children in the Movies*, London, Batsford, 1992.

Sloman, Tony, 'Jack Clayton: The Bespoke Cinéaste', National Film Theatre programme, March 1996, pp. 15–17.

Spark, Muriel, *Memento Mori*, London, Macmillan, 1959.

Stephenson, Ralph and Debrix, J. R., *The Cinema as Art*, London, Penguin, 1965.

Tibbetts, John C., 'The Illustrating Man: The Screenplays of Ray Bradbury', *Creative Screenwriting*, Vol. 6, No. 1, January–February 1999, pp. 45–54.

Trevelyan, John, *What the Censor Saw*, London, Michael Joseph, 1973.

Walker, Alexander, *Hollywood, England: The British Film Industry in the Sixties*, London, Michael Joseph, 1974.

West, Jessamyn, *The Massacre at Fall Creek*, New York, Harcourt, Brace, Jovanovich, 1975.

Williams, Tennessee, *Memoirs*, New York, Doubleday & Co., 1975.

Index

Page references in *italics* relate to illustrations

'Abstract on Vision' (Jack Clayton), 239–40
Accident, 12, 138, 157
Adjani, Isabelle, 212–13
Adrian, Rhys, 89
Agutter, Jenny, 134
'Ain't We Got Fun?', 150–1, 156
Albee, Edward, 212
Aldgate, Anthony, 13, 40
Aldredge, Theoni, 150
Aldrich, Robert, 220
Aldridge, James, 215
Alice Adams, 180
Alien, 221
All Quiet on the Western Front, 51
Allied Artists, 175
Altman, Robert, 220
Ambler, A. G., 100
American Tragedy, An, 44, 57, 159
Amis, Kingsley, 38
Anderson, Lindsay, 10, 13, 38, 62
Anderson, Robert, 218
Andrews, Nigel, 206
Antonioni, Michelangelo, 5, 15, 110–11, 114, 118, 160
Apocalypse Now, 218
Archibald, William, 84–5, 88, 90–1
Arden, John, 210–11
Armes, Roy, 3, 8
Ashcroft, Peggy, 22, *69*
Asherson, Renée, 2, 192–4, 197
Aspern Papers, The, 84
Asquith, Anthony, 23
Atlantic Ferry, 262
Augustus, 216
Auric, Georges, 5, 23–4, 34, 92, 204
Ayres, Lew, 51

Babenco, Hector, 186
Baddeley, Hermione, 49
Baird, Roy, 212, 216
Baker, Peter, 34
Bancroft, Anne, 6, 18, 60, 109–11, 114, 117, 120, 124, 178, 225–6
Barr, Charles, 13
Bart, Lionel, 239
Bass, Alfie, 31–2, 34, 190–1

Batalov, Alexei, 30
Baxter, Warner, 145
Bayldon, Oliver, 193
Bayliss, Peter, 27
BBC, 191–3
Beat the Devil, 24–5, 31, 91, 191, 263
Beauty and the Beast, 5, 92
Beckett, Samuel, 32
Beerbohm, Max, 132
Ben-Hur, 26
Bennett, Arnold, 54
Bergen, Candice, 149
Bergman, Ingmar, 14–15, 110, 114, 192
Bergman, Ingrid, 88, 208
Bergson, Philip, 175, 206
Bernstein, Elmer, 135
Bernstein, Leonard, 17
Bespoke Overcoat, The, 23–5, 30–5, 38, 92, 115, 191, 225, 264
Billington, Michael, 112, 116–17
Black, Karen, 153–4, 164
'Black Ferris', 161
Black Narcissus, 57
Blackwood, Roger, 224
Blade Runner, 171
Blees, Robert, 217
Bloom, Claire, 88
Blue Lamp, The, 5
Bogarde, Dirk, 12–14, 57, 78, 130–41 *passim*, 182, 225
Bogdanovich, Peter, 188
Bolt, Robert, 213, 216
Bond Street, 23, 262
Bordwell, David, 15–16
Born Yesterday, 174
Boulting, Ingrid, 148
Bourne Identity, The, 214
Boyer, Charles, 195

Bradbury, Ray, 161–3, 167–70
Bragg, Melvyn, 21
Braine, John, 37–43 *passim*, 46–7
Brazzi, Rossano, 25
Bridge on the River Kwai, The, 47
Brief Encounter, 37, 41, 45, 51, 118, 123, 125
Brimstone and Treacle, 25
Brinton, Ralph, 57
British Academy of Film and Television Arts (BAFTA), 193, 225–6
British Academy Awards, 31, 187, 193
British Board of Film Censors, 40–1, 55
British Broadcasting Corporation (BBC), 191–3
British Film Institute, 13–14
Britten, Benjamin, 94
Brook, John, 144
Brook, Peter, 131
Brooks, Jeremy, 133–4, 139
Brooks, Margaret, 134
Brooks, Mel, 226
Brooks, Richard, 3
Bruccoli, Matthew J., 145
Burton, Richard, 34, 133

Calderon, Alvarez, 215
Calvert, Phyllis, 57
Campbell Dixon, S., 31
Cannes Film Festival, 76, 82
Cannon distributors, 186–7
Capote, Truman, 91, 146, 148, 191
Cappotto. Il – The Overcoat, 30
Cardiff, Jack, 209
Carlino, Lewis, 218
Carson, Shawn, 164
Casablanca, 152

Casino Royale, 210
Cassavetes, John, 209
Castaway, 111
Castell, David, 168, 206
Casualties of War, 208, 218–22
Charge of the Light Brigade, The, 11
Charisma Films, 215
Chartoff, Robert, 161
Chayefsky, Paddy, 61, 218
Chekhov, Anton, 127, 217
Cherry Orchard, The, 217
Child is Waiting, A, 208–9
Chiles, Lois, 149–50, 153, 156
Christie, Agatha, 201, 203
Christie, Julie, 149
Church, Michael, 194, 206
Cinemascope, 82
Clark, James, 82, 86
Clavell, James, 209
Clayton, Haya *see* Harareet,
     Haya
Clément, René, 5, 133
*Close Encounters of the Third
     Kind*, 162
Cocteau, Jean, 5, 27–8, 92
Cold Spring Harbour, 216
Cole, Stephanie, 195, 198
Color Purple, The, 135
Columbia Pictures, 209–10
Comedians, 164
Conquest of the Air, The, 261
Conroy, David, 212
Conway, Harold, 61
Copland, Aaron, 227
Coppola, Francis Ford, 148–9,
     157, 159
Cornelius, Henry, 25, 191
Count Your Blessings, 91
Coveney, Michael, 185
Cowan, Tony, 226
Cox, John, 100

Craig, Wendy, 57
Crawford, Joan, 25
Crichton, Charles, 57, 217
Crist, Judith, 190
Cristofer, Michael, 213, 220–1
Cropper, Anna, 204
Cukor, George, 195
Cusack, Cyril, 192, 194, 198
Cuthbertson, Allan, 45

Daily Express, 39
Daily Herald, 58, 61
Daily Sketch, 56
Daily Worker, 54
Dam Busters, The, 47
Damned, The, 135
Danger Within, 47
Danischewsky, Monja, 217
Dano, Royal, 169
David and Lisa, 133
Davidson, Claire, 138
Davies, Rudi, 182
Davis, Colin, 239
De Palma, Brian, 218–19
Dead, The (John Huston), 6,
     176, 183, 199
'Dead, The' (James Joyce), 175,
     199
Dearden, Basil, 5
Death in Venice, 135, 148
Debrix, J. R., 114
Deer Hunter, The, 218
Degermark, Pia, 210
Dehn, Paul, 94
Delerue, Georges, 5, 79, 110, 113,
     117, 125, 135, 164–5, 171,
     187, 204, 225
Denham, Maurice, 193–4, 198
Dern, Bruce, 125, 152, 178
Devlin, Alan, 181
Dewey, Donna, 215–17

Dick, Philip K., 171
Dickens, Charles, 44
Dickinson, Thorold, 10, 23, 35, 92, 104
Diller, Barry, 162, 212
Disenchanted, The, 145
Disney Corporation, 162–6, 169–71
Divided Heart, The, 91
Divorce of Lady X, The, 261
Dock Brief, 90
Dostoevsky, Feodor, 30
Douglas, Kirk, 161–2
Douglas, Melvyn, 212–13
Douglas, Peter, 161–2, 206
Driving Miss Daisy, 192
Dry Rot, 190, 263
Dubliners, 175–6
Dumbo, 163
Dunaway, Faye, 144, 149
Durgnat, Raymond, 13, 135, 137, 140
Dyer, Lee, 164, 166, 168
Dyer, Richard, 16

Eastman, Carol, 148
Eclipse, The, 114
Edinburgh Film Festival, 31
Eggar, Samantha, 210
Elgar, Edward, 13
Eliot, George, 18
Eliot, T. S., 153, 159, 241
Elvira Madigan, 210
Enchanted April, 193
Enchantment', 'The (Jack Clayton), 18, 215, 241–60
Enfants terribles, Les, 137
Evans, Robert, 144–5, 212
Ewell, Tom, 150
Eyre, Peter, 196

Fahrenheit 451, 12
Fallen Idol, The, 85–6
Farrow, Mia, 78, 125, 149, 152, 157
Fat City, 188
Fellini, Federico, 15, 31
Ferrer, Jose, 24
Field, Sally, 214
Finch, Peter, 2, 109, 111, 125
Findlater, Richard, 34
Fiskin, Jeffrey Alan, 214
Fitzgerald, F. Scott, 9, 22, 144–8, 153–60 *passim*, 215
Fitzgerald, Zelda, 215
Five Easy Pieces, 149
Flemyng, Robert, 193
Flesh and Blood, 263
Ford, Ford Madox, 159
Ford, John, 13–14, 220
Forster, E. M., 147
Fox, Michael J., 218
Framework (magazine), 13
Francis, Freddie, 82, 86, 91, 225
Franklin, Pamela, 4, 7, 78, 85, 91, 134–5, 139
Fraser, George MacDonald, 215
Frears, Stephen, 59, 224
Free Cinema movement, 10, 38, 61
Freeman, John, 239
French, Philip, 14, 206
Frost, Robert, 202
Full Circle, 213

Garland, Judy, 209
Garner, Jane, 191
Gaslight, 195
Gates of Paradise, 134
Genevieve, 25
Ghost Story, 213
Giler, David, 218, 221

Gilliat, Penelope, 9, 86, 154–5, 158
Girardet, Christophe, 5
Glenville, Peter, 39, 84
Gloag, Julian, 133–4
Go-Between, The, 90
Godard, Jean-Luc, 13, 15
Godfather, The, 148, 155
Goetz, Ruth and August, 84
Gogol, Nicolai, 18, 30, 35
Golden Toy, The, 22, 69
Goldfinger, 94
Golding, William, 131
Goldman, William, 218
Goldsmith, Jerry, 165
Good Die Young, The, 263
Good Soldier, The, 159
Gow, Gordon, 24, 39, 84, 87, 96, 100, 135, 150–1, 157
Grabe, David, 218
Graham, Peter, 110
Graham, Winston, 210
Granger, Stewart, 39
Grant, Cary, 89
Gray, Janine, 116
Great Expectations, 39, 44
Great Gatsby, The, 2–4, 7, 9, 22, 25, 30, 43, 50, 67, 78, 142–61, 180, 191, 207, 212, 219, 225–7, 267–8
Green Berets, The, 219
Greene, Graham, 20
Grier, Pam, 166, 170
Griffiths, Trevor, 164
Grobel, Lawrence, 130–1
Guerany, 213
Gugolka, John, 137

Hale, John, 211
Hall, Stuart, 59–60
Hall, Willis, 48

Hamill, Peter, 218
Hamlet, 52, 164
Hampton, Christopher, 148, 212
Handford, Peter, 126
HandMade Films, 176, 186–7, 215
Hand-Me Downs, 214
Hannah, 215
Harareet, Haya, 22, 26, 76, 83, 91, 126, 133, 136, 139, 149, 160, 221, 224–7
Harcourt, Peter, 13
Hardwicke, Sir Cedric, 115
Hardy, Thomas, 57
Harrison, Wilham, 216
Hartley, L. P., 90
Harvey, Laurence, 40–1, 47–8, 51–2, 55, 71–3, 145
Hay Fever, 217
Heiress, The, 84
Hellfire Club, The, 91
Hemingway, Ernest, 145, 154, 215
Hemmings, David, 94, 210
Henry, Gustav, 137
Hepburn, Katharine, 175, 180
Herrmann, Edward, 156
Hibbin, Nina, 54
Hicks, Barbara, 193
High Tide at Noon, 62
Higson, Andrew, 84
Hill, Arthur, 170
Hill, John, 52, 54
Hillary, Richard, 215
Hiller, Wendy, 184
Hinxman, Margaret, 56–7
Hird, Thora, 193–4, 197–8
Hiroshima Mon Amour, 82
Hitchcock, Alfred 5, 113, 117, 140, 165, 201
Holliday, Judy, 174
Holt, Seth, 11
Homecoming, The, 112

Hook, 141, 170

Hopkins, Anthony, 210

Hordern, Michael, 192, 195, 197, 200

Horner, James, 165

Hoskins, Bob, 4, 176, 182–3, 187

Houston, Donald, 42, 72

Houston, Penelope, 38, 60, 82, 110, 118, 145, 147

Howard, Trevor, 51

Howe, Geoffrey, 239

Hunted, 57, 138

Huntley, Raymond, 41

Huston, Anjelica, 130–1

Huston, John, 3, 6–8, 24–5, 28, 31, 48, 63, 68, 107, 131, 161, 175, 183, 188, 191, 199, 216

Hutson, Lee, 213

Hyams, Joe, 85

I Am a Camera, 25, 94, 191, 263

'I Only Saw Him in a Café in Berlin', 94

Ice Cold in Alex, 47

Ideal Husband, An, 23, 262

If You Could See Me Now, 213, 239

Imperial War Museum, 28

Innocents, The, 4–5, 7–8, 15–16, 20, 23–4, 30, 32, 36, 51, 60, 74–5, 81–109, 115, 118–19, 123, 131, 134, 142, 163–4, 168, 180, 190–1, 226, 239, 265–6

Invitation to a Dance, 161

Ironweed, 186

Jackson, Frank, 61

Jackson, Shirley, 214

James, Henry, 4, 8–9, 20–1, 81–4, 89, 93, 96, 101, 180, 184

James, Sid, 26

Jarrott, Charles, 211

Jenkins, Megs, 91

Jessop, Clytie, 87

Jeux Interdits – Forbidden Games, 5, 133

John, Augustus, 216

Johnson, Celia, 51, 123

Johnson, Richard, 124

Jones, Christopher, 210

Jones, Evan, 215

Jones, Katherine Ann, 217

Jones, Quincy, 135

Jordan, Neil, 176

Joyce, James, 44, 175–6

Joyce, Yootha, 109–10, 119, 136

Jude the Obscure, 57

Judgement at Nuremberg, 209

Jules et Jim, 110, 204

Julia, 213

Kael, Pauline, 32, 107, 114, 178, 180, 183–4

Kanter, Jay, 221

Kath, Katherine, 25

Katz, Ephraim, 206

Katzka, Gabe, 214

Kazan, Elia, 148

Kean, Marie, 183–4

Kelley, Alan, 193

Kelly, Gene, 161, 185

Kemplen, Ralph, 24

Kent Messenger, 40

Kerr, Deborah, 4, 23, 60, 74, 86, 88, 175, 225

Kershner, Irvin, 175

Kid for Two Farthings, A, 31

Kidnappers, The, 62

Kind Hearts and Coronets, 192

Kind of Loving, A, 62

King and Country, 12

Kingsley, Ben, 212
Kohan, Rhea, 214
Korda, Alexander, 20, 22–3, 261
Kossoff, David, 18, 31–2, 34, 225
Kotcheff, Ted, 39
Kozintsev, Grigori, 30
Kramer, Stanley, 208–9
Kubrick, Stanley, 3, 207
Kurosawa, Akira, 14

L-Shaped Room, The, 60, 207
Ladd, Alan, 145
Lady Chatterley's Lover, 142
Ladykillers, The, 192
Laing, Stuart, 45–6, 62–3
Lamb, Irene, 2, 197
Lambert, Gavin, 59
Lamorisse, Albert, 35
Lancaster, Burt 209
Lang, Daniel, 218
Last Enemy, The, 215–16
Last Tycoon, The, 148
Lattuada, Alberto, 30
Laughton, Charles, 140, 171
Laurel, Stan, 181
Lawrence, D. H., 142
Lawson, Wilfrid, 22, 44
Le Carré, John, 209–10
Leacock, Philip, 62
Lean, David, 11, 13–14, 45, 47,
    147, 157, 207
Leavis, F.R., 12
Lee, Bernard, 25
Lee Thompson, J., 47, 55, 57
Lehmann, Rosamond, 59
Leigh, Vivien, 39
Lejeune, C. A., 54
Lemmon, Jack, 220–1
Lennon, John, 62–3
Lester, Mark, 134, 136
Lester, Richard, 3, 53, 110

Life at the Top, 39
Lindfors, Viveca, 111
Lion, The, 209
Little Big Man, 220
Liverpool Daily Post, 61
Lockwood, Preston, 193
Lodge, David, 43–4
Lofficier, Randy and Jean Marc,
    171
Lom, Herbert, 57
London Evening Standard British
    Film Awards, 187
London Films, 22, 261
*Lonely Passion of Judith Hearne,
    The*, 4, 6, 9–10, 15–16, 18,
    35, 51, 60, 80, 174–88,
    195–6, 201–4, 207, 269–
    70
*Long and the Short and the Tall,
    The*, 48
Look Back in Anger, 38
Looking-Glass War, The, 209–10
Lord of the Flies, 131
Los Angeles Star, 186
Los Angeles Times, 187
Losey, Joseph, 12, 90, 110, 138,
    157
Love Bug, The, 170–1
Lovell, Alan, 8, 11
Lucky Jim, 61
Ludlum, Robert, 214
Luke, Michael, 217
Lumet, Sidney, 3

McArthur, Colin, 12
Macbeth, 48
McCabe and Mrs Miller, 220
McCormick, Donald, 211
McCoy, Horace, 22, 207
MacDonald, Richard, 164
McFarlane, Brian, 8, 23

McGraw, Ali, 144–5
McIlroy, Brian, 9
McKee, Robert, 217
Mackendrick, Alexander, 10, 57, 133, 211
MacLaine, Shirley, 175
McMurtry, Larry, 219–20
McNeice, Ian, 183–4
McQueen, Steve, 144–5
McVay, Douglas, 50–1, 110, 125
Magnificent Ambersons, The, 159
Mahler, Gustav, 17, 202
Main, The, 213
Major Barbara, 23, 262
Maltese Falcon, The, 48
Man Who Would Be King, The, 48
Mandy, 57
Mankowitz, Wolf, 31–2
Mann, Abby, 208–9
Mann, Roderick, 177
Manteau, La, 30
Marceau, Marcel, 30
Marchand, Colette, 24
Marks, Louis, 192–3
Mary, Queen of Scots, 210–11
Masina, Giulietta, 174
Maslin, Janet, 7, 157–8
Mason, James, 15–16, 76, 109, 114, 120, 122–3, 125
Massacre at Fall Creek, 208, 219–20, 221, 222, 227
Medavoy, Mike, 219
Melly, George, 239
Memento Mori, 2, 16, 35–6, 190–204, 207, 225–6, 270–1
Men Are Not Gods, 261
Merrick, David, 4, 213, 219–20
Metz, Christian, 2
MGM, 133
Middlesex County Times, 110
Milius, John, 218

Miller, David, 25
Miller, J. P., 218
Minghella, Anthony, 193
Minnelli, Vincente, 31
Moby Dick, 161
Mona Lisa, 176
Monaco, James, 159
Monsey, Derek, 55
Monthly Film Bulletin, 7, 139
Moon Shadows, 214
Moore, Brian, 9, 175–6, 183–4
Morgan, Terence, 57
Morris, Oswald, 25
Mortimer, John, 90–1, 148, 168, 199–200, 225
Mortimer, Penelope, 109, 112–13, 118, 126–7, 131
Moss, Stirling, 239
Moulin Rouge, 24–5, 31, 92, 263
Movie (magazine), 11
Movie Mail (magazine), 53
Müller, Matthias, 5
Murphy, Robert, 118–19, 126, 132

Naples is a Battlefield, 23, 26–30, 229, 264
Nasatir, Marcia, 219
Nash, Roy, 31
National Film Theatre, London, 225
National Gallery of Art, Washington, 225
Naughton, John, 197
Naylor, Phyllis, 213
Neill, Nigel, 89
Nelson, Peter, 175–7, 185
Nesbitt, Darren, 49
New Statesman, 31
New Yorker, The, 218
Newell, Mike, 193
Ni Mhuiri, Aine, 181

Nicholls, Anthony, 134
Nicholls, Sarah, 134
Nichols, Mike, 175
Nicholson, Jack, 149, 186
Night of the Hunter, The, 140, 171
Nightcomers, The, 89
Niven, David Jr, 220–1
No Trees in the Street, 57
Norman, Leslie, 48
North, Alex, 84
Novak, Kim, 208
Nunnerley, Leslie, 122–3

Oakes, Philip, 61, 110
'Obituary' (Jack Clayton), 226
O'Brien, Edna, 210
Observer, The, 221
Oliver!, 134
Olivier, Laurence, 34, 197
'On the Prevention of War' (Jack
    Clayton), 234–7
One Foot in the Grave, 192
One Last Glimpse, 145, 215
O'Neal, Patrick, 217
O'Neal, Ryan, 188
Oscars, 30, 40, 86, 134, 148,
    150–1, 167, 186, 209, 226
Our Mother's House, 4–5, 7, 30,
    35, 77, 130–42, 145, 180,
    182, 191, 204, 267
Over the Moon, 261
Oxford Guide to Film Studies, 16
Oxford Mail, 12

Page, Geraldine, 175
Papp, Joseph, 150
Paramount, 148, 162, 212–13
Parker, Dorothy, 154
Parry, Gordon, 23
Pascal, Gabriel, 23
Passage to India, A, 147

Passport to Pimlico, 25
Paterson, Neil, 49, 62
Patton, 148
Pavlow, Muriel, 193
Peach, Mary, 57, 72
Pearson, Allison, 201
Peckinpah, Sam, 13, 161, 219
Peeping Tom, 56, 62
Peer Oppenheimer Productions,
    217
Penn, Arthur, 220
Perry, Eleanor, 133
Peter Pan, 141
Peterson, Vidal, 164, 214
Petrie, Daniel, 175
Petulia, 110
Phillpotts, Ambrosine, 45
Phoenix Tapes, The, 5
Picker, David, 162
Pierson, Frank R., 210
Pinewood studios, 3, 82, 150
Pinocchio, 163
Pinter, Harold, 32, 89, 110–27
    passim, 148, 225, 228
Place in the Sun, A, 57, 159
Plaschkes, Otto, 6, 17, 25, 35,
    109
Poe (The Dark Angel), 217
Polanski, Roman, 212–13
Porter, Eric, 113
*Portrait of the Artist as a Young
    Man, A*, 44
Potter, Dennis, 20–1, 25
Powell, Dilys, 31, 37–8, 57–8
Powell, Michael, 23, 56–7, 62
Previn, André, 150
Prison Without Bars, 261
Pryce, Jonathan, 79, 164, 167, 170
Psycho, 113, 117, 137–8
Pumpkin Eater, The, 2, 5–6, 15–
    16, 25, 30, 60, 76, 109–

27, 131, 134, 142, 160,
176–80, 187, 191, 201,
204, 209, 228, 266–7
Pushkin, Alexander, 23, 35

Q Planes, 262
Quatre Cents Coups, Les, 82
Queen magazine interview with
Jack Clayton, 237–8
Queen of Spades, The, 10, 23, 35,
92, 104, 262
Quintero, José, 175

Racing Pigeon, The (magazine),
226
RAF Film Unit, 23, 26
Raggedy Man, 214
Rama Rau, Santha, 147
Ramsay, Peggy, 210–11
Rank Organisation, 55
Ransohoff, Martin, 133
Rattigan, Terence, 23
Rawlings, Terry, 225–6
Reach for the Sky, 47
Rebello, Stephen, 92
Red Balloon, The, 35
Red Desert, The, 111
Redfern, Stephen, 226
Redford, Robert, 78, 125, 149,
152, 155–7
Redgrave, Michael, 84, 89–90,
95
Redgrave, Vanessa, 176, 211
Reed, Carol, 31, 85, 134
Reeves, Saskia, 174–5, 181, 196
Reid, Sheila, 184
Reinhardt, Max, 25
Reisz, Karel, 2–4, 10, 13, 20, 23,
38, 62, 81, 83, 110, 225–7
Relph, Michael, 4–5
Resnais, Alain, 82, 110–11

Revelations, 162, 213–14
Revolutionary Road, 217
Reynolds, Burt, 214
Reynold's News, 61–2
Richard III, 34
Richards, Dick, 60
Richards, Jeffrey, 13
Richardson, Ralph, 210
Richardson, Tony, 10–11, 38, 62
Richler, Emma, 226
Richler, Mordecai, 4, 39, 133,
148, 209–10, 217, 226
Riddle, Nelson, 150–1, 226
Robards, Jason, 18, 161, 167–70
Roberts, Jerry, 207
Roberts, Rachel, 175
Roeg, Nicolas, 10, 12, 62, 111,
131, 209–10
Rome – Open City, 28
Romney, Jonathan, 111
Romulus Films, 24
Room at the Top, 1–2, 4, 10–11,
14–16, 22, 24–6, 29–30,
37–63, 71–3, 82, 91, 111,
118, 131, 142, 145, 180–1,
187, 190–1, 207, 224, 237,
264–5
Rose, Reginald, 218
Ross, Katharine, 149
Rossen, Robert, 3
Rudkin, David, 216
Russell, Ken, 13, 62
Russell, Rosalind, 175
Russell, Shirley, 150
Ryan's Daughter, 11, 14, 121, 157
Rydell, Mark, 161

Sailor Beware, 38, 190, 263
Salt, Waldo, 213
Samuelson, Sir Sydney, 226
Sanders, Dennis, 35

Sarris, Andrew, 3, 6, 11, 110
Saturday Night and Sunday Morning, 60, 62, 207
Scales, Prunella, 57, 181, 184
Scarlet and the Black, The, 44, 57
Schickel, Richard, 163
Schlesinger, John, 10, 13, 38, 62
Schulberg, Budd, 145
Scott, Ridley, 171
Screen Writers' Guild, 91
Sears, Heather, 25, 40, 42, *73*
Seastrom, Victor, 23
Seckerson, Edward, 17
Sellars, Elizabeth, 57
Servant, The, 12, 121, 131–2, 138
Seventh Seal, The, 192
Shadow of a Doubt, 165
Shakespeare, William, 48, 52
Shapiro, Robert, 225
Sheffield Park, 96
Sheldon, Louis, 135
Shepherd, Cybill, 149
Shepperton studios, 177
Shinel – The Overcoat, 30
Shipman, David, 146, 154
Sight and Sound, 6, 38, 81
Signoret, Simone, 2, 40, 51–62 *passim*, 71, 224
Silence (unmade film), 26, 208, 213, 220–2
Silence, The (Ingmar Bergman), 110
Sim, Gerald, 121, 136
Simmons, Jean, 39
Simpson, Philip, 13
Sims, Jeanie, 2, 24, 193–4, 199, 213–17
Sinatra, Frank, 209
Slocombe, Douglas, 148
Smith, Maggie, 18, 22, 60, *80*, 123, 142, 109–10, 115, 174,

176, 180–1, 185–7, 193–8 *passim*, 225
Smith, Scottie, 146, 149
Snow White, 163
Some Like It Hot, 190
Something Wicked This Way Comes, 14, 18, 35, 51, 79, 142, 160–71, 202, 204, 206, 213–14, 225, 268–9
Sons and Lovers, 60, 86, 207
Soundtrack (magazine), 204
Spacek, Sissy, 214
Spanish Gardener, The, 138
Spark, Muriel, 190–5, 199
Spielberg, Steven, 135, 141, 162, 170, 187
Sporting Life, This, 62
Spy in Black, The, 23, 262
Spy Who Came in from the Cold, The, 94, 210
Stagecoach, 220
Stark, Ray, 176, 188
Stendhal, 44, 57
Stephens, Martin, 85, 91
Stephenson, Ralph, 114
Stern, Milton R., 146
Stern, Stewart, 148
Stevens, George, 57, 159, 180
Stirling, Joyce, 30
Stone Virgin, The, 216
Story of Esther Costello, The, 25–6, 40, 263
Strada, La, 31, 174
Straight, Beatrice, 84
Stratton Smith, Tony, 215–16
Straub, Peter, 213
Streep, Meryl, 186
Strick, Philip, 198, 202–3
Strindberg, August, 114
Sulitzer, Paul-Loup, 215
Susskind, David, 218

Sweet Autumn, 210
Syms, Sylvia, 57

Taste of Honey, A, 62
Taylor, John Russell, 32
Tea and Sympathy, 31
Tenant, The, 212–13
Tennyson, Alfred, 87
Thain, Paul, 214–15
Thesiger, Ernest, 22
They Shoot Horses, Don't They?, 22, 154, 207
Thief of Baghdad, The, 23, 262
Thomson, David, 140
Three Men in a Boat, 38, 190, 263
Thurber, James, 155
Till, Eric, 210
Tilvern, Alan, 32
Time Out of War, A, 35
Times, The, 54, 86, 110, 207
Titfield Thunderbolt, The, 192
To Kill a Mockingbird, 135
To Sir With Love, 209
Todd, Richard, 48
Topor, Roland, 212
Tower, The, 197
Towne, Robert, 148
Toye, Wendy, 22
Tracy, Spencer, 176
Trauberg, Leonid, 30
Treasure of the Sierra Madre, The, 48
Trevelyan, John, 55–6
Tron, 164
Truffaut, François 11–12, 56, 81–2, 110, 130, 204, 225
Truly Madly Deeply, 193
Turn of the Screw, The, 22, 82–4, 92, 94
Turner, Adrian, 216

Twentieth Century Fox, 82, 84, 88–9, 133, 220–1
Twilight Zone, The, 165

Ulzana's Raid, 220
Under the Red Robe, 23, 261
Under the Volcano, 6
United Artists, 219–20
United British Artists, 176
Universal Pictures, 211–12
Unsworth, Barry, 216
Uses of Literacy, The, 61

Variety, 90
Varley, Beatrice, 44
Venice Film Festival, 31
Vertigo, 140
Victim, 5
Vidal, Gore, 148
Viertel, Peter, 88
Village of the Damned, 92
Visconti, Luchino, 135, 148, 154
Vista Films, 214
Voight, Jon, 144

Waiting for Godot, 32
Wajda, Andrzej, 134
Walbrook, Anton, 23, 104
Walkabout, 131
Walker, Alexander, 1–3, 6, 37–8, 40, 44, 51, 53–4, 61, 99, 110, 179
Walking Stick, The, 210
Wallace, Parnum, 138
Walter, Bruno, 202
Wanamaker, Zoë, 193, 195, 198, 225
Warner Brothers, 218
Washington Square, 84, 180, 184
Waste Land, The, 153, 159
Waterston, Sam, 152, 155, 225, 227

Watkins, Peter, 13
'We Are Seven', 132
We Have Always Lived in the Castle, 214–15
Weather in the Streets, The, 59
Webb, Alan, 115
Weld, Tuesday, 149
Welles, Orson, 87, 152, 208
West, Jessamyn, 219
Westbrook, John, 42, 45
Whannel, Paddy, 54, 59–61
'What'll I Do?', 150–1
While the Sun Shines, 23, 262
White, Frances, 120
Whitemore, Hugh, 212
Whole Truth, The, 264
Who's Afraid of Virginia Woolf?, 34
Wigan, Gareth, 221
Wilde, Oscar, 23
Wilder, Billy, 190
Wilder, Thornton, 164
Wilhite, Tom, 164
Williams, Tennessee, 144, 160, 225
Williamson, W. Lambert, 92
Wilson, Edmund, 93, 101, 147
Wilson, Scott, 154, 225
Wings of the Morning, 261
Winkler, Irwin, 161

Winner, Michael, 89
Winters, Shelley, 212–13
Withers, Margery, 195, 198
Wolfit, Donald, 46
Wollen, Peter, 1, 17
Woman's Mirror, 56
Wood, Natalie, 149
Woolf, James, 10, 24, 31, 39
Woolf, John, 10, 24, 31, 39, 134, 225
Wordsworth, William, 132
'Working Class Hero', 62–3
Wyatt, Woodrow, 39
Wyler, William, 28, 85, 87, 184
Wyngarde, Peter, 86, 101

X certificates, 55–6, 131

Yates, Peter, 13
Yates, Richard, 216–17
Yeats, W. B., 197
'You Can't Declare Peace' (Jack Clayton and A. Calder-Marshall), 229–33

Zaharoff Pedlar of Death, 211–12
Zavattini, Cesare, 30
Zed Zed, 212
Zinnemann, Fred, 1–2, 16, 224–5
Zuckmayer, Carl, 22, *69*